The Laughing
Jesus

The Laughing
Jesus

RELIGIOUS LIES

AND

GNOSTIC WISDOM

TIMOTHY FREKE AND PETER GANDY

 Harmony Books /New York

ISBN 1-4000-8278-1

Printed in the United States of America

Design by Sarah Maya Gubkin

This book is dedicated

to all those who love

their enemies

Contents

∞

PART I

The Bathwater

GNOSTIC SPIRITUALITY AND LITERALIST RELIGION

The letter kills but the spirit brings to life.
— PAUL, LETTER TO THE EPHESIANS[1]

Wake up! Rouse yourself from the collective coma you mistake for 'real life'. See through the illusion of separateness and recognize that we are all essentially one. Although we appear to be isolated individuals, in reality there is one awareness dreaming itself to be everyone and everything. This is our shared essential nature. The simple secret to enjoying this dream we call 'life' is to wake up to oneness. Because, knowing you are one with all, you will find yourself in love with all. You will fall in love with living. This is the message of the original Christians, who symbolised this awakened state with the enigmatic figure of 'the laughing Jesus'.[2]

Have you ever seen a picture of Jesus laughing? Probably not, because we have inherited a distorted form of Christianity created by the Roman Church in the fourth century, which focuses exclusively on Jesus the 'man of sorrows'. The image that has dominated our culture is that of a man being tortured to death on a cross. But the original Christians didn't see Jesus as an historical man who 'suffered for our sins'. They viewed Jesus as the mythical hero of a symbolic teaching story, which represents the spiritual journey leading to the experience of awakening they called 'gnosis', or 'knowing'.

The original Christians were inspired men and women who saw how good life could be if we would just wake up and live in love. They imagined a new world that would no longer be divided into slaves or citizens, men or women, Gentiles or Jews. But inadvertently, this band of non-conformists gave birth to a totalitarian regime that would rule Europe with an iron fist for over a thousand years. The result was not Heaven on Earth, but the Holy Roman Empire. The dream became a nightmare.

The Roman Church did all it could to suppress the teachings of gnosis and the image of the laughing Jesus. It succeeded so well that it now seems strange to even suggest that Christianity was originally about awakening. But in the middle of the twentieth century some of the texts of the original Christians were found in a cave near Nag Hammadi in Egypt. In these texts the message of awakening is proclaimed loud and clear.

Those who have realised gnosis have set themselves free by waking up from the dream in which they lived and have become themselves again.[3]

How can you bear to be asleep, when it's your responsibility to be awake?[4]

You are asleep and dreaming. Wake up.[5]

Listen to my teachings, which are good and practical, and end the sleep which weighs so heavily upon you.[6]

People are caught up in many vain illusions and empty fictions, which torment them like sleepers prey to nightmares. When they wake up they see that all those dreams were nothing. This is the way it is with those who have cast ignorance aside, as if waking from sleep. They no longer see the world as real, but like a dream at night. They value gnosis as if it were the dawn. Whilst they exist in a state of ignorance it is as if everyone is asleep. Experiencing gnosis is like waking up.[7]

Such teachings of awakening are not exclusively Christian. Throughout history men and women of all faiths have woken up to oneness and love. We use the broad term 'Gnostic' meaning 'knower' to refer to all such individuals because, although they express their insights in the various languages of their diverse cultures, they all talk about the experience of awakening or gnosis.

These charismatic individuals often inspired the formation of small communities dedicated to waking up. But, ironically, the more successful such groups become the more they turn into their opposite. What begins as a loose alliance of free-thinking non-conformists degenerates over time into an organised, authoritarian religion, and people end up completely misunderstanding the original message. We refer to this degenerate form of Gnosticism as 'Literalism'.

Gnosticism is sometimes called 'the perennial philosophy' because it has been found in all cultures and all times. It is not that Gnostics all say exactly the same thing. They don't. It is rather that their teachings are like fingers pointing from different perspectives to the same experience of gnosis. Unfortunately, most people focus on the finger and miss the point. This is Literalism. Literalist religions are clubs for people who want to worship the finger of their founder as the One True Finger, but who have no understanding of the experience of awakening towards which it points.

This book is a damning indictment of Literalist religion and a passionate affirmation of Gnostic spirituality. Let's start by clearly discriminating Gnosticism from Literalism:

Gnostics teach that the important thing is to wake up and experience gnosis for ourselves.	Literalists teach that the important thing is to blindly believe in religious dogmas.
Gnostics interpret their teachings as signposts pointing to the experience of awakening.	Literalists see their teachings as literally the truth itself.
Gnostics use symbolic parables to communicate the way to wake up.	Literalists mistake Gnostic myths for literal accounts of miraculous historical events and end up lost in irrational superstition.
Gnostics know that all books contain the words of men.	Literalists believe that sacred scripture is the Word of God.
Gnostics understand that the way the wisdom of awakening is expressed must constantly evolve to address the ever-changing human condition.	Literalists want a fixed canon of scripture which has absolute authority for all time.
Gnostics want us to think for ourselves, so that we become more conscious and wake up.	Literalists want us to believe what they believe, so that we will join their cult.

Gnostics understand that life itself is a process of awakening.	Literalists believe their particular religion is the only way to the truth and condemn everyone else as lost in diabolical error.
Gnosticism is about waking up from the illusion of separateness to oneness and love.	Literalism keeps us asleep in an 'us versus them' world of division and conflict, inhabited by the 'chosen' and the 'damned'.
Gnosticism unites us.	Literalism divides us.

Throughout history Gnostics have ceaselessly exposed Literalist religion as a pernicious source of ignorance, division and suffering. This Gnostic message has never been more relevant than today. The three great religions of the West—Judaism, Christianity and Islam—are on a collision course that threatens the security of the whole world. Taking religious myths literally is the root cause of the problems in the Middle East which led to 9/11 and a host of other atrocities since. But there is nothing new about religious violence. The present conflict is just the continuation of a long and gruesome history of killing and dying for God.

The burning of Christians by Pagans as flaming torches to light their games. The brutal Christian revenge on the Pagans. The relentless persecution of the Jews by Christians. The violent expansion of the Muslim empire and the bloody conquest of India. The barbaric crusades by Christians against the Muslims. The horrors of the Inquisition. The genocide of indigenous people in the New World. The mass burnings of witches. All were motivated by the desire to please God. All were justified with reference to sacred texts that not only condoned such behaviour but demanded it. These evils have not occurred because the perpetrators were bad people, but because they were in the grip of very bad ideas.

The Baby and the Bathwater

The time has come to say enough of this madness and consign Literalist religion to the garbage can of history. But we must be careful not to throw out the baby with the bathwater. Religion isn't all bad. It has answered the profound human yearning to understand the mysteries of life and death. It has inspired people of all cultures to create sublime works of art, glorious cathedrals and temples, transcendental music and songs. It has this power because at its heart is Gnostic spirituality. In this book we want to rescue the teachings of gnosis from under the accumulated debris of religious dogma, so that we can jettison outdated religious Literalism but retain and revivify the perennial wisdom of awakening.

Let's stop blindly believing in old books and listen instead to those heretical voices that have been drowned out by the cacophony of Literalist war cries. Just imagine for a moment that what Gnostics have been telling us throughout the ages is true. We appear to be separate, but essentially we are all one. The awareness that is conscious in you is the same awareness that is conscious in everyone. And if you recognise this, you will find yourself in love with all.

Imagine what would happen if we actually began to wake up and live by the Gnostic teachings of oneness and love. If we started to truly love our neighbours, and even our enemies, because we recognise that they are actually expressions of our own deeper self. If we saw through to the reality that there are no Jews, Christians or Muslims. There is no 'us versus them'. There is only us. This is the Gnostic vision that has inspired us to write this book.

In Part 1, 'The Bathwater,' we undertake a religious detox to flush the poison of Literalism out of our system. We take a good hard look at the supposedly 'sacred' scriptures of Judaism, Christianity and Islam, and demonstrate that these texts are far from divine. We show that they were not written or inspired by God, but created by men. And often by the worst kind of men. Politicians dressed up as priests.

In Part 2, 'The Baby,' we bring ancient Gnostic teachings to life, using modern language free from worn-out religious jargon. We give the timeless wisdom of awakening a make-over for the twenty-first century, so that you can experience gnosis, here and now, as you read this book. We want you to get the joke and understand for yourself why the Gnostic Jesus laughs.

2

A RELIGIOUS DETOX

The inhabitants of the earth are of two sorts.
Those with brains, but no religion,
and those with religion, but no brains.
— ABU'L-ALA AL MA'ARRI, TENTH-CENTURY ISLAMIC POET[1]

'Allahu Akbar'! The *muezzin* cries a wake-up call to the world. The prayer reverberates through your head as the plane plunges towards the earth. 'There is no God but Allah'. Oh the divine ecstasy of final surrender to the holy, triumphant, glorious will of Allah! 'Surrender' is the true meaning of 'Islam.' A true Muslim is one who has surrendered his entire being to Allah. And what greater surrender could there be than to shed one's blood in the great *jihad*? To become a martyr for Muhammad, may blessings be upon him! One last thought before the inferno of hell explodes around you. The unbelievers who deserve to die will boil in the flames, but you will be transfigured in glory! Noise. Screams. Pain. It is done. 'God is great!'

The Nightmare of Religion

9/11 was a wake-up call to the world. We need to wake up from the nightmare of religion. Because it was not just Islamic Literalism which led to the horrors of 9/11 and its brutal aftermath. Jewish and Christian Literalists also played their part. Let's look at the religious madness that has led to our present world crisis:

- On September 11, 2001, Islamic Literalists, believing they would each be rewarded by God in the afterlife with seventy-two virgins plus free passes to Heaven for their entire family, martyred themselves and murdered thousands of other people by crashing jets into the twin towers in New York.

- These Islamic Literalists were angry about the appropriation of Palestine by Jewish Literalists, whose sacred texts declare that God bequeathed this land to them.

- The Palestinian uprising was provoked when the Israeli prime minister walked around the Al-Aqsa mosque in Jerusalem. This is a sacred site to Islamic Literalists because Muhammad stopped there one night to meet Abraham, Moses and Jesus, whilst on a trip to Heaven on a magic flying horse.

- To support the Palestinian uprising, Islamic Literalists attacked the U.S. because Christian Literalists in America strongly support the expansion of Israel. These Christian Literalists believe that only when the Jews have returned to the 'Holy Land' will Christ come again to bring about the end of the world, which they fervently hope will happen soon.

- In response to the brutal attack by Islamic Literalists, the Christian Literalist president of America, ignoring the New Testament injunction to 'love your enemies' and 'turn the other cheek', announced a 'crusade' to protect the 'civilised world'. Terrifying their people with thoughts of crazed religious extremists armed with weapons of mass destruction, crazed religious extremists who actually *were* armed with weapons of mass destruction unleashed Biblical 'shock and awe'.

- In reaction Islamic Literalists, ignoring Mohammad's advice to 'repay evil with good because then someone who was your enemy will become your friend', started cutting people's heads off on the Internet.

- And on and on it goes. Yet, in the midst of this tragic farce which is tearing the world apart, all these different religious Literalists find consolation in something wonderful that allows them to withstand the endless cycle of suffering. They are absolutely certain they are pleasing God.

Literalist religion is the greatest threat to world peace in the twenty-first century. In all of the world's trouble hotspots—the Balkans, Chechnya, Cyprus, East Timor, Kashmir, Indonesia, Northern Ireland, Nigeria, Palestine, the Philippines, Sudan, the Middle East—religion is either the root cause of the trouble or one of the main contributing factors. In the West, we are told the danger is 'Islamic Fundamentalism', but it is religious Fundamentalism in all its forms that is the problem. And 'Fundamentalism' is no more than a new name for the extreme religious Literalism that has bedevilled us for centuries. The divinely sanctioned violence that threatens our world today is not a new phenomenon. Throughout history religious terrorism has been the norm.

Religion Is the Devil's Greatest Achievement

In our previous book *Jesus and the Lost Goddess*, we concluded that religion is the Devil's greatest achievement. We were being deliberately provocative, of course, because we certainly don't think there is some evil mega-being out there orchestrating all this chaos. But our point was serious. In our Western spiritual mythology the *diabolus* or Devil is the divider. He symbolises all that separates us in strife and prevents us uniting in love. And nothing is more horrendously divisive than Literalist religion. It is now, and always has been, a diabolical force of evil in the world.

It is easy to blame the current crisis on mad Muslims and to forget the horrors the West has perpetrated throughout history in the name of Christianity. Let us not forget the unspeakable suffering inflicted on Muslims and Jews during the Crusades. When Jerusalem fell to the crusaders they butchered more than seventy thousand Muslims in the Al-Aqsa mosque alone. They also burnt thousands of Jews alive in their synagogues. A Christian chronicler records 'our troops boiled adults in cooking-pots and impaled children on spits and devoured them grilled'.[2]

Let us recall the thousands of men, women and children condemned for heresy and burned alive by the Inquisition. Let us hold in our hearts those placed in the Torture Chair, with its wrought-iron mechanism for clamping the head still to enable the inquisitor to remove the heretic's tongue or teeth with ease, and its cunningly designed seat that allowed the insertion of torture instruments into the anus or vagina of the victim.

Let's not forget that the Catholic Church created the Inquisition in order to ethnically cleanse Spain of hundreds of thousands of Muslims and Jews, which it did with unimaginable brutality. The Inquisition then planned to put to death the three million inhabitants of the Netherlands simply because they had become Protestants, but fortunately it failed. One writer of the time declared the Inquisition to be a 'wild monster of such terrible mien that all of Europe trembles at the mere mention of its name'.[3]

But it was not just Europe that trembled before the torturers of the Holy Inquisition. When Columbus set out in his little boat he had red crusader crosses stitched to his sails. Columbus may have discovered the New World, but this was just a happy accident. He was actually looking for a way to sail around the world and attack the Muslim empire in the rear. When he discovered the Americas instead, Columbus wrote that he had found enough gold to recapture Jerusalem. In the New World the Spanish Inquisition repeated on an even grander scale the genocide they carried out so effectively in Europe. Hundreds of thousands, probably millions, of innocent indigenous Americans perished in unimaginable pain and suffering. They were burnt alive or tortured to death as a glorious testimony to the triumph of Christianity throughout the world.

Let us remember the relentless persecution of the Jews by Literalist Christians. Throughout Christian history Jews have been routinely burnt alive by zealous mobs with the full blessing of priests and popes. It was the Catholic Church in the thirteenth century who first forced the Jews to live in ghettos and to wear a yellow badge, a policy that the Vatican was still enforcing in the nineteenth century. In Eastern Europe the Inquisition used ovens to burn heretics, who were rubbed with grease and roasted alive. All that changed in the twentieth century was that the process was industrialised.

When the Fascists and Nazis started persecuting the Jews by humiliating them, depriving them of all rights, herding them into ghettos, killing and burning them, they were only doing what the Church had done for centuries. When they introduced their racial purity laws they argued that they were merely following the lead of Catholicism's most respected religious order, the Jesuits. As a member of the Fascist Grand Council in Italy announced:

> It comforts our souls to know that if, as Catholics, we became anti-Semites, we owe it to the teachings that the Church has promulgated over the past twenty centuries.[4]

Let's not forget that the Nazi SS who exterminated the Jews had emblazoned on their belt buckles the words 'God is with us'.

To those of us not afflicted with the insanity of religious Literalism, it seems impossible to understand how human beings could inflict such horrors on other human beings. But to those unfortunate enough to be in the grip of religious madness, these terrible crimes against humanity are seen in an entirely different way. They are righteous acts, required by God and justified by sacred scripture.

The burning to death of heretics was justified by a passage in *The Gospel of John*, which states:

> He who does not abide in me is cast off as a withered branch; men gather these branches, throw them into the fire and they are consumed.[5]

The persecution of the Jews was legitimised by the New Testament, which makes it quite clear that the Jews were responsible for killing Christ, were born of the Devil and constituted a synagogue of Satan.[6] The planned destruction of all Europe's Protestants and the mass murder of indigenous Americans was legitimised by the Old Testament, in which God orders his chosen people to butcher all those who stand in their divinely ordained way. God approves of ethnic cleansing. It says so in the Bible!

Fundamentalism

In 2000 we wrote in the concluding chapter of our book *Jesus and the Lost Goddess:*

> Feeling threatened and vulnerable, both Christian and Islamic Fundamentalists are growing edgy and excitable, and could do with a divinely sanctioned scrap to relieve the tension. There is nothing like holy conflict to galvanise support for religion—and Fundamentalists know it.

Our book hit the shelves as planes hit the twin towers. We are not prophets. It had been glaringly obvious for years that the great religions of the Western world were set on a collision course, because these faiths are becoming increasingly Fundamentalist.

Islamic Fundamentalists consider *none* of the existing Muslim states to be Islamic enough, not even Saudi Arabia, where Shari'a law demands amputation for simple theft, public beheading for adultery and sentences corrupters of the state to partial beheading followed by crucifixion. Some Christian Fundamentalists have aligned themselves with the Fascists and White Supremacists and advocate the wholesale murder of Jews, blacks and homosexuals. The born-again Christian Timothy McVeigh belonged to this particularly nasty strand of Christian Literalism and until 9/11 held the record for the largest peacetime bombing of civilians in America.

Some Jewish Fundamentalists condemn the very existence of modern Israel as sacrilege because they believe that only the Messiah should found a new Jewish state. They have made several attempts to bomb the Al-Aqsa Mosque in Jerusalem, because they want to build the Third Temple on its ruins. Their hero is a Jewish settler who entered the shrine of Abraham at Friday prayers and opened fire on Muslims with a machine gun. Another Jewish Fundamentalist gunned down the Israeli prime minister for even daring to talk about swapping some of the Jew's sacred land for peace with the Palestinians.

What causes Fundamentalists of all religions to be so extreme is that they have an absolute certainty that they are right and everyone else is wrong. And their absolute certainty comes from the fact that they believe that their opinions are God's opinions. Human opinions are relative, but God's opinions must, by definition, be absolute. There can be no argument with God. God's laws must be enforced. End of debate. This is why Fundamentalism, like Fascism, has nowhere to go but war.

The great irony is that Fundamentalists of different persuasions share much in common. Their vision of life and how to live it is driven by the same needs and neuroses. What they hate in the other is a projection of what they hate in themselves. If they had been brought up in a different culture they would be Fundamentalists of another persuasion. This was dramatically illustrated after 9/11, when Christian Fundamentalists declared that the attack on the twin towers was divine retribution on America for tolerating feminism and homosexuality. It became immediately obvious that these so-called Christians had more in common with the Taliban than with the majority of compassionate people in their own country.

Two of the most prominent voices of America's religious right, televangelists Jerry Falwell and Pat Robertson, declared live on TV that God allowed 9/11 to happen because he was 'mad' at America. Falwell declared:

> Pagans and the abortionists and the feminists and the gays and the lesbians . . . all of them who have tried to secularize America, I point the finger in their face and say 'you helped this happen'.

At the end of Falwell's rant, Robertson responded, 'Well, I totally concur'.[7] So if you were wondering where God was on the morning of

9/11, now you know. He was up there in those planes helping Islamic extremists commit mass murder because he's mad at America for being so tolerant!

Fundamentalists hate the modern world. But this should not surprise us. Literalists have consistently opposed progress. The Church opposed the abolition of slavery because it is legitimised in both the Old and New Testaments. It opposed the introduction of anaesthetic during childbirth because the Bible says that women are meant to suffer whilst giving birth. It opposed the introduction of inoculation because it is up to God to decide who lives and who dies. Today the Catholic church condemns the use of condoms, which has led to millions contracting AIDS, a dogma which is the cause of so much avoidable suffering that it must rank as one of the greatest evils of all times.

Yet Fundamentalists aren't opposed to all that modernity offers. After all, Fundamentalists of all persuasions are more than happy to arm themselves to the teeth with the poison fruit of modernity: deadly weaponry. The Taliban may have detested video players, tape recorders and televisions, but they liked nothing better than riding into battle on the back of a Toyota pick-up armed with a Kalashnikov rifle.

Religious Fundamentalism is an irrational pathology which leads otherwise decent men and women to become enemies of open-mindedness and big-heartedness, and enlist in the service of divinely sanctioned bigotry. Fundamentalism creates dangerously self-righteous people who turn against those who espouse the truly spiritual values of love, tolerance and understanding. Fundamentalists particularly loathe members of their own faith who suggest dialogue with the other. A Hindu Fundamentalist murdered Mohandas Gandhi. An Islamic Fundamentalist murdered Malcolm X. A Christian Fundamentalist murdered John Lennon. A Jewish Fundamentalist murdered Yitzhak Rabin.

But Fundamentalists aren't just monsters. They are often moved by their strong religious convictions to great generosity and compassion. But this is strictly limited to 'us' and not 'them'. Before the Israeli army assassinated him, the wheelchair-bound Sheikh Ahmed Yassin was the 'spiritual' inspiration of Hamas, the Palestinian terrorist/liberation group (delete according to your prejudices), and a well-respected figure within his own community responsible for setting up schools and social programmes. But he was also responsible for the murder of Israeli children.

Fundamentalism is a fundamental misunderstanding of history, spirituality and the nature of reality, which causes ordinary people to commit terrible acts for pious reasons. This is the story of a kind and thoughtful gentleman called Anwar Shaikh. Now in his seventies, he is known for his books that criticise the Qur'an. For this brave work he has been branded an apostate who 'deserves to be killed' by Islamic Fundamentalists.[8] But in 1947, during the partition of India and Pakistan, Anwar was himself a young Islamic Fundamentalist possessed by religious zeal. Determined to please Allah by revenging the murder of his Muslim brothers, he went into the streets of Lahore and battered to death three innocent Sikhs, two with a club and the third with a spade. He writes:

You know a madness gripped us in 1947. A madness. I was a part of it. When I was killing them all I could think of was revenge. I knew I was destined for the Islamic paradise, where scores of Houris were waiting for me. Seventy virgins with upright breasts and Allah would give me enough virility for eighty-four years. What more could a young man want? So you see, not only was I unafraid, but even looking forward to continuous sex in Heaven. You don't believe me. Please believe me. I believed it at the time. I was young and impressionable.

I kept thinking, as I still do, that I have destroyed three innocent lives. They might have been alive had it not been for me. I don't even know who they were. And I began to think. All this happened because of religion. I had never given up reading the Qur'an. Now I read it with wide-open eyes. One day I read something I had read hundreds of times before: 'O Believers, do not walk in front of the prophet. Do not raise your voice above his,' And I asked myself why? Why should Allah raise one human above others? Well, once you ask why, you can never stop. The spell was broken.

Whatever happens now I will die confident in my humanist and rationalist beliefs, and if my writings have weaned even a few dozen people away from religious hatred and fanaticism I feel I will have partially redeemed myself, even though nothing, nothing can bring my three victims back to life. I don't worry for myself. I worry for others. Look what we did to each other with our bare hands. With nuclear weapons they could destroy everything in the name of religion. They might, you know. They might.[9]

Armageddon

Anwar Shaikh's plaintive warning needs to be heard, because Fundamentalists could indeed destroy the world. In Pakistan Islamic Fundamentalists boast that in ten years time they will control the army and so command nuclear weapons.[10] But we don't need to wait for Fundamentalists to get their fingers on the nuclear button, we've had that for decades in the U.S., where Christian Fundamentalists sincerely believe that their divine mission is to co-operate with God's great plan for the end of the world, which they interpret as a coming nuclear holocaust.

One week before announcing his candidacy for president in 1980 Ronald Reagan told a reporter, 'We may be the generation that sees Armageddon'. Jerry Falwell told a reporter that President Reagan agreed with him on Bible prophecy and had said, 'Jerry, we are heading very fast for Armageddon now'. Reagan's Secretary of Defence, Caspar Weinberger, told students at Harvard University: 'I have read the Book of Revelation, and, yes, I believe the world is going to end . . . and every day I think that time is running out'.[11] At the time Weinberger was head of the Pentagon and second in command of America's nuclear weapons. Such beliefs by those in possession of such diabolical power raises the alarming possibility of the Biblical warning of the end of the world becoming a self-fulfilling prophecy.

A recent report showed that almost four out of ten Americans believe that when the Bible prophesies that the Earth will be destroyed by fire, it's predicting a nuclear war.[12] But, according to some Christian Fundamentalists, this glorious day can't come until the Jews who were scattered throughout the world are re-established in the Old Testament Kingdom of David. Then a pleasant plain outside Jerusalem called Armageddon will become the site of the last great battle between good and evil and Jesus will come again to wrap things up.

The desire to help fulfil Biblical prophecy has led Christian Fundamentalists in the U.S. to form an unholy alliance with Jewish Fundamentalists intent on re-establishing the mythical Kingdom of David. But this alliance only goes so far. For Fundamentalist Christians, once the Kingdom of David is re-established the news is not so great for the Jews. When the End Days come it is only Christians (of the right denomination of course) who will ascend to Heaven. The Jews, like the rest of us, must convert or burn.

Christian Fundamentalists are increasingly apocalyptic. *Left Behind* is one of a series of books that exploit the Fundamentalist belief that we are heading for 'The Rapture'. This is the moment when all born-again Christians will be lifted off planet Earth to Heaven. While this may sound like the plot of a sci-fi B Movie, the authors are deadly serious and have sold over sixty million copies in the U.S. On what remains of the blasted and radioactive planet Earth 'gentle Jesus' will set up his torture camp called Hell. Here those of us who are unfortunate enough to have been 'left behind' will be tormented for eternity. In the light of this it comes as no surprise that Christian Fundamentalist politicians see no point in cooperating to prevent global warming. They believe it is going to get a lot hotter than even the environmentalists can imagine!

It seems incredible that people can get away with such nonsense in this day and age, especially as Christianity has been bleating on that 'The End is Nigh' for two thousand years and it still hasn't happened. In the gospels Jesus repeatedly assures his disciples that the end of the world will come in their lifetime. But here we are two thousand years later and none of the things that Jesus predicted have happened.[13] To continue to peddle this prophecy when Jesus himself got it wrong doesn't make sense. But, then, Fundamentalists don't need things to make sense. They have willingly abandoned rationality in favour of blind faith in old books.

Literacy, Literature and Literalism

Fundamentalism manifests in many different forms, but it can be reduced to one very simple idea. Sacred scripture is the infallible Word of God. The name 'Fundamentalism' was coined after the publication of a book called *The Fundamentals*, by a group of conservative American priests in the early twentieth century.[14] The book's central axiom is that everything the Bible says is true, historical and has literally happened as described. It is not possible to believe anything less and still be a Christian. Viewed in this way Fundamentalism is clearly not new, for this could hardly be described as a novel way of viewing the Bible.

Christian Literalists have taught for centuries that the Bible is literally true. For nearly two millennia the Church controlled every aspect of an individual's life, right down to what they were allowed to think, and justified this with reference to 'sacred scripture'. As every other way of looking at life had been violently suppressed, there was no alternative to the Christian worldview. There was no way out of the circular thinking that states: 'Everything in this book is true. How do I know? Because it says so in this book'.

Prior to the invention of books, in oral cultures traditions underwent subtle changes as they were transmitted, just as in the game of Chinese Whispers. Change was inevitable if only because of the imperfection of human memory. Outdated, inappropriate or irrelevant ideas could be discreetly dropped and new ones incorporated. But with the invention of writing this flexibility was lost. When traditions came to be 'written in stone', they became immutable.

No sooner had humans begun writing than God Himself started publishing. Literalism's big idea was born. God writes books. He might occasionally use a secretary, such as Moses or Muhammad, but nonetheless he likes to communicate with his subjects via the written word. A new genre called 'sacred scriptures' was created. Sacred scriptures are special and off-limits to the kind of criticism that might be applied to any other piece of literature.

Human beings had long known that words were power, but when they invented writing they learnt that the written word can wield power for eternity. Literalist religion is fixated by the written word. Moses came down the mountain with written laws. The Jews are known as the People of the Book. Christianity famously declares, 'In the beginning was the Word, and the Word was with God and *the Word was God*'. Muhammad was illiterate, but Allah brought him a written message, and taught him to read and write.

It soon became compulsory for every religion to have its sacred text and they quickly multiplied. As long as people lived inside a hermetically sealed culture, with only one religion and one sacred text, everything was fine. But wherever cultures collided it soon became apparent that there were many different sacred scriptures inspired by many different gods saying a variety of contradictory things. By definition only one of these religions can be the one true religion. But which one?

It is to prevent people asking such questions that Fundamentalists want to enforce the reading of only their special book. This is an old ploy that has been used by Literalists for millennia. The Roman Church made huge bonfires of Pagan libraries and destroyed all the works of those 'heretics' who had the audacity to challenge them. It continued to use Latin for centuries after it ceased to be the language of the people to ensure that no one spotted the inconsistencies with which the Bible is riddled. To guarantee that the Church's interpretation of the Bible would not be questioned it was made illegal for anyone but clergy to read it. Any layperson caught in possession of a Bible was executed.

It was only after the Protestant Reformation that the Bible was translated into the common tongue, due to the heroic struggle of brave individuals who faced torture and execution for their efforts. The foundation stone of the Reformation was the right of all men and women to read the Bible in their own language. The outcome was exactly as the Church had feared. When people began to study the texts for themselves the idea that the Bible was the infallible Word of God became increasingly questioned. Now, after three centuries of careful scholarship, it has become obvious that the Bible is actually just another eclectic, contradictory and quirky piece of archaic literature.

Therapy for the Western Soul

It is time to break the spell of the written word. Sacred texts are meant to be just the media, but with Literalism the media has become the message. These so-called 'sacred scriptures' are dangerous documents that have held us under their thrall for too long. Devotion to a book is simply another form of idolatry. These books are not the Word of God, they are the words of men, and often men with a patently political agenda. It is time we woke up from the nightmare of Literalism, and even some within the Christian Church are beginning to admit as much. The Reverend John Shelby Spong, Bishop of Newark, writes:

> I look at the authority of the Scriptures as one who has been both nurtured by and then disillusioned with the literal Bible. My devotion to the Bible was so intense that it led me into a study that finally obliterated any possibility that the Bible could be related to on a literal basis. . . . A literal Bible presents me with far more problems than assets. It offers me a God I cannot respect, much less worship. [15]

Our sacred texts purport to be the collective memories of our deepest past. They claim to tell us who we are and where we came from. They represent our collective identity as surely as our individual memories represent our individual identity. Now imagine for a moment that you woke up one morning and everything you thought you knew about yourself was untrue. Your name was not your true name. Your parents were not your real parents. Your whole identity was a fabrication. This is how it is with our so-called sacred texts, for they are not what they purport to be. They have been wilfully distorted, badly remembered and wrongly interpreted. They have mangled our memories and the outcome has been disastrous. We are victims of an enormous 'False Memory Syndrome' and are in desperate need of collective therapy.

People go into therapy because they can no longer go forward in their lives. They often discover that their present problems arise out of past trauma, and that in order to go forward they must first go back. We suggest that the same holds true for cultures. We must face up to the truth about our past. We have a terrible history of religious intolerance and have inflicted the most atrocious sufferings on our neighbours in the name of God. If we don't learn from our mistakes, we will most certainly repeat them.

The horrors of 9/11 revealed that Literalism remains rife in the world. Our response is to mount a full-scale assault on the pernicious idea that God writes books. Armed with the latest discoveries from modern historians and archaeologists, we intend to undermine the very foundations of Literalist religion. In the next three chapters we will demonstrate that the 'sacred scriptures' of Judaism, Christianity and Islam are not special 'holy' books. They are just *books*.

THE WORD OF GOD?

God's Bible? Look at it.
It was made as a lie by the false pen of scribes.
—*THE BOOK OF JEREMIAH*[1]

Six thousand years ago God created the universe in six days and then took a day off. He made Adam out of dust and breath, and then he made Eve from Adam's rib to keep him company. God kept Adam and Eve in a garden, but one day they broke the rules so he had to kick them out. Adam and Eve had kids, but one of them killed his own brother. This was just the start of a series of disappointments for God. In fact, human beings turned out to be such a bad idea that God sent a flood to destroy them. Noah and his family were saved, and when the flood receded they went forth and peopled the Earth.

In 2000 BCE Noah's descendant Abraham moved to Canaan, where he became the founding patriarch of the Jewish people. But a few centuries later the Jews were enslaved by the Egyptians. Then, in an event called the Exodus, they miraculously escaped from Egypt under the leadership of Moses. The Jews now wandered around the desert for forty years before finally arriving back at the land that God had promised them in Palestine. Unfortunately, this was occupied by Canaanites, but with God's help the Jews managed to clear the land under the leadership of Joshua.

The Jews went on to create a powerful state under King Saul and his successor, King David, who ruled a united monarchy that included both the north and south of Palestine. David's kingdom reached all the way to Egypt in the south, the Euphrates in the east and Samaria and Galilee in the north. David's son Solomon built a lavish temple to the God who had made the Jews such a big success. Solomon was really clever. But sadly he forgot that the Jews were special because they only worshipped the one true God. Angry at Solomon for worshipping other gods, God punished the Jews by allowing the Babylonians to enslave them. About fifty years later he relented and the Jews returned to Jerusalem where they built another temple. And here they lived in happy prosperity right down to the time of Alexander the Great.

The sacred scripture that Jews call the Tanakh and Christians call the Old Testament tells the story of the Jews from Adam to Alexander. The message is clear. The Jews are an extremely ancient nation with a well-documented history going back millennia. This claim is confirmed by the Jewish calendar. In Europe at the time we are writing it is the year 2004, but in Jerusalem it is a whopping 5764. To put this date into perspective, this puts the beginning of Jewish history over thirteen hundred years before the Egyptian pyramids. It's all very impressive, until you start looking for the evidence to justify it.

Travellers to Egypt will have seen the vast temples and impressive monuments that litter the landscape. Texts, sculpture and artefacts testify to a sophisticated culture that really did endure for millennia. Much the same can be said for Mesopotamia, the so-called 'cradle of civilisation'. So, what have we discovered in Palestine that dates from these early periods? Nothing but the typical garbage and potsherds of a few wandering nomads and pastoralists.

It has sometimes been argued that Palestine was invaded so often that nothing aboveground has survived. However, sub-surface investigations have also revealed nothing of significance. No grand palaces, temples or dressed stone buildings that would justify the claims of a grand empire centred in Jerusalem have been found. If they had they would now be on the immensely lucrative Bible-tourist trail. But they aren't.

It has been obvious for centuries that stories such as Adam and Eve are myths with no basis in history. But what about the rest of the Tanakh? Is that history? The evidence suggests not. Rather the Tanakh is a collection of myths and legends. And to be fair to the Tanakh it never actually claims to be history. In fact you won't find the word *history* anywhere in its pages, because the word did not even exist in Hebrew. We have projected back onto these ancient texts our modern idea of history as distinct from mythology, a concept that simply did not exist at the time.

Thomas Thompson, professor of Old Testament studies at the University of Copenhagen, writes:

> Today we no longer have a history of Israel. Not only have Adam and Eve and the flood story passed over to mythology, but we can no longer talk about a time of the patriarchs. These images have no place in descriptions of the real historical past. We know them only as story and what we know about such stories does not encourage us to treat them as if they were or were ever meant to be historical. There is no evidence of a United Monarchy, no evidence of a capital in Jerusalem or of any coherent, unified political force that dominated western Palestine, let alone an empire of the size the legends describe. We do not have evidence for the existence of kings named Saul, David or Solomon; nor do we have evidence for any temple at Jerusalem in this early period.[2]

Israel Finkelstein, director of archaeology at Tel Aviv University, and his co-writer, Neil Silberman, describe the Bible as 'no more historical that the Homeric saga of Odysseus or Aeneas's founding of Rome. The biblical narrative is so thoroughly filled with inconsistencies and anachronisms . . . that it must be considered more of an historical novel than an accurate historical chronicle'.[3]

The Tanakh's A-List Celebrities

Let's have a look at some of the heroes of the Tanakh to see if there is any evidence of them actually being real historical people.

Abraham

Abraham is considered to be the great patriarch of the Jewish nation. He is also an important figure for Christians and Muslims. Evidence for his existence is crucial to the idea that these three religions might all be 'Sons of Abraham', as is often claimed. According to Biblical chronology Abraham moved to Canaan about 2100 BCE. But this is impossible as Abraham is said to have come from the Chaldean city of Ur that did not exist until after 1000 BCE. Prior to this date there were no Chaldeans. *Genesis* tells us that Abraham's son Isaac sought help from Abimelech, the king of the Philistines, yet the Philistines were not a presence in the area until after 1200 BCE. And although the camel is mentioned frequently in the stories of Abraham and the other patriarchs, the domestication of the camel did not happen until around 1000 BCE. The camel caravan described frequently in the Tanakh, with its cargo of 'gum, balm, and myrrh', did not become widespread until the eighth century BCE.

Moses

There is no evidence for the existence of Moses. Although he is portrayed as an influential member of the Egyptian royal household, he is not mentioned in any Egyptian record. Nor is there any evidence to support the idea that the Jews were ever held captive in Egypt or that they made an exodus from the country under Moses' command. The Egyptians chronicled their history in great detail but make no mention of any captive Jews. Amongst the hundreds of thousands of Egyptian monumental inscriptions, tomb inscriptions and papyri, there is complete silence about the '600,000 men on foot, besides women and children' who *The Book of Exodus* tells us escaped from Pharaoh's armies.[4]

The story of Moses, with its many miracles, has all the hallmarks of a myth. The account of Moses' birth is a retelling of the myth of the birth of Sargon the Great, the king of Akkad, which is known in a number of variations from the early sixth century BCE. Like Moses, the child Sargon is 'set in a basket of rushes' and 'cast into the river', from which he is later rescued by an influential woman. Similar Greek stories tell of the child Dionysus confined in a chest and thrown into the river Nile. These probably all go back to Egyptian stories which tell of Osiris confined in a chest and thrown in the Nile.

Joshua

According to the Tanakh Joshua is the great general who leads the devastating invasion of the 'Promised Land' of Canaan, but evidence for this is non-existent. Indeed, the invasion of Canaan by Jews escaping the Egyptians is an historical impossibility. From the fourteenth to the twelfth centuries BCE, when the exodus is supposed to have occurred, Canaan was a province of Egypt, so the Jews would not have escaped from Egyptian rule at all, but merely passed from one Egyptian territory to another. *The Book of Joshua*, which relates the Jews supposed invasion of the Promised Land, makes no mention of Egyptians in Canaan, when the area should have been crawling with them.[5]

In 1999 Professor Ze'ev Herzog of the University of Tel Aviv's Institute of Archaeology published an article in the Israeli newspaper *Ha'aretz*, entitled 'Deconstructing the Walls of Jericho'.[6] In it he declares that the exodus from Egypt, the invasion by Joshua and the famous walls of Jericho are all without historical foundation. He laments:

> These facts have been known for years, but Israel is a stubborn people and nobody wants to hear about it.[7]

Although his views are widely shared in the academic community, Herzog's article caused a furore, with secular Israelis responding the most violently. The reason is simple. They immediately recognised that the modern state of Israel would be seriously compromised if its claim to the land turned out to be based on a mere myth.

David

What about David? Did he exist? In 1993 an inscription was found at Tel Dan that referred to a 'king of the dynasty of David'. No previous reference to David had ever been found outside of the Tanakh. The finding became world news and made the front page of the *New York Times* and the cover of *Time* magazine. Here, at last, was the first ever independent verification of one of the Bible's leading players. Here was evidence for the historical existence of King David, who ruled over the united monarchy of Israel and Judea. The famous singer of psalms, slayer of Goliath and forefather of Jesus. But ten years of careful investigation has revealed that the inscription is not evidence for the existence of David at all.

For a start, the translation 'king of the dynasty of David' gives you an impression of an imposing inscription that might have adorned a mighty palace. In fact it is a scribbling of six letters on a piece of stone—*bytdwd*. The first word claimed to be 'king' has been reconstructed from just one letter, so it could actually mean any number of things. As there are no vowels in written Hebrew these have to be inserted, which leads to many possible translations of the inscription. The word translated 'David' could also be translated 'beloved', 'uncle' or even 'kettle'![8] It could equally be the name of a place called *Beth Dod*. Another recently discovered inscription has also been declared to refer to the 'House of David', but the Hebrew on this inscription is different from the one at Tel Dan.[9] What is going on here?

The problem is that when something is discovered that could, at a stretch, be seen as corroborating something in the Bible, a whole bunch of a priori beliefs ensure that the evidence is made to fit the theory. One modern scholar considers the idea that the Tel Dan inscription refers to David as just wishful thinking, a classic case of scholars working back from the Bible rather than forward from the evidence.[10] Another scholar is 'convinced that the published fragments in fact belong not to one but to two different, related inscriptions'.[11] Other scholars have found indications that the inscriptions are forgeries and the whole subject is now under investigation by the Israeli Department of Antiquities. The antiquities market is littered with such fakes because there are so many wealthy and powerful groups with a desperate desire to prove that the Bible is true. Any discovery that appears to validate the Bible is guaranteed to make world news, but when it is later debunked it rarely makes the back pages.

Even if David did exist he cannot possibly have been the mighty king described in the Tanakh. At the time when he is said to have ruled over a large and sophisticated civilisation, the real world of archaeology has revealed 'only a few dozen very small scattered hamlets and villages' supporting farmers who 'numbered hardly more than two thousand persons'.[12] If David existed at all he can have been little more than a hill country chieftain. As one recent commentator observes:

> The chief disagreement nowadays is between those who hold that David was a petty hilltop chieftain whose writ extended no more than a few miles in any direction, and a small but vociferous band of 'biblical minimalists' who maintain that he never existed at all.[13]

Solomon

So what about David's son Solomon? He is said to have had a harem of three hundred concubines and seven hundred wives, which included Egyptian, Moabite, Ammonite, Edomite, Zidonian and Hittite princesses. According to the Bible he ruled a vast empire. He had a fleet of ships that traded with the Egyptians and Mesopotamians on equal terms. He was so wealthy that his soldiers had shields of gold. He was so famous for his wisdom that even the Queen of Sheba paid him a visit. He spent thirteen years building a palace to house the Ark of the Covenant, and embellished it with gold and precious jewels. Surely somebody somewhere should have heard of him.

Yet there is no evidence for the existence of Solomon. It is said that he was married to the daughter of an Egyptian pharaoh, but no reference to this dynastic alliance has been found in any of the Egyptian records. His name is not mentioned in any contemporary Middle Eastern text. But none of this should surprise us, as at this time Jerusalem was not the capital of a vast empire. It was actually just a small village.

Around 1000 BCE the highlands of Judea contained no public buildings, palaces, store-houses or temples. Signs of any sophisticated kind of record keeping, such as writing, seals and seal impressions are almost completely absent. Almost no luxury items, imported pottery or jewellery have been found. The population of the entire region can have been no more than forty-five thousand people. Whoever was living in the Palestinian highlands at this time, they were not the people the writers of the Tanakh have put there.

The Myth of Return

The Tanakh would have us believe that there once was a mighty kingdom of Israel with its great capital Jerusalem. But there is very little evidence concerning either Israel or Jerusalem. The first we hear of Jerusalem is in Egyptian curse texts dated from 1810 to 1770 BCE, where it is listed among several towns in Palestine together with the names of their chieftains. Our earliest mention of Israel is in the so-called 'Israel Stele' of Pharaoh Merneptah, dated from 1207 BCE. It says simply: 'Israel is desolate; its seed is no more'.[14] There is a dispute about whether the name 'Israel' refers to a people or simply a person, but it is ironic that our earliest mention of Israel tells us that Israel no longer exists!

A little later we have an inscription from the time of Pharaoh Sheshonq, c. 945 to 924 BCE, and a little later an inscription of Shalmaneser III, c. 853 BCE, which refers to a land of *sir-il-la-a-a*.[15] This meagre handful of inscriptions might as well be about *la-la-land* for all that they can tell us about the Israel of the Tanakh. Additionally, none of these inscriptions was found in Palestine or was written by the people to whom they refer, which would at least be evidence of their own high culture. Instead they were written by their traditional overlords and describe villages in impoverished regions under their control.

There is a further problem with the names 'Jerusalem' and 'Israel'. Their derivation tells a history that is completely at odds with the Tanakh. The word *Israel* means 'fighter for El' who was a Canaanite god. Jerusalem is named after another Canaanite god called Shalem. But according to the Tanakh, the Canaanites were the deadly enemies of the Israelites. What is going on here? The answer is simple but shocking.

All the evidence now points to the Israelites being indigenous inhabitants of Canaan. The Biblical story that they arrived in Palestine from Egypt is a myth. The Israelites did not come from somewhere else, they were already there. This view is now widely shared by scholars. One modern archaeologist states:

> The Israelites never were in Egypt. They never came from abroad. The whole chain is broken. It is not an historical one. It is a later legendary reconstruction . . . of a history that never happened.[16]

Reliefs at Karnak in Egypt do not show any distinction of hairstyle or clothing between Israelites and Canaanites, so the Egyptians clearly did not discriminate between the two. The evidence from digs all over Palestine has revealed a seamless continuity between the two cultures. We cannot point to a Canaanite layer here superseded by an Israelite layer there. The Israelites emerged from the indigenous Canaanites and were not invaders, as the Tanakh claims.

The story of the Jews return from captivity in Egypt is a myth. And so is the story of their return from captivity in Babylon. Although we now consider the Jews and Israelites to be the same, in ancient times they were two distinct peoples and bitter enemies. The Israelites lived in northern Palestine and had their capital at Samaria. The Judeans (a.k.a. Jews) lived in southern Palestine and had their capital at Jerusalem.

When the Assyrians invaded Palestine in 733 BCE the Israelites resisted and were ruthlessly punished. Their city of Samaria was levelled to the ground and the population taken into slavery. The Judeans, however, offered the Assyrians their support, and after Israel was liquidated Judea began to flourish as a new Assyrian province. The population of Jerusalem increased to some fifteen thousand people.

A century and a half later Assyrian power began to crumble and the Babylonians took control of the Assyrian empire, including Palestine. In 587 BCE the Babylonians destroyed Jerusalem and its inhabitants were deported into slavery. The Judeans (a.k.a. Jews) met exactly the same fate as the Israelites (a.k.a. Samaritans). The state of Judea ceased to exist as totally as that of her former rival Israel.

In the mid-fifth century the Persians succeeded the Babylonians and took control of Palestine. The Bible recounts that the Persian king allowed the Israelites to return from exile in Babylon to Jerusalem, but this cannot be true. If the Israelites had returned 'home' it would have been to their capital city of Samaria and not Jerusalem! As a modern scholar writes:

> Whatever people were transported or returned to Palestine they certainly were not Israelites.[17]

No empire would have allowed a people to return home, as this would have defeated the whole purpose of deportation. Removing whole peoples and resettling them elsewhere was a brutal but routine practise in the ancient world that allowed empire builders to exercise total control over their subjects. There is historical evidence of 157 acts of deportation from the Assyrian period and 36 from Babylonian records. A total of over a million displaced people has been calculated for this brief period.

The 'Return of the Israelites' is a legend. The Israelites and the Jews were both deported around the ancient world during this period and where they went we have no idea. Other peoples were settled in the area and adapted some of the indigenous mythology to legitimise their claims to the land. Their descendants would later come to think of themselves as Israelites and Jews, but originally they were neither.

The Jews and the Greeks

At the end of the fourth century BCE Alexander the Great conquered Palestine and the Persian overlords were replaced by Greek overlords. Prior to this, in the fifth and fourth centuries BCE, survey data from settlements shows that the population of Judea was only thirty thousand people. The great scholar Bickerman described Jerusalem at the time of Alexander as 'the obscure abode of an insignificant tribe'.[18] This explains why there is no mention of the Jews in all of the Greek texts prior to Alexander. The Greeks were fascinated by 'barbarians', and delighted in recording their funny little habits in numerous works. They would undoubtedly have recorded something about the Jews had they been significant, but as one scholar writes:

> Nothing so far has disproved the contention that the classical Greeks did not even know the name of the Jews.[19]

Even in the first century CE the Jewish historian Josephus was unable to find references to Jews in Greek literature before Alexander the Great. As a modern scholar explains:

> In reality, we may conclude from this that the political and economic significance of the little temple state of Judea in the hill-country between the Dead Sea and the coastal plain was too slight to attract the attention of historians. Why should a Greek author, at a time when the whole fabulous Orient was open to his inquiry, concentrate on a Lilliputian place in the arid mountains?[20]

After the death of Alexander in 325 BCE his general Ptolemy ruled Palestine from Egypt. The next century and a half saw momentous change in Palestine as Greek technology and customs were introduced into the region. Coinage replaced barter. Agriculture was revolutionised by artificial irrigation, waterwheels, the plough, the wine-press and other similar implements. Now Jerusalem really did become a city 'skilled in many crafts', as one of the Jewish writers of the time puts it.[21] In this same period there was an explosion of Jewish literature. For the first time in the history of this region we have the beginnings of a high culture capable of creating and sustaining a literate class.

As befits a flourishing Hellenistic city there was a gymnasium, or Greek university, in the middle of Jerusalem from at least the second century BCE. *The Book of the Maccabees* tells us that it was so popular that the priests would hurry off to study there, ignoring their priestly duties.[22] In the gymnasium Jews received the standard Greek education, copying out passages from Homer and Plato, and studying the histories of Thucydides and Herodotus. The eastern Mediterranean was fast losing its status as a cultural desert.

From the beginning of the second century BCE Palestine produced many famous philosophers, poets, satirists and rhetoricians, some of whom even became friends and advisors to influential Roman statesmen, such as Pompey, Brutus and Cicero. The Jews had finally arrived on the world stage as a sophisticated people. But, ironically, they had only achieved this through an education that was thoroughly Greek.

Almost all of the Jewish literature produced in this period is written in Greek. The Jews wrote in Greek and thought in Greek. And yet the Jews were not Greeks and never could be, no matter how hard they aspired. The Greeks had divided the whole world into two mutually exclusive categories: Greeks and barbarians. In response, the Jews divided the world into Jews and Gentiles, and produced a body of literature that proved, at least to their own satisfaction, that the Jews were not only equal to the Greeks, they were better.

The Jewish Fantasy Factory

No sooner had the Jews assimilated their Greek education than they began to give a novel account of how they had come by it. They had not learnt from the Greeks. It was the other way around. In 220 BCE the Jewish writer Hermippus recorded his opinion that Pythagoras, the first man in the Greek world to be called a philosopher, had actually acquired all his wisdom from the Jews.[23] Aristobulus, writing in the middle of the second century BCE, added that Plato had borrowed his ideas from Moses.[24] In the first century CE Josephus claimed that 'the wisest of the Greeks', including Plato, Pythagoras, Anaxagoras and the Stoics, had 'learned their conceptions of God from principles with which Moses supplied them'.[25]

But how could Greek philosophers have had access to the Hebrew

Scriptures centuries before they were translated into Greek? Aristobulus assures his readers that these books were available in Greece, but there is no evidence of this.[26] The first quotation of the Tanakh by a Greek writer can be dated to no earlier than the middle of the first century CE.[27] Indeed, the Tanakh says itself that Greece was one of the nations that had not heard of the fame of the Lord.[28]

According to the Jewish writer Eupolemus, however, the Greeks even owed their knowledge of the alphabet to Moses. He had taught it first to the Jews, who then taught it to the Phoenicians, who in turn taught it to the Greeks.[29] Artapanus, another Jewish writer, tells us that Moses acquired the name Mousaios from the Greeks, became the teacher of Orpheus and conferred a whole host of benefits upon mankind, including the invention of ships, mechanisms for stone construction, weaponry, hydraulic engines, implements of warfare and, of course, philosophy.[30] In Egypt Moses' achievements were even more spectacular. He taught hieroglyphics to the Egyptian priests, divided the nation into the thirty-six nomes, assigned to each the god it was to worship, and was named 'Hermes' because of his ability to interpret sacred writings.[31]

During the Hellenistic period there was no end to the Jews' delight in rewriting history and playing one-upmanship with the Greeks, Egyptians and their other powerful rivals. The whole of the Hellenistic world was obsessed with astrology, and according to Eupolemus it was Abraham who discovered it. He taught it to the Phoenicians, explaining to them the movements of the sun and the moon and a host of other matters.[32] Abraham also journeyed to Egypt and dwelt with the priests of Heliopolis, where he taught them about astrology and a range of additional subjects.[33] In Artapanus' version of this tale, Abraham becomes the mentor of the Pharaoh himself.[34]

These are not the only fantastic stories cooked up by Hellenistic Jews to make themselves feel good. Josephus tells the wonderful story of how, when Alexander arrived in Jerusalem, he was so dazzled by the sight of the Jewish people clad in their white garments that he fell to his knees in front of the High Priest. Turning to his astonished generals he explained that here was the man he had seen in his dream in Macedonia who had first urged him to conquer Persia.[35] The dumbstruck Alexander is then shown *The Book of Daniel*, which had miraculously predicted the fall of Persia at the hands of a Greek.[36] It's a cracking tale and has been believed to be true throughout Christian history. But it is entirely without historical foundation. Nowadays no scholar has a good word to say about it, with verdicts ranging from 'silly' to 'outright fabrication'.[37]

In fact Alexander never went to Jerusalem. Greek historians make no mention of any such visit.[38] And Alexander could not have been shown *The Book of Daniel*, as it was not written until a century and a half after his death![39] Although *Daniel* claims to be written in the sixth century BCE, it was actually composed centuries later. The Pagan scholar Porphyry first demonstrated this in the third century CE. Using careful textual analysis he demonstrated that *Daniel* was written in the second century BCE, during the Jewish Maccabean revolt.[40] Today it is accepted that Porphyry was right.

The Book of Daniel is a typical example of a genre called 'prophecy after the event'. In this genre the appearance is created that a text has uncannily predicted the future, in this case the triumph of Alexander, but actually the prophecy has been written centuries after the events it pretends to predict have actually happened. The real reference of such 'prophecies' is to the present. They are meant to impress the readership of the time and give a brand-new text an aura of antiquity and supernatural legitimacy. This genre became extremely popular in the Jewish fantasy factory, and was later used by Christians to great effect.[41]

Another famous story created by Hellenistic Jews relates how the Greek version of the Hebrew Scriptures came to be written. A Jewish text called *The Letter of Aristeas* explains that Ptolemy I sent a message to the Jews saying that he wished to add a Greek translation of the Tanakh to his illustrious new library at Alexandria. The Jews responded by sending seventy-two famous sages who immediately set to work and miraculously produced seventy-two identical Greek texts, thus demonstrating how faithful the translation was to its Hebrew original. It came to be called the Septuagint, after the seventy sages. At the conclusion of a week of banquets held by Ptolemy in honour of the seventy-two Jewish sages, the Greek philosophers erupted into applause proclaiming that the Jews far exceeded them in education and eloquence.[42]

Although it has been believed to be true throughout Christian history, this story is now considered by scholars to be no more than a 'picturesque legend'.[43] Indeed, not only is this story a myth, the text that first recounts it is a forgery! *The Letter of Aristeas* was attributed to a Jewish scholar of the third century BCE but was actually written c. 130 BCE by an Alexandrian Jew.

Like all the Jewish literature produced in this period, the myth of the creation of the Septuagint demonstrates a newfound Jewish self-confidence and self-consciousness, and a delight in setting fantasy and propaganda in the guise of history. In fact, as one scholar notes about Jewish literature of the period:

> It is precisely where the story presents itself as the most 'history-like' that it is actually most fictional—a point well worth remembering![44]

It is absurd to treat the myths and legends turned out in this Jewish fantasy factory as having anything to do with history. And this should make us think twice about the veracity of those other Jewish texts that we now think of as 'sacred scripture'. Because the Tanakh, which still commands the respect of millions, was put together in the same period and probably by the same authors.

When Was the Tanakh Created?

After centuries of foreign rule the Jews saw an opportunity to achieve their independence. In 161 BCE the Jewish leader Judas Maccabeus made an alliance with the Romans and led a rebellion against the Jews' Greek rulers. This alliance with Rome would eventually turn Judea into a vassal state of Rome, when the Romans under Pompey took control of Palestine in 67 BCE. But in the intervening century, there was a tremendous outburst of Jewish nationalism.

Judas Maccabeus and his sons established the Hasmonean dynasty that ruled Judea for the next century. In 164 BCE the temple in Jerusalem was rededicated, after which a whole new era was declared, a new calendar created, and a military programme for the expansion of Jewish territory began. During this period, the collection of texts we know as the Tanakh (a.k.a. Old Testament) was written, compiled and extensively edited, to serve as the mythological justification for the Hasmonean desire to rule all of Palestine.[45]

The Hasmoneans constructed a history that portrayed themselves as descendants of an ancient people who were bequeathed this whole area by God himself. They were the heirs of King David, who had once ruled over both northern and southern Palestine. Their ancestor Solomon was an emperor as important as Alexander. Josephus relates the legend that the Hasmonean leader Hyrcanus found the money to pay his army by opening the supposed tomb of King David, where he miraculously discovered three thousand talents of silver.[46] So if David himself was paying for the re-establishment of his mythical kingdom from beyond the grave, what 'Israelite' worthy of the name could refuse to join his army?[47]

It is in this period that the term 'Israel' first acquires a political and religious connotation. What marks the language of the Tanakh is its self-conscious ethnicity and narrow sectarianism, both of which were pronounced features of the Hasmonean dynasty. Several scholars now consider that the Tanakh was produced by a 'Taliban-like Fundamentalist core of religious bigots'.[48]

When the Hasmoneans invaded their neighbours they forced non-Jews to convert, requiring adult males to be circumcised in order to become 'true Israelites'.[49] The whole of Galilee was forcibly converted in 100 BCE. In the same period they conducted campaigns in Transjordan, Idumaea and Samaria, butchering the populations or forcibly converting them into Jews. At this same time thousands of Greeks and Hellenised Jews fled Palestine in the face of the Jewish Taliban, which is why so many Jewish philosophers ended up teaching in Rome.

The Hasmoneans created the stories in the Tanakh to justify their brutal behaviour. The ethnic cleansing of Canaan by Joshua, during which 'the Israelites left no breathing thing alive', legitimised the kind of practises that were actually being carried out on the ground. Josephus relates stories of the military conquests of the Hasmonean leader Hyrcanus in language that perfectly echoes the stories in *2 Kings* about the forced conversion of entire populations by the Jewish King Josiah.

The Hasmonean capacity for cruelty was legendary, especially when it involved religion. Alexander Jannaeus, for example, had eight hundred religiously liberal Pharisees crucified, whilst their women and children were butchered in front of them. Alexander Jannaeus is said to have enjoyed the spectacle while 'reclined amidst his concubines'.[50] The repellent cruelty of large chunks of the Tanakh makes perfect sense when seen as a product of this kind of environment. For example, the Tanakh has Moses flying into a rage when a returning Israelite war party has slaughtered only the adult male Midianites. Moses orders them to return, saying:

> Now kill all the boys, and kill every woman who has slept with a man, but save for yourselves every girl who has never slept with a man.[51]

Could this really be the same Moses who had been told by God to prohibit murder? Or is this really Alexander Jannaeus in disguise?

The New Age

The Book of Maccabees, written in the Hasmonean period, makes no mention of any existing definitive and authoritative collection of scriptures. It refers only to various collections of texts, mentioning that one of these collections had been lost in the wars, but that a new collection had begun.[52] Although *The Book of Maccabees* claims to be written in the second century BCE, it was actually written in the first century BCE. This is further evidence that there was no such thing as the Tanakh until as late as the first century BCE.

The evidence suggests that the Hebrew Tanakh and the Greek Septuagint originated in the same nationalistic frenzy of bookishness that generated all the hundreds of other texts we possess. Far from developing as a coherent whole over a period of centuries, the Tanakh appeared as an incoherent mishmash of texts, cobbled together by a bunch of religious extremists in a few generations.[53] A further compelling piece of evidence that supports this claim is the carefully crafted chronology of the Tanakh.

In the seventeenth century CE James Ussher, Archbishop of Armagh and Primate of All Ireland, calculated the date of the creation of the world to be Sunday, 3 October 4004 BCE. Ussher's conclusion was included in the Authorized Version of the Bible printed in 1701 and came to be regarded as Bible Truth. The Archbishop further concluded that Adam and Eve were driven from Paradise on Monday, 10 November 4004 BCE, and that Noah's ark had landed on Mount Ararat on 5 May 1491 BCE, which was 'a Wednesday'. Archbishop Ussher made his 'discovery' by adding together the time periods that are carefully recorded throughout the texts of the Tanakh. So carefully, in fact, that it is as if someone had deliberately left a trail that might, fairly easily, be followed. Why would someone do that?

Hellenistic historians of the period believed that a 'Great Year', four thousand years in length, was coming to an end and a New Age was soon to begin. Heraclitus, Plato and the Stoic philosophers had predicted it. Virgil and Cicero lamented that the world had become so awful it was long overdue. The Tanakh, being a product of this environment, also conceives of a 'Great Year' of four thousand years in length.[54]

The Tanakh's Great Year begins with Adam and culminates in the New Age of Jewish independence initiated by the Hasmoneans. Archbishop Ussher had followed the trail back to what he believed was the date of the creation, but this was not the purpose of the Tanakh's compilers. The creators of the chronology wanted their readers to follow it forward from the dawn of creation to their own time, which they considered to be the 'Year Zero'. Here is the chronology of the Tanakh as calculated by modern scholars:

Adam	4164 BCE
Birth of Abraham	2218
Entry into Egypt	1928
Exodus from Egypt	1498
Solomon's temple	1018
Exile to Babylon	588
Return to Jerusalem	538
Rededication of the temple	164 BCE—Year Zero[55]

The 'Great Year' of the Tanakh terminates in the very year that the temple in Jerusalem was rededicated after Judas Maccabeus seized power. The Hasmoneans began a new calendar in this period because they saw themselves as the creators of a New Age.

Contradictions in the Tanakh

The Tanakh draws together fragments from a common fund of Palestinian, Egyptian and Mesopotamian folk traditions that had originated in Palestine over centuries. These fragments were then assembled and edited into an extended pseudo-historical narrative by a group of nationalistic, religious sectarians. But the Hasmoneans, like all creators of prophetic literature, were only interested in history if it could be made to serve their interests in the present, and so they fabricated a past that made the present appear inevitable. But their casual disregard for history bequeathed us a collection of texts that are riddled with problems and inconsistencies.

Take the first five books of the Tanakh, known as the Books of Moses. As early as the twelfth century CE Jewish rabbis had expressed grave doubts that these texts could actually have been written by Moses. The Jewish scholar Isaac ibn Yashush noted that a list in *Genesis* named kings who lived long after Moses was supposed to have lived. Abraham ibn Ezra pointed out that several passages referred to Moses in the third person, used terms that Moses could not have known, described places that he didn't visit and used language from an entirely different period.[56] Later on Hobbes and Spinoza made similar observations. Spinoza was thrown out of his synagogue for observing that Moses could not possibly have written the account of his own death!

By the late nineteenth century the school of Biblical study known as 'Higher Criticism', relying on linguistic and textual analysis, came to the conclusion that the Books of Moses could not have been written by Moses. In the first eleven chapters of the Books of Moses scholars found two creation stories, two stories of the flood and two different accounts of how the nations spread over the face of the Earth. They then noted that these doublet stories had two different names for God: El and Yahweh. Clearly two originally separate traditions had been combined. The thesis that the Books of Moses were created by merging separate documents is now almost universally accepted. As one modern scholar writes:

> There is hardly a biblical scholar in the world actively working on the problem who would claim that the Five Books of Moses were written by Moses—or by any one person.[57]

There are other serious problems with the traditional interpretation of the Books of Moses. For example, God tells Moses that the early patriarchs knew him only under the name *El Shaddai*, which is a reference to the god El and means 'El the Almighty'.[58] And El was the god of the Canaanites, who were the supposed enemies of Moses and Joshua! The Bible redactors found this embarrassing and created their own story to explain it. After the exodus God explains to Moses that he no longer likes the name El and would rather be called Yahweh from now on. But if the name Yahweh was unknown to the Israelites until after the exodus, how do we explain the name 'Joshua', which means 'Yahweh is Salvation'? Joshua was born before the exodus began, so could not have been called by a name that refers to 'Yahweh'.

As scholars continued to study the Tanakh in ever-greater detail, the repetitions and contradictions multiplied to absurd proportions. Moses climbs Mount Sinai at least eight different times. He receives the Ten Commandments at Sinai in *Exodus* and then again at Horeb in *Deuteronomy*. The stone tablets are written by God in *Exodus* chapter 31, but engraved by Moses in chapter 34. There are three variants of Moses' farewell speech. We have three different stories of Jerusalem's conquest in three different books, and only one is under the leadership of David. There are three accounts of Saul's death and three of Goliath's. *The Book of Jeremiah* gives an account of the entire population going into exile three times! According to one scholar, without all these variants, the text would be half its present length.[59]

The Ark Was Never Lost!

Understanding the haphazard way in which the Tanakh was composed solves one of the perennial mysteries that has needlessly engaged the popular imagination for centuries. The so-called 'lost' Ark of the Covenant. There are two hundred references to this mysterious ark which supposedly contained the two tablets of Moses. The Israelites are said to have carried the ark about with them on their wanderings from Egypt, and installed it in their temple when they arrived in Jerusalem. Later, however, the Tanakh describes the sanctuary as empty and the ark appears to have vanished without explanation. The mystery of where it went has spawned more mad theories than Bigfoot and the Loch Ness monster put together. But we don't actually need to go looking for the ark like demented Nazis, because the ark was never lost.

The key to solving this mystery is to understand the troubled history of Palestine. This small region was a permanent battleground. The great powers of the ancient world, Egypt, Assyria, Babylon, Persia, Greece and eventually Rome, all fought in Palestine and garrisoned it as a buffer zone. As the balance of power swung wildly back and forth between different empires over the millennia, the tribes living in this no-man's-land had no choice but to constantly shift their allegiances.

At a point in history when the Egyptians were in the ascendant, the people living in Palestine created a story about their religious sanctuary designed to please Egyptians, who were well known for carrying their gods around in a boat or an ark, and placing sphinxes nearby to guard it. So the people of Palestine also had a sanctuary with an ark and two sphinxes or cherubim to guard it. At another period, when the Persians were in the ascendancy, the people of Palestine changed the story to please their new overlords. The Persians made no images of their gods as they considered this to be the height of blasphemy. Lo and behold, we find that the people of Palestine also have a sanctuary empty of images.

The solution to one of the maddest goose chases in history is simple. We know it will disappoint lovers of Indiana Jones, but in truth the ark was never lost, just deleted from the record by an editorial hand when it became a liability. In time, both stories came to be incorporated into the Tanakh and the contradiction between them went unresolved.

Exactly the same considerations led the creators of Biblical mythology to construct two great leaders to be patriarchs of the Jews. Abraham comes from Mesopotamia and Moses from Egypt. Both were useful to have in the archives to please either Babylonians or Egyptians, depending on who was in the ascendancy. In the same way, when Rome began breathing down Judea's neck and an alliance with Greece seemed like a good idea, a diplomatic correspondence was produced from the archives showing that the Jews and the Greek Spartans were related, as both were descended from Abraham.[60] It was absolute nonsense, of course, but desperate times call for desperate measures.

The First Monotheists?

Traditionally we are told that Judaism brought the doctrine of monotheism to a poor benighted humanity for the first time. But this is merely Jewish and Christian propaganda. Nowhere in the whole of the Tanakh is there an unequivocal statement of monotheism. Cunning editorship and translation has disguised the fact that there are an embarrassing number of gods running around the Bible. The stories told in the Books of Moses refer to the gods El and Yahweh, but El is sometimes masculine, sometimes feminine and sometimes plural. The famous opening words of *Genesis*, for example, speaks of gods in the plural: 'In the beginning the *gods* created the earth'. Archaeologists have also discovered a plurality of Yahwehs. We know a Yahu or Yau of Nebo, as well as the Yahwehs of Teman and Samaria.[61] As one scholar states:

> The names used for God in the Bible are a strange mixture of things. It's as if the biblical authors attempted to assimilate all the different names from the local Canaanite culture and translate them into Jewish terms.[62]

The Jewish prophets repeatedly condemned their people for worshipping other gods than Yahweh, such as Baal, Ammon, Chemosh and

Tammuz. Archaeology has discovered that Greek deities such as Athena, Heracles and many others were also worshipped in the region.[63] Jeremiah laments that the number of gods worshipped in Judea equalled the number of her cities, and the altars in Jerusalem equalled the number of stalls in the bazaar.[64] No wonder Yahweh was such a jealous god. He was up against a lot of competition.

So how did we ever come to think of the Jews as monotheists? The Tanakh was put together in the Hellenistic world when the most important idea shaping men's perception of the divine was Greek monotheism. It was Voltaire who first suggested that there was a secret monotheistic cult amongst the Greeks that predated Jewish monotheism.[65] He was both right and wrong. There was such a cult, but it was hardly a secret.

In the sixth century BCE Heraclitus wrote about the one God who some call Zeus, but who does not mind being called by other names.[66] Pythagoras, Parmenides, Xenophanes and a multitude of others made similar statements. Much of Plato's literary output is an extended eulogy and defence of what he calls 'the One', which he equates with God and defined as 'Being'. The Stoic and Cynic philosophers also argued that the popular gods were many, but the true God was One.[67] In a way, to call this Greek philosophy monotheism is misleading, because it is actually more sophisticated than that. It is Monistic Polytheism. The belief that all gods are merely the many masks of the one supreme and universal God.

This philosophy was streets ahead of the Jews, who were still mired in the primitive mind-set that the name of one's god should be disguised for fear that one's enemies might do magic with it. When the god of the Hebrew Tanakh gives his name to Moses, he refers to himself cryptically as YHVH, which is elaborated by the insertion of vowels into either Yahweh or Jehovah. The production of the Septuagint offered the Jews an opportunity to bring Yahweh into line with Greek conceptions of God. In the Septuagint God now spoke in Greek and called himself 'I am who I am'. This is a clever word-play on the first-person singular of the verb *to be*, which equates Yahweh with the God of the philosophers who is Being. The Septuagint 'Platonized the Lord himself', as the Jewish scholar Bickerman puts it.[68]

Josephus claims that Moses talked of God in thoroughly Platonic terms as the 'One, uncreated and immutable to all eternity, in beauty surpassing all mortal thought'.[69] But these noble sentiments are impossible to reconcile with the jealous, partisan and cruel Yahweh we actually find in the Tanakh. Despite Josephus' attempts to Platonise Yahweh, he is really just a tribal deity who represents the crude self-interest of a nationalistic people. Whereas Plato had genuinely elaborated an impersonal, universal God, the Jews had merely elevated their tribal deity into the only face of God, complete with all his rather unpleasant personality problems. This was not a great step forward from Pagan philosophy, as we are traditionally told. It was a monumental step backwards that has left us with a god who resembles the Devil.

Mrs God

A final nail in the coffin for the idea that the Jews gave us monotheism has been the discovery in recent years of Mrs Yahweh. The commonest religious objects found in archaeological sites throughout Israel are small female figures, of which some three thousand have been found. In the late 1960s at Khirbet el-Kom near Hebron an inscription from the eighth century BCE was discovered that talked of Yahweh 'and his Asherah'. In the 1970s another was discovered in Kuntillet Ajrud in the Sinai. These inscriptions confirmed that the statuettes were depictions of Yahweh's female consort called Asherah.[70]

It seems astonishing that the Israelites were worshipping Mr and Mrs God because the Tanakh seems to make no mention of a Goddess. But actually Asherah is mentioned almost forty times, although one would never suspect these were references to a Goddess. As a modern archaeologist writes:

> The later Bible scribes have systematically written Asherah out as a goddess. They disguised her presence in the text.[71]

Wherever the original text referred to 'Asherah' translators have rendered this as 'the Asherah', as if the name referred to a sacred object, not a personal Goddess. They turned her into it. This problem was compounded by the translators of the King James Bible, who had no idea what the word 'Asherah' referred to and assumed it was some kind of sacred grove.[72]

Some scholars have suggested that a trace of the Asherah cult lived on in the female figure of Wisdom, who appears in several books of the Tanakh. The Goddess 'Wisdom' is the Jewish version of the Greek Goddess Sophia, whose name means 'Wisdom'. She was the Goddess honoured by the 'philosophers', or 'lovers of Sophia'. But the figure of Wisdom in the Tanakh is a mere shadow of the mighty figure of the great Goddess who was worshipped throughout the Mediterranean as Asherah or Aphrodite or Ishtar. The creators of the Tanakh set out to diminish the importance of the Goddess. For example, turning the great myth of Ishtar and her consort Marduk into a simple story about a Jewish couple called Esther and Mordecai.

The 'Good' Book?

Modern research has now shown that the Tanakh (a.k.a. Old Testament) is not an accurate account of historical events. But can we still continue to see it as the 'Good Book', as we have for centuries, and use it as the basis for a moral code? Surely the answer is emphatically 'no'. Do we really want to carry on worshipping a God who legitimised the clearing of Canaan by the total extermination of every man, woman, child and animal? The Tanakh is rarely moral or spiritually uplifting. It is a bizarre and contradictory collection of texts assembled by the immoral, brutal and bigoted Hasmoneans, and it reflects their values perfectly.

Dubious ethics and loose morals are littered throughout the Bible. Take the story of Noah, whom God saves after drowning the rest of humanity but who turns out to be nothing but a vindictive drunk! After the flood, Noah, always partial to a drink, passes out naked on the floor. One of his sons, Ham, accidentally comes across his father and goes off to tell his two brothers, Shem and Japheth, who return and respectfully cover their father's nakedness. When Noah regains consciousness he curses Ham's son Canaan, declaring that his offspring would ever after be slaves to Shem, Japheth and their descendants. So the moral of the story is that the Canaanites deserve to be punished because their ancestor's father saw Noah naked! The modern conflict between Jews and Palestinians is rooted in the spiteful behaviour of a drunk for whom God had an inexplicable fondness. That's not moral. It's mad.

And what exactly is the moral lesson of the story of Abraham? His son Isaac was conceived when Abraham was a hundred and his wife ninety-nine. But after the miraculous birth of their much-longed-for child, God tells Abraham to build an altar of wood, tie up his son, lay him on the pyre and slit his throat. As if that wasn't sick enough, just as Abraham is about to carry out this dreadful instruction, God tells Abraham that it was all just a trick to test his fidelity! What kind of God is this? Fortunately, if anyone today declared that they were about to slit their child's throat on the instructions of the Lord they would be immediately arrested.

But God was hardly more pleasant to Abraham's other child Ishmael, whom the patriarch had previously fathered on Sarah's maidservant Hagar. Jealous of Hagar and Ishmael, Sarah urges Abraham to abandon them in the desert. Incredibly God thinks this is a good idea. Abraham takes Hagar and Ishmael into the wilderness where he leaves them to die. A miracle saves them and Ishmael goes on to become the ancestor of all the Arabs. We could look long and hard to find any moral sense in any of this and still come up empty-handed. But as a way for Jews to denigrate Arabs its message comes across loud and clear. The Arabs are descendants of an outcast bastard whom God himself abandoned to his fate in the desert.

What about God's beloved King David? The Jews regard him as the greatest king of Israel. The Christians consider Jesus to be of David's line. The Qur'an says David was an exalted prophet, given command by God over the mountains, the birds and the rising and setting of the sun.[73] Yet David's moral standards are decidedly dubious. One day, as David arose from his afternoon nap and wandered up onto the roof of his palace, he spotted Bathsheba, the wife of one of his generals, bathing in her house. Despite the Biblical injunction against adultery, David seduces her and she falls pregnant. David then sends Bathsheba's husband to the battlefront with express orders that he be exposed to maximum danger and he is duly slain.

The prophet Nathan denounces David for his behaviour and, although David at first explodes with rage, he subsequently repents. But what does he do to cleanse his guilt? He sleeps with Bathsheba again! Yahweh did not allow Bathsheba's first child to live as a way of punishing David. But the second child, Solomon, lived to become a great king. So God kills an innocent baby to punish its father, but blesses David's other bastard child by giving him a life of luxury. This is not ethics. Its infanticide. And it hardly supports the 'family values' that religious Fundamentalists so vigorously espouse!

Immorality is rife throughout the Tanakh. God goes to the extraordinary lengths of destroying the cities of Sodom and Gomorrah because of their infamous degeneracy, and only Lot and his family are thought worthy of saving. But immediately after this we are told how Lot's daughters get their father drunk, seduce him, become pregnant, and Lot then raises his daughter's sons as his own. If this is the new standard of morality that God wanted to raise out of the ashes of Sodom and Gomorrah, why did he bother destroying these cities in the first place?

What about the Ten Commandments? These are held up as some of the greatest moral statutes of all time. Yet they appear embarrassingly naïve and simplistic when set beside the great Law Codes of Hammurabi in Mesopotamia or the Negative Confession of the Egyptians. They begin with the declaration 'Thou shalt have no other God but me', but as this God is the capricious tribal deity Yahweh who legitimises the genocide of all who oppose him, this rather precludes trying to derive any kind of moral sense from the other nine.

The reason we should have no other God but Yahweh is because, as he openly admits, Yahweh is prone to jealousy. But isn't jealousy a mortal sin? The commandment not to kill appears to have had no effect on the majority of the Tanakh's leading characters. But, then, we can hardly expect consistency from them when God himself ignores his own commandment on a regular basis. That still leaves us with a few salvageable commandments, such as not coveting one's neighbour's ox or ass, but thankfully such crimes are no longer a major problem in the modern world.

Nationalist Propaganda and Gnostic Myths

The Tanakh (a.k.a. Old Testament) has been a part of our culture for so long that we are incapable of applying the same critical standards to this collection of old books that we would to any other piece of ancient literature. After all, if we found these texts today, would we for a moment believe that Noah and his wife had really herded all the world's animals onto their little boat? Or that Joshua had brought down the walls of Jericho with a trumpet? Surely not! We would read them as we do the epic of Gilgamesh or the story of Beowulf, with the understanding that anything that is remotely historical is almost completely buried beneath layers of mythological accretions. We would certainly not be in the absurd situation we are today, where the Holy Land is crawling with well-funded expeditions intent on finding lost arks or magical trumpets!

Two thousand years ago a Jew born of the tribe of Benjamin, who had been circumcised on the eighth day, and was once a zealous Pharisee, described the sacred texts of Judaism as 'crap' that were so outdated they would soon be redundant.[74] We know him as Saint Paul. But sadly, although Paul was right about the Tanakh being crap, he was wrong about it becoming redundant. Instead, the Christian movement he helped inspire degenerated into a Literalist cult that adopted this crap as its Old Testament. This disaster was further compounded when another religion arose called Islam, which based itself on the same old crap. As now almost half of the world's population calls itself Jewish, Christian or Muslim, this has left us up to our waists in crap.

Yet Paul didn't see Jewish Scripture as just 'crap'. Jewish Gnostics, such as Paul of Tarsus and Philo Judaeus, viewed important sections of the Tanakh as profound allegorical myths. They were able to interpret these texts in this way because parts of them were originally Gnostic teaching stories, which answered the human need to understand where we have come from and what life is all about. The Tanakh, like so many sacred texts, offers us distorted versions of allegorical myths overlaid with other material included by religious Literalists for political purposes.

Jewish Gnostics interpreted the books of *Genesis* and *Exodus*, for example, as complementary symbolic stories. *Genesis* was seen as an allegory of how human beings became lost and exiled in the world, whilst *Exodus* was seen as an allegory of awakening to gnosis. *Genesis* was interpreted as a mystical cosmology, in which eating of the fruit of the Tree of Good and Evil represents the fall from a primal oneness into a state of duality. *Exodus* was understood as an allegory of awakening in which captivity in Egypt symbolises being lost in the world, the crossing of the Red Sea represents the process of initiation, the forty years wandering in the desert represents the spiritual work of waking up and the arrival in the Promised Land represents the experience of gnosis.

It is typical of Gnostics to try and re-awaken their religious tradition by bringing out the mystical meaning hidden within sacred scripture. The Pagan philosophers did this with the myths of Homer and Hesiod. Jewish Gnostics did it with the Tanakh. Sometimes Gnostics may have projected onto texts mystical meaning that was never there, but often they recovered ancient truths encoded by other Gnostics before them. The Gnostic agenda throughout history has been to show Literalist interpretations of sacred scripture to be 'crap' and to revivify the teachings of gnosis that these myths originally articulated.

THE MOST FAMOUS MAN
WHO NEVER LIVED

Things that you're liable,
To read in the Bible,
It ain't necessarily so.
—GEORGE GERSHWIN

Once upon a time a bright new star appeared in the heavens. It trav-
elled across the sky and came to rest over a little stable. An angel appeared to shepherds in a nearby field and told them that the Son of
God was about to be born. When they went to the stable they found
a baby who had just been born to a Jewish girl who was still a virgin.
The miraculous baby was called Jesus.

At the age of thirty Jesus was baptised and the voice of God announced to everyone that he was God's only son and God was very
proud of him. Jesus set out to teach people about God and chose
twelve people to be his special disciples. Jesus performed many miracles. He turned water into wine at a marriage. He walked on water,

stilled great storms, created food for thousands out of nothing, healed many people and even brought some back from the dead.

Jesus rode into Jerusalem on a donkey surrounded by his cheering supporters. In the city he criticised the Jewish religious leaders as hypocrites. They were furious and reported him to the Romans who put him to death. But after three days he resurrected. Later he ascended into Heaven, but not before promising that he would come back soon to punish the baddies and take the goodies to Heaven, where they would live happily ever after.

Imagine, if you can, that you had never heard this story before. Archaeologists have just discovered an ancient text which tells this miraculous tale in a cave in Palestine. Do you think it would be read today as an historical record of things that had actually happened? Wouldn't it be treated as another ancient myth, like Adam and Eve or Jason and the Argonauts? The Jesus story has all the hallmarks of a myth. And the reason for this is quite simple. It is a myth. Indeed, not only is it a myth, it is a Jewish version of a Pagan myth!

The Dying and Resurrecting Pagan Godman

The earliest religious texts in the world come from ancient Egypt and tell the story of Osiris. Osiris is a god who became a man and wandered through Egypt teaching the people about religion and the right way to live. He was put to death by the forces of evil, but was magically restored to life and ascended into Heaven to become the judge of souls in the afterlife. Egyptians believed that by worshipping Osiris and following his teachings they too would enjoy eternal life.

Over the next two thousand years cultures throughout the Mediterranean adopted this myth, with its promise of immortality, and made it their own. They synthesised sophisticated Egyptian spirituality with their own indigenous mythology to create the various 'mystery religions' of the ancient world. Each mystery religion taught its own version of the myth of the dying and resurrecting Godman, who was known by different names in different places. In Egypt, where the mysteries began, he was Osiris. In Greece he becomes

Dionysus, in Asia Minor he is known as Attis, in Syria he is Adonis, in Persia he is Mithras, in Alexandria he is Serapis, to name a few.

The mystery religions were immensely popular in the ancient world. Most of the great philosophers and statesmen of antiquity were initiates, including a number of Roman emperors. Initiates of the mysteries learned that the myth of the Godman was a giant allegory, every element of which could be decoded to reveal profound spiritual truths that lead to the experience of gnosis. These are some of the allegorical stories told about the Pagan Godman in his many different guises. We think they will sound familiar:

- His father is God and his mother is a virgin girl.

- He is hailed by his followers as the saviour, God made flesh and Son of God.

- He is born in a cave or humble cowshed on the twenty-fifth of December in front of shepherds.

- He surrounds himself with twelve disciples.

- He offers his followers the chance to be born again through the rites of baptism.

- He miraculously turns water into wine at a marriage ceremony.

- He rides triumphantly into town on a donkey while people wave palm leaves to honour him.

- He attacks the religious authorities who set out to destroy him.

- He dies at Easter time as a sacrifice for the sins of the world, sometimes through crucifixion.

- On the third day he rises from the dead and ascends to Heaven in glory.

- His followers await his return as the judge during the Last Days.

- His death and resurrection are celebrated by a ritual meal of bread and wine, which symbolise his body and blood.

- By symbolically sharing in the suffering and death of the Godman, initiates of the mysteries believed they would also share in his spiritual resurrection and know eternal life.

This is, of course, the story that we now think of as the life of Jesus. But although the similarities between Pagan myths and the story of Jesus often come as a shock to people today, in the ancient world they were obvious to Pagans and Christians alike. Pagans repeatedly accused the Christians of plagiarising the myths of the mysteries. The way early Christians responded to this criticism is highly revealing.

By the end of the second century we find the Christian movement divided into two opposing camps, which we call Gnostics and Literalists. What divides Gnostic Christians and Literalist Christians is the different ways they explain the similarities between the Jesus story and Pagan mythology. The Gnostic explanation is straightforward. Jesus is the Pagan dying and resurrecting Godman under a new name. The Gnostics even refer to Jesus using the names of the Pagan Godman, equating him directly with 'Attis'.[1] For the Gnostics the Jesus story is an allegorical initiation myth, based on ancient Pagan myths.

Early Literalist Christians, such as Justin Martyr and Tertullian, have a much more convoluted explanation. They claim that Jesus was a real man who actually lived out the myths of the Pagans. While the Pagan stories of the Godman are just myths, the Jesus story is a factual account of miraculous events. The Literalists explain that the Devil, knowing that Jesus was going to come in the flesh, created the Pagan myths of the Godman in advance in order to deceive the faithful and lead them astray. Justin informs us that the Pagan stories about the Son of God, who was born of a virgin, rode on an ass, and who died and ascended to Heaven, had been put about by 'wicked demons'.[2] Tertullian agreed that the Devil, 'whose business is to pervert the truth', had copied the sacraments, the blessing of the bread, baptism for the forgiveness of sins and even the symbol of the resurrection itself.[3]

From the late second century onwards there was an almighty battle for the soul of Christianity. On one side were Gnostics who argued that the Jesus story was a giant allegory, every detail of which could be decoded to reveal profound mystical teachings about gnosis. On the other side was a vociferous band of Literalists who taught that the Jesus story was history. So who is right? The Gnostic Christians or the Literalist Christians? Is Jesus a myth or a man?

The Invisible Man

Is there any historical evidence to make us believe that the fantastical stories of Jesus in the gospels are fact rather than fiction? Jesus is said to have miraculously fed thousands of people and raised the dead. When he was crucified a great unnatural darkness is said to have covered the land, the whole earth quaked and split open and the dead came out of their graves. If such dramatic occurrences had actually happened they would surely have been mentioned by one of the many historians of the time. Yet none of them does.

The Romans kept detailed legal records, but no record of the trial or crucifixion of Jesus has ever been found. Later Christians forged such documents, but these have long been known to be fakes. In fact, from the hundreds of books written during this extremely literate period in history, only a few fragments of text are brought forward as possible evidence for the historical Jesus. But none of them stands up to scrutiny.

From all the Roman authors there are three small passages in Pliny, Suetonius and Tacitus, which Christian apologists claim as proof of the existence of Jesus. But these authors were writing in the second century, long after the supposed life of Jesus, and all they actually tell us is that a few Christians existed in the Roman world at this time, which has never been in doubt. The reference in Pliny is a trivial footnote in a letter about some Christian trouble-makers, Suetonius actually refers to someone called 'Crestus' and the Tacitus passage is now considered by many scholars to be a forgery.

So what about Jewish writers of the time? They should be more interested in such a famous Jew as Jesus, but here the situation is even worse. Philo should mention him, as he lived at exactly the same time that Jesus is claimed to have been stirring up trouble in Jerusalem. And yet in his numerous books he makes no mention of Jesus or any of the events described in the New Testament. The one Jewish historian who does mention Jesus is Josephus.

In a single paragraph in his many works he makes what at first sight seems to be a glowing reference to Jesus 'the Messiah'. But over two hundred years ago the great scholar Edward Gibbon in *The Decline and Fall of the Roman Empire* dismissed this passage as a 'vulgar forgery'.[4] He demonstrated that the passage was not to be found in Josephus at the beginning of the third century and must have been inserted into the text early in the early fourth century, after Christianity had been made the religion of the Roman Empire.

The passage is an obvious interpolation because when it is removed the original text flows easily and makes more sense. The sentiments it expresses are entirely out of keeping with Josephus' views on the Jewish myth of the Messiah. Josephus wrote his works after the destruction of Jerusalem in 70 CE by the Romans, which he blamed entirely on the many would-be Messiahs running around Palestine in the years leading up to the disaster. Josephus damned these Messiahs as 'religious bandits' who had whipped up the people into a Messianic frenzy and deluded them into believing that they could defeat the might of Rome.

After Jerusalem was destroyed Josephus abandoned the Jewish religion completely and went to live in Rome. There he wrote books that were sponsored by wealthy Romans and were intended as a warning to the East against further pointless resistance, and especially about the dangers of listening to that well-worn Jewish prophecy that the Messiah would arise out of Israel. Josephus even provokes Jewish religious zealots by stating that in his opinion the myth of the Messiah had indeed been fulfilled, not by a Jew but by the Roman general Vespasian, who was made emperor whilst besieging Jerusalem! So it is simply impossible that Josephus could have said the things about Jesus that the forger of the Josephus passage claims.

Outside of the fabulous tales in the New Testament, these are the only pieces of 'evidence' that scholars have ever found to testify to the supposed life of Jesus. As the Protestant scholar Albert Schweitzer wrote in his book *The Quest of the Historical Jesus:*

> There is nothing more negative than the result of the critical study of the life of Jesus . . . it has fallen to pieces, cleft and disintegrated by the concrete historical problems which came to the surface one after another.[5]

In the 1970s a Carmelite nun called Phyllis Graham left her order and wrote a book called *The Jesus Hoax* in which she explained why she had come to the conclusion there was no historical Jesus.[6] Sadly, like the vast majority of converts, she did things the wrong way round. She spent a lifetime as a believer and *then* went looking for evidence to support her faith in the existence of Jesus the man. She found none. For her the Josephus passage is a vital piece of evidence, but not in the way that its creator meant. Rather than proving the existence of the historical Jesus it is actually damning evidence that he never existed. The forger only succeeded in proving that even at this very early date Christians could find no more evidence for Jesus than scholars can today, and so they made it up. Making things up is something Literalist Christians are very good at.

In 2002 it was announced that an ossuary had been discovered which claimed to have once housed the bones of 'James son of Joseph brother of Jesus'. Jesus is said to have had a brother called James who ran the Jerusalem Church. The ossuary became world news. For Literalist Christians, aware of the lack of evidence for the existence of Jesus, it was almost too good to be true. And, indeed, it was. When independent experts studied the ossuary they discovered that, whilst it was indeed from the first century and belonged to someone called James, the words 'brother of Jesus' had been added to the inscription in the third century.[7] The ossuary was a creation of the holy relics industry, which traded endless sacred artefacts, such as splinters of the 'true cross', nails used in the crucifixion, a large number of foreskins purporting to have once been belonged to Jesus and even his umbilical cord! The ossuary was announced to be a fake. But this, of course, did not become front-page news around the world.

Paul's Mythic Christ

The traditional history of Christianity cannot convincingly explain why the Jesus story is so similar to ancient Pagan myths. Nor can it explain why there is no evidence for the historical Jesus. However, there is a solution that disposes of both these problems in one stroke. The Gnostics were right. The Jesus story is an allegorical myth. This simple explanation also solves another problem that has troubled scholars for centuries. Why does Paul never mention an historical Jesus in his letters?

Although scholars have now dismissed almost half of Paul's letters as forgeries, his authentic letters are the earliest Christian documents we possess and predate the gospels by many decades. They should be full of stories about the life of Jesus. But they aren't. Paul never quotes Jesus and never mentions any details about his life. He never refers to Jesus' miraculous birth. He doesn't tell any anecdotes about Mary and Joseph. There is no mention of any miracles. No water into wine, no walking on water, no miraculous meals or extraordinary catches of fish. There is no Sermon on the Mount or Lord's Prayer. There is no agony in Gethsemane, no trial, no flogging, no crown of thorns, no thieves crucified with Jesus, no weeping women, nothing about the place or time of execution and no Judas or Pilate.

Many Christian scholars have pondered over the 'scantiness of Paul's Jesus tradition', which they have described as 'surprising', 'shocking' and a 'matter of serious concern'.[8] We agree that it is inconceivable that Paul would not have talked about the life of Jesus if he had known of one. In our experience of cults, followers of a recently dead teacher can't help but enthuse about how wonderful the master was, what he did and what he said. But as one scholar writes, Paul's complete silence on the historical Jesus 'remains a problem only for those who insist that there was an historical Jesus to be silent about'.[9]

From the Literalist perspective the absence of an historical Jesus in Paul's letters is a major problem. But from the Gnostic perspective it makes perfect sense. Paul is a Gnostic and his Jesus is the hero of an initiation myth. This idea seems shocking because today Paul is regarded as a bastion of Literalist orthodoxy. But in the first two centuries Paul was honoured by Gnostics as their 'Great Apostle' and revered as the founding father of Christian Gnosticism. The Gnostic master Valentinus tells us that his teacher had received the teachings of gnosis directly from Paul. Indeed, several previously unknown Gnostic works attributed to Paul were found in the library of Gnostic texts discovered at Nag Hammadi.

Paul's authentic letters are full of thoroughly Gnostic ideas and terminology. He tells us he experienced Jesus as a vision of light and everything he knows about Jesus came through 'revelation'.[10] When Paul tells us 'the secret' of Christianity, it has nothing to do with an historical Jesus. The great secret of Christianity, Paul declares, is the mystical revelation of 'Christ in you'.[11] For Paul, as for later Gnostics, the Christ represents the one awareness that is the true identity of all of us. Paul's message is the perennial Gnostic message. We are all one. He teaches that when we are 'baptised into union with Jesus . . . there is no such thing as Jew and Greek, slave and freeman, male and female, for we are all one person in Christ Jesus'.[12]

The only elements of the Jesus myth that Paul mentions are Christ's death and resurrection, which Paul understands as symbolising the process of initiation. By sharing in Jesus' death and resurrection initiates symbolically die to their 'old self' and resurrect 'in Christ'.[13] Paul reminds his students 'the person you once were has been crucified with Christ'.[14]

The Christian Gnostics repeatedly attacked Jewish Literalism, declaring that the God of their spiritual Jesus is not the God of the Tanakh, who they derided as a false god and called an 'exterminator'.[15] Paul also displays contempt for Jewish Literalism, declaring Jewish law to be a curse that has served only to keep the people down.[16] He opposes the very idea of Literalism, declaring, 'The letter kills but the spirit gives life'.[17]

Genocidal Joshua Becomes Gentle Jesus

It's not looking good for the Literalists. The story of Jesus is extremely similar to ancient Pagan myths. There is no evidence for the existence of Jesus as an historical figure. And Paul, whose letters are the earliest Christian documents we possess, is clearly a Gnostic who regards the Jesus story as a mythical allegory encoding mystical teachings. The Gnostics are clearly right to claim that the Jesus story is an allegorical myth. But how and why was it created?

In the same way that authors today write novels to communicate profound ideas, authors in the ancient world composed mythological stories to communicate ideas. Myths were not seen as untrue as they are today. Rather myths were a way of conveying spiritual truths in a form that worked on many levels. The Greeks had brought myth-making to a high art, and Hellenised Jews had become equally fluent in the medium.

Jewish Gnostics of the first century CE were extremely influenced by Pagan spirituality. The Therapeutae, for example, were a group of mystical Jews who practised their own Jewish mysteries based on an allegorical interpretation of the myths of Moses and Joshua. But the Therapeutae were also followers of the great Pagan sage Pythagoras. Philo, who tells us about the Therapeutae, was known as both Philo the Jew and Philo the Pythagorean.

Synthesising Pagan and Jewish mythology obsessed Jewish Gnostics, such as Philo and the Therapeutae. We possess a large number of texts by Jewish writers that combine themes from Pagan and Jewish mythology. It is out of this eclectic environment that a new myth arises which synthesises the Pagan myth of the dying and resurrecting Godman with the Jewish myth of the Messiah. Two centuries earlier a Jewish author had written the first-ever novel, which is an allegorical story that portrays Judaism as a mystery religion.[18] Now the Jesus story was created as an allegorical novel which portrays the Messiah as the hero of a Jewish mystery religion.

Many Jews of this period were anxiously awaiting the return of their great Messiah Joshua, the nationalistic hero of the Tanakh who led his people to the Promised Land. They hoped that Joshua would deliver them from the oppressive Romans who now ran Israel. The word 'Messiah' means 'anointed' and refers to a king or spiritual leader. Translated into Greek 'Messiah' becomes 'Christ' and 'Joshua' becomes 'Jesus'. So these Jews were waiting for the return of their Messiah Joshua or Christ Jesus.

Translators of the Bible always use the Hebrew name 'Joshua' to refer to the hero of the Old Testament, but the Greek translation 'Jesus' when referring to the hero of the New Testament. This sleight of hand has prevented us from realising that the Jesus of the New Testament is simply the Joshua of the Old Testament in a new disguise. In the second century BCE the Hasmoneans had created the Jesus of the Tanakh to fit their nationalistic agenda. In the first century CE mystical Jews created an alternative Jesus to fit their Gnostic agenda.

The original Christians were Jewish Gnostics reacting against the fanatical Jewish Literalism of the Hasmoneans. Hasmonean religious bigotry had made the Jews extremely unpopular in the ancient world. At the time Paul was travelling through the Mediterranean with his message of love, hatred of the Jews had become widespread. Greek and Roman authors at that time routinely described the Jews as the most anti-social of all races. They were said to despise the rest of humanity, from whom they separated themselves with the most ridiculous dietary laws and superstitions.[19] Cicero described Judaism as a 'barbarous superstition'.[20] In the face of this rampant anti-Semitism Jewish Gnostics such as Paul hoped that their Jesus mystery religion would break down the walls that divided Jews and Gentiles.

In the hands of the Gnostics the genocidal Jesus of the Tanakh is transformed into the gentle Jesus of Christianity. Their new Jesus is a free-thinking, compassionate Gnostic superhero, who is both the Jewish Messiah and the Pagan Godman. He is not a xenophobic patriot who conquers his enemies with extreme brutality, like the genocidal Jesus. He is a pacifist advocating non-violence. He does not invoke the law of Talion found in *The Book of Exodus*, which demands 'an eye for an eye and a tooth for a tooth'.[21] Instead he proclaims the message of Socrates that we should love our enemies. This Jesus comes to bring personal not national salvation. His God is not a narrow sectarian bigot who loves only Jews, but a universal God of Jews and Gentiles alike. A God of love. A Gnostic God.

The gospel story is a critique of Literalist Judaism. Its hero is a Jewish heretic who is forever criticising the religious authorities, calling them vipers, and declaring the God of the Tanakh to be the Devil.[22] He constantly breaks Jewish religious laws and encourages his disciples to do likewise. He hangs out with all the wrong people, such as prostitutes, tax collectors, lepers and the dispossessed. He accuses the 'teachers of the Law' of having the 'keys to gnosis' but of not entering in themselves, and not allowing others to enter in either.[23] This Jesus speaks and acts like a Gnostic, because he is their literary mouthpiece.

The new Jesus story was not created all at once but grew organically over time. In the early first century Paul has a simple myth of Jesus. From the same periods we have *The Gospel of Thomas*, which consists of wisdom sayings put into the mouth of Jesus. Within a generation the Jesus story had become progressively fleshed out with more and more allegorical motifs drawn from Jewish and Pagan mythology. Other characters, such as Mary, Peter and Judas, were introduced, all of whom the Gnostics regarded as playing a symbolic role in their great parable of initiation. By the middle of the second century the story had developed into a profound and complex allegorical novel set in Palestine. But once the symbolical story of Jesus had become a quasi-historical narrative, it was only a matter of time before people started taking it literally as a record of actual events.

The Literalist Heresy

In the first century CE the Jews were consumed by a crisis created by religious extremism. Judea was now a Roman province and Jewish zealots claiming to be the Messiah were constantly leading futile revolts. In 70 CE the Roman army laid siege to Jerusalem and destroyed the temple. In 135 CE another revolt broke out that spread to cities throughout the Greek and Roman world, where Jews rose up and massacred their neighbours. This time Roman revenge was total. Jerusalem was dismantled stone by stone and another wave of enslaved Jews was dispersed throughout the Roman Empire.

After the destruction of Israel it was obvious what Jewish religious exclusivity had really achieved. The genocidal Jesus of the Tanakh had not returned to lead the Jews to victory over their enemies. In fact he had not appeared at all! Belief in the Messiah had not delivered the Jews from oppression. Quite the opposite. It had led them to be exiled from their Promised Land into slavery amongst the Pagans. Jewish Literalism had failed.

In the face of this desperate predicament, the cult of the Gnostic

Jesus provided some hope and reassurance. Gnostic Christianity began to take off amongst Jews, who were now dispersed around the ancient world. And Gentiles increasingly embraced it as well, just as Paul had hoped. But when Christianity reached Rome, it underwent a dramatic transformation.

In the second century the Romans finally felt secure enough to tolerate diversity and Rome witnessed the proliferation of a bewildering variety of cults and philosophies. The city became a magnet for wandering prophets from all over the Near East. There was money to be made out of the mysteries and soon satires of wandering miracle-workers making a mint out of the gullible became a popular literary genre.

Strange beliefs and exotic religions were no longer the preserve of the poor. Just as Hollywood stars today traipse from one new cult to another in search of something more than money and fame, so rich Romans also liked to spend their leisure time dabbling in the mystery religions of the mystic East. Wealthy aristocrats, politicians and even emperors became initiates of various cults of the dying and resurrecting Godman. Mark Antony chose Dionysus as his patron deity. Claudius favoured Attis. Vespasian worshipped Serapis. Domitian honoured Osiris. Even a god worshipped by the Persians, Rome's bitterest enemies, found imperial favour when the emperor Commodus was initiated into the Mysteries of Mithras.

Many Gnostic masters moved to Rome in the middle of the second century to set up schools of philosophy. At this time a Christian philosopher called Justin also moved to Rome. He had been rejected by both Pythagorean and Platonic schools of philosophy before he moved to the big city and, desperate to be accepted as a philosopher, he set up his own Christian cult. It is in his writings we hear for the first time that Jesus was a real man who had been put to death by Pontius Pilate. Justin is the first of the Literalist Christians.

Literalist Christianity was just another minor cult competing for adherents in the overcrowded spiritual marketplace. But it came up with a new marketing angle that gave it an edge over the other cults of the dying and resurrecting Godman. It claimed that while the Pagan stories were just myths, Jesus had actually come and lived out these myths in the flesh. The Son of God, so lovingly described by the Pagan philosophers, and the Messiah, so desperately awaited by the Jews, had incarnated in one man, in one place, at one time. This was a revolutionary new claim.

Pagans, of course, continued to complain that the Jesus story had been plagiarised from Pagan myths, but this only drove the Literalists to rebut such charges by fleshing out the narrative of the Jesus story with more and more pseudo-historical details. Of course, it helped that there was no way of knowing what had really taken place in Jerusalem more than century and a half ago. Jerusalem was an insignificant place a long way from Rome. No one could check the Literalists' wild claims against the facts on the ground, because the ground had been utterly razed. Just a few years before Justin arrived in Rome the city of Jerusalem had been re-founded as a Roman city from which Jews were forbidden on pain of death.

Justin not only gives us the first evidence of Literalist Christianity, he also gives us the first indications of a rift between Gnostics and Literalists. Gnostics were a problem for Literalists because they kept undermining their new cult's advertising campaign by claiming that Jesus wasn't really a man, but the hero of an allegorical myth. Justin puts down Gnostics by accusing them of a variety of dirty tricks, such as gaining adherents by seducing women. He even accuses the Gnostics of cannibalism!

Literalists do all they can to portray the Gnostics as fringe heretics and themselves as the Catholic, or 'universal', Church, but this is actually a complete reversal of the truth. For the first three centuries CE Literalist Christianity was the fringe sect and Gnostic Christianity was far more popular, which is why Literalists spent so much time attacking Gnostics. And why Gnostics could rarely be bothered to fight back.

By the time Justin was writing in Rome, Gnostic Christianity had spread throughout the ancient world. In Egypt, Syria and Asia Minor, the first Christians we know of are all Gnostics. In 110 CE Carpocrates founded a Gnostic sect in Alexandria. In 117 CE Basilides began another school in Alexandria. Around 120 CE, Cerinthus was writing in the city of Ephesus. Valentinus studied in Alexandria before going to Rome in 136 CE to set up his school. In 144 Marcion, who already had thousands of followers in the East, also came to

Rome, followed in 150 by Marcus. By the third century Mani had founded a Gnostic church whose influence would eventually reach from Spain in the West to China in the East.

Pagan writers testify to the popularity of Gnostic Christianity. The philosopher Celsus tells us about many different Gnostic Christian groups and their texts, but he knows nothing of Literalist Christians and the books of the New Testament. The Pagan philosopher Plotinus tells us that some of his friends are Gnostic Christians and mentions their texts, some of which have been found at Nag Hammadi, but he also has no knowledge of Literalist Christianity or any of the New Testament gospels.

The popularity of Gnostic Christianity is attested to by Literalist Christians themselves. A letter attributed to Polycarp admits that 'the great majority' of Christians don't believe that Jesus existed 'in the flesh'.[24] Tertullian bemoans the fact that Gnostics fill 'the whole universe'.[25] Even the great heroes of early Literalist Christianity were just going through a phase. Justin's star pupil Tatian gave up on Literalism and went off to join the Gnostics. As did Tertullian, who eventually condemned the Literalist Roman Church as an organisation of 'a number of bishops' rather than 'a spiritual church for spiritual people'.[26]

Mathew, Mark, Luke and John

In Rome a generation after Justin, the Literalist Bishop Irenaeus was hard at work composing his massive work *Against Heresies* to discredit his Gnostic rivals. He rambles on for volume after volume deriding their allegorical interpretations of the Jesus story as 'craftily-constructed plausibilities' designed to 'draw away the minds of the inexperienced and take them captive'. Gnosticism is a conspiracy to deceive the faithful by 'drawing them away under a pretence of superior *gnosis*'.[27] In response Gnostics accuse Literalists of setting up an 'imitation church', because they had replaced the Gnostic understanding of the Jesus myth as a spiritual parable with something utterly banal, but beguilingly simple.[28]

According to Literalists all you needed to do was believe the Jesus story was true and you would be saved. The problem was that there were dozens of Christian gospels in circulation, many of which have now been found at Nag Hammadi, which clearly portrayed Jesus as a mythical figure. In response Irenaeus suddenly produces four gospels which tell the Jesus story as an historical narrative. He claims to have four eye-witness accounts of the life of Jesus, which he attributes to Matthew, Mark, Luke and John, and he rejects all the other Christian gospels as spurious.

No one before Irenaeus had ever claimed that there were only four genuine gospels. A generation earlier Justin never mentions *Matthew*, *Mark*, *Luke* and *John*. But Irenaeus sets out to establish these four gospels as the definitive Christian canon and the basis for what will become the New Testament. His arguments, however, are somewhat tortuous:

> It is not possible that the gospels can be either more or fewer in number than they are. For, since there are four zones of the world in which we live, and four principal winds, while the Church is scattered throughout all the world, and the 'pillar and ground' of the Church is the gospel and the spirit of life; it is fitting that she should have four pillars, breathing out immortality on every side, and vivifying men afresh.[29]

Irenaeus' rhetorical gymnastics may well have convinced other Literalists, but all they really tell us is that his 'four gospel' project was a novel idea that needed some desperate defending. It still needs desperate defending today because scholars have demonstrated that not one of these gospels is an eye-witness account of the life of Jesus.

Scholars regard *The Gospel of Mark* as the earliest of the gospels. But careful analysis of the text has revealed that it is not one man's account of historical events. It is a cut-and-paste creation put together over time from pre-existing sayings and teaching stories.[30] In *Mark* these fragments have been woven together into a narrative that has been sexed up with some seemingly historical and geographical details. But whoever did this made all sorts of mistakes due to what one scholar calls 'a lamentable ignorance of Palestinian geography'.[31]

Matthew and *Luke* are likewise not eye-witness accounts of Jesus' life. When scholars first put *Matthew*, *Mark* and *Luke* alongside one another they noticed that large sections of *Matthew* and *Luke* had simply been copied verbatim from *Mark*. Other sayings and stories have been added from other sources, for example the virgin birth and the resurrection, but basically *Matthew* and *Luke* are just *Mark* with extra fries.

The Gospel of John is written in a completely different style from the other gospels and tells a significantly different version of the life of Jesus. This gospel is actually attributed to the 'Beloved Disciple'. Based on a childhood memory Irenaeus claims the Beloved Disciple is John. But is this right? In other Christian texts found at Nag Hammadi it is Mary Magdalene who is referred to as Jesus' Beloved Disciple. And scholars have shown that crude alterations have been made to the gospel to make John rather than Mary the supposed author. In the original text it was not John who was portrayed as intimately lying across Jesus' lap at the last supper, but Mary.[32]

Irenaeus has changed the sex of the Beloved Disciple to meet the marketing needs of his Literalist cult in Rome, because the misogynist Romans would never be impressed by a book written by a mere woman! At the same time that Irenaeus is writing, the Pagan philosopher Celsus only knows of Christian gospels which are all attributed to women.[33] But Irenaeus claims there are only four gospels and they are written by men!

The author of the misnamed *Gospel of John* attributed this work to the Beloved Disciple who is Mary. In the ancient world spiritual literature was routinely attributed to mythical figures. Mary is an immensely important figure in Gnostic mythology, because she is Jesus' consort and represents the Christian Goddess Sophia. Literalist Christians have completely erased Sophia from Christianity, but she was once as important a figure as Jesus himself.

None of Irenaeus' four gospels are actually eye-witness accounts of historical events. The great scholar Rudolf Bultmann devoted his whole life to studying these gospels, but he eventually concluded that they could tell us 'almost nothing concerning the life and personality of Jesus, since the early Christian sources show no interest in either and are, moreover, fragmentary and often legendary'.[34] Now we are in a position to go further than Bultmann and conclude they can tell us nothing at all about an historical Jesus because no such man ever existed. The four gospels are literary creations designed to serve as the foundation texts for the Literalist Church of Rome. They are Gnostic myths embellished later by Literalists to fit their agenda of creating an authoritarian religion.

The Acts of the Apostles?

If Jesus really was an historical figure, what happened to his disciples? To answer this question Irenaeus produces another new text which no one has previously mentioned, called *The Acts of the Apostles*. And what do the apostles do? They attack Gnostics of course! Many Gnostics traced their tradition to the first-century sage Simon Magus. *Acts* portrays Jesus' disciple Peter humiliating Simon. Irenaeus quotes from *Acts* as proof that Simon had been shown to be a fraud by Peter. A generation earlier, Justin had also attacked Simon, but he didn't bolster his arguments by quoting from *Acts*.[35] Why? Because *Acts* didn't exist in Justin's time. Gnostic Christians refused to acknowledge *Acts* as scripture and you can see why. It is a crude piece of anti-Gnostic propaganda forged in the late second century.

Although its title suggests that it is going to tell us what happened to Jesus' disciples, *The Acts of the Apostles* actually tells us nothing about nine of them except their names.[36] That is because the real Literalist agenda in forging *Acts* is to establish the identity of Peter, who they want to claim as the founder of their Literalist Church. Literalists needed an apostle of their own with the clout to rival the Gnostics' 'great apostle' Paul.

The Literalists could not ignore Paul because he was too well known, so in *Acts* they set about turning him into a Literalist and making him subordinate to Peter. They did this by making use of the fact that Paul says himself that he had never met Jesus. *Acts* now makes it a condition of being an apostle that you need to have met Jesus.[37] It was a simple ploy but it effectively put Paul and all those misguided Gnostics who followed him firmly in their place. So now Peter, the supposed founder of the Literalist Church, is a true apostle, although in fact he is not an historical figure at all. And Paul, the hero of the Gnostics, is not a true apostle, although in fact he was one of the founders of Christianity.

Acts was fabricated to suggest that Paul and Peter had met in Jerusalem and that Paul had accepted Peter's authority. Actually, however, almost everything *Acts* says about Paul conflicts with what Paul says about himself in his letters.[38] And Paul never mentions meeting anyone called Peter. The Literalists' solution was two clever pieces of editorial tampering. One with Paul's *Letter to the Galatians* and one with *The Gospel of John*.

In his *Letter to the Galatians*, Paul mentions a Christian he met in Jerusalem called Cephas. With a simple interpolation one of these references to Cephas was changed to 'Peter'. It is clearly an addition to the text because in the next sentence Paul immediately reverts back to talking about Cephas. Nonetheless, it was enough to identify Cephas and Peter as the same person.

Peter was a central fictional character in the Jesus myth. There are over 150 references to 'Peter' in the New Testament. In *The Gospel of John* one of these has been changed to read 'Cephas' and an editorial voice helpfully points out 'that is Peter'.[39] From then on Cephas is never mentioned again.

The name Cephas appears only once in the whole of the New Testament and the name Peter appears only once in all the letters of Paul, but these two simple interpolations were enough to identify the mythical figure Peter with the historical person Cephas. This connection then formed a foundation for *Acts*, which shows the Gnostic apostle Paul as subordinate to the Literalist apostle Peter.[40]

Other adjustments were made to Paul's letters that also achieved a great deal with the minimum of tampering. Irenaeus and Tertullian both quote *Galatians* but omit the word *not* in a key passage. In the original letter Paul says that he does 'not' subject himself to the authority of the Christians he met in Jerusalem, but in the new version he accepts their authority, which fits the Literalist agenda perfectly.[41] Now they could claim that Paul met Peter (a.k.a. Cephas) in Jerusalem and accepted the authority of Peter. It is a story that is still believed today, but none of it is true.

In the years following the creation of *The Acts of the Apostles* legends about Peter multiplied exponentially. Dramatic stories were composed relating how Peter founded the Literalist Church in Rome and was martyred by being crucified upside down. But despite their creativity and entertainment value, these fantasies were invented too late to be included in the New Testament.

The Literalist Paul

Not only is Irenaeus the first person in history to mention *Matthew, Mark, Luke* and *John,* and *The Acts of the Apostles,* he also claims to be in possession of a number of letters by Paul which have not been heard of previously. In these letters, which are knows as the 'pastorals', Paul has been transformed from a Gnostic into a Literalist. Of the thirteen letters attributed to Paul in the New Testament, the three letters that are most widely dismissed by scholars as forgeries are the pastorals, which Gnostics at the time also refused to acknowledge as authentic.[42]

The pastorals received their name because their purpose is to provide 'pastoral' rules for guiding the organisation of the Church. But the genuine Paul shows no interest in such matters, because when he was writing there was no church of bishops and deacons to organise! What the pastorals actually show us are the aims and ambitions of second-century Literalists, such as Irenaeus, who were desperate to set up as an authoritarian church, and prevent their members from wandering off and joining those dreadful Gnostics.

Irenaeus' massive work against heretics quotes from the pastorals where Paul, the great hero of the Gnostics, is supposed to have given a warning against 'the gnosis falsely so-called'![43] Although the genuine Paul only ever refers to a mythical Jesus, the Paul of the pastorals has a very concrete Jesus proudly laying out his legal defence in front of Pontius Pilate.[44] The forger of the pastorals also took the opportunity to have a swipe at women.

The Gnostics were famous, or infamous if you were a Literalist, for the equality they afforded women. Not only did Gnostic women preach, baptise and celebrate the Eucharist, many Gnostic groups were even named after women, as were many Gnostic gospels. Literalists, such as Irenaeus and Tertullian, were outraged. They found it shocking that Gnostic women could 'engage in discussion' and even act as bishops.[45] Their misogynistic opinions are now put into the mouth of Paul in the pastorals:

Let the woman learn in silence with all subjection.

I suffer not a woman to teach, nor to usurp authority over the man, but to be in silence.[46]

The pastorals effectively Romanise Paul. In Roman society the idea that women were equal to men was simply unthinkable. The notion that a woman might be the leader of a religious sect was nothing less than sacrilegious. The rights of Roman women with regard to religion were simple. They had none. They were forbidden from officiating in religious rites and Roman law demanded that even those Eastern cults that were traditionally led by a priestess put a man in charge instead. By creating the misogynist Paul of the pastorals, Irenaeus makes his Literalist Christianity acceptable to a Roman audience.

There still remained the problem that the real Paul doesn't mention an historical Jesus. But once again the solution was simple. Place Paul's letters after the gospels. Now when readers come to Paul they naturally assume that he is talking about the historical Jesus portrayed in the earlier books. Modern spin-doctors could learn a thing or two from these Literalists! You've got to admire their ingenuity.

The 'Holy' Bible?

In the battle for authority texts were weapons. In the third century CE the holy forgery mill of Literalist Christianity continued to churn out documents to add to the New Testament. More letters were created that portray Paul as a Literalist, such as *2 Thessalonians* and *3 Corinthians*.[47] Letters were also forged in the names of Peter and John. *The Second Letter of John* gives up all pretence that it is trying to communicate anything about Jesus. Its sole purpose is to attack the 'many deceivers' who 'do not acknowledge Jesus Christ as coming in the flesh'.[48]

During the first three centuries CE every book that now makes up the New Testament was hailed by someone as sacred scripture and derided by someone else as a forgery.[49] Nevertheless, over time, the New Testament came to be seen as the definitive Christian canon. Literalist Christians also adopted the Tanakh, which had been so vociferously rejected by the original Gnostic Christians, and made it their Old Testament, albeit with an important change to suit their own purposes.

The Tanakh is arranged in three sections: the Pentateuch, the Prophets and the Writings. Literalist Christians reversed the order of the Prophets and the Writings so that the Old Testament appears to be one long preparation for Jesus, who was 'born of David's line'. The Old Testament ends with the prophecy of Malachi, 'Lo, I will send the prophet Elijah to you',[50] which leads into the appearance in the New Testament of John the Baptist, who is claimed to be Elijah come again to prepare the way for Jesus.

Adopting the Tanakh as their Old Testament served two purposes for Literalist Christians. It made Christianity appear to be the continuation of a venerable tradition, which was vital when Roman law would allow the practice of a faith only if it could be shown to be ancient. And later, when the Church became the official religion of the Roman Empire, it provided scriptural justification for the brutal repression of all opposition, just as it had for the sectarian Hasmoneans who created it.

The process that created the New Testament was uncannily like that which produced the Old Testament. Both were put together by sectarian Literalists intent on creating and maintaining their own power and authority. Both contain the remains of Gnostic myths which have been buried beneath accretions of blatant political propaganda. Both are riddled with contradictions and anomalies because they have been altered and amended by so many editorial hands. The Literalists' Bible is not holy scripture. It's an unholy mess.

Glorious Gore

By the middle of the third century the Roman Empire was on the verge of collapse. The Persians threatened from the east and the barbarians from the north. For the first time in history a Roman emperor was killed in battle and another was captured and died in captivity. Plague devastated entire regions. In this 'Time of Chaos' all manner of superstitions spread widely, including Literalist Christianity, which claimed that the end of the world was nigh. This now seemed not only possible but extremely likely.

Eventually the emperor Diocletian imposed order on the empire. To appease the gods, whose neglect he believed had caused the chaos, the emperor decreed that everyone in the Roman army should make a sacrifice for the health of the emperor and the empire. Many Christians, who now formed a sizeable minority in Diocletian's army, refused. In response Diocletian ordered the destruction of all churches throughout the empire, the imprisonment of leading Christians, and decreed that all Christians were to offer sacrifice to the Roman gods or be put to death.

This was not the first time that Christians had been persecuted by the Romans, but previous persecutions had been short-lived and not widely enforced. Under Diocletian the persecutions were brutal, but counterproductive. As the modern world is discovering, there is nothing like persecution to whip up religious fanaticism. Taking out religious extremists may seem like an easy solution, but every martyr's death inspires a hundred more with the desire to emulate their devotion. As Tertullian had written at the time of the persecutions a century before Diocletian:

> The more you mow us down, the more we grow. The blood of the martyrs is the seed of the Church.[51]

Literalist Christians, like so many other religious extremists since, embraced the opportunity for martyrdom enthusiastically. They idealised their martyrs as spiritual athletes and holy warriors. They believed that 'through suffering for one hour' it was possible to 'purchase eternal life'. The Literalist Cyprian vividly describes the delight of the Lord with 'the sublime, the great, the acceptable spectacle' of 'flowing blood which quenches the flames and the fires of Hell with its glorious gore'.[52]

Gnostic Christians saw Literalists as fanatics leading the gullible to pointless suffering with false promises. They viewed it 'foolish' to actively seek out martyrdom as a quick way into Heaven, because they believed that salvation comes only through the realisation of gnosis. *The Testimony of Truth* declares that those who teach that God desires 'human sacrifice' are making God into a cannibal. Literalist Christians are 'the ones who oppress their brothers' by encouraging naïve fellow believers 'to the executioner'.[53] *The Apocalypse of Peter* expresses particular horror at Literalist delight over the suffering of 'the little ones'.[54]

Gnostic protests made little impact. Once martyrs were guaranteed a place in Heaven, Literalist Christianity became a mass-suicide cult, with adherents actively seeking death. It is interesting, however, that two of the most vocal exponents of martyrdom, Irenaeus and Tertullian, managed to avoid this fate themselves. Funny how it is always the foot soldiers of a movement from whom martyrdom is required, not the leaders who are urging others on to this glorious sacrifice.

The Unholy Roman Empire

When the emperor Diocletian died, Literalist Christians experienced a complete reversal of fortune. The bishops suddenly found themselves out of jail and running the empire. There was a new military dictator in charge called Constantine. And he adopted Christianity as the religion of the empire. What made Constantine choose Christianity and not one of the other cults of the dying and resurrecting Godman adopted by his predecessors? Perhaps it was because his mother was a Christian. After all, one should never underestimate the influence of a mother! Perhaps, as an autocrat himself, he was attracted to the authoritarian nature of the Literalist Church. We can at least dismiss the fantasy created later by Literalists that Jesus had appeared to Constantine the night before a great battle and guaranteed him victory over his enemies. It seems unlikely that Jesus, the 'prince of peace', would approve of a vicious tyrant like Constantine.

Constantine planned to use the organisation of the Literalist Church to help him unite and control his empire. The problem was that Christians had been disagreeing with one another since the beginning of Christianity. His solution was to invite Christian bishops to the first ever Christian conference in Nicea to fix the dogmas of Christianity. But no sooner had the bishops arrived than they began to bombard the emperor with petitions complaining about their fellow Christians. Constantine simply burnt all the petitions. He wanted unity and he enforced it.

A Literalist creed was composed at Nicea and imposed on the troublesome bishops with cynical use of carrot and stick. Those who agreed to sign up to the new creed were invited to stay on for months of lavish entertainment as Constantine's guests. Those who refused were banished from the empire as criminals. The Nicean Creed was designed by a despotic Roman emperor and imposed on Christianity by force. Yet, incredibly, it is still repeated in churches throughout the world today.

Bishop Eusebius arrived at the conference in opposition to many of the ideas that became the creed, but he could see the way the wind was blowing and left Nicea as Constantine's right-hand man. Eusebius became Constantine's biographer and wrote *The Oration*, which praises the emperor as a living saint. Almost a god. Certainly God's representative on earth. But in reality Constantine, like most Roman emperors, was a monster. He returned home from Nicea to have his wife suffocated and his son murdered. He remained unbaptised until his deathbed, so he could keep on assassinating all those who challenged his authority and yet still receive forgiveness at the end. But you would never know any of this from reading Eusebius.

Bishop Eusebius also wrote the hugely influential *History of the Church*. But his 'history' is as accurate an account of the origins of Christianity as his *Oration* is a true portrait of Constantine. It is a complete flight of fantasy, designed to meet the needs of the authoritarian Roman Church. Yet Eusebius' book forms the basis of our traditional understanding of Christian history, because for centuries all historians have had to rely on it as their most important source. Why? Because all alternative accounts were banned and burned.

From the beginning of the fourth century CE, with the backing of the Roman Empire, Literalist Christians set about persecuting their Gnostic and Pagan rivals out of existence. Armed with the New Testament that repudiated heretics and the Old Testament that legitimised a scorched-earth policy against all opposition, the Holy Roman Empire enforced Christianity with unholy violence. But Literalist Christians did much more than eradicate all other religions. They destroyed civilisation itself. Christians had long dreamt about the apocalypse and they now succeeded in making it a reality.

Everyone knows that the barbarians destroyed Rome, but few know that these barbarians were Christians. In the fifth and sixth centuries bands of black-robed Christian monks roamed unchecked throughout the disintegrating empire, laying waste to the wonders of Pagan civilisation. A Pagan writer of the time described them as 'monks who resemble men but live like pigs' and laments that 'anyone who had a black robe had despotic power'.[55]

Like the Taliban, who dynamited ancient statues of the Buddha in Afghanistan, Christian monks destroyed ancient Pagan temples that had stood for thousands of years. Their priests and priestesses were exiled, murdered or simply chained in their sanctuaries and left to starve. The wealth of the temples was shared out between the emperor and the bishops. Philosophers and heretics were murdered or exiled. Great libraries were torched. And while the literature of antiquity was being consigned to the flames, Augustine declared the triumph of Literalism writing:

Nothing is to be accepted except on the authority of scripture, since greater is that authority than all powers of the human mind.[56]

Literalist Christians believed that by revering the Bible as the infallible Word of God they would usher in a new age of Christian enlightenment. But they were completely wrong. In fact the lights went out all over Europe and the West reverted to a brutish life of ignorance and superstition. Literalist Christians hoped to bring about the Kingdom of God, but they actually created the thousand years of misery that we call the 'Dark Ages'.

A Question of Competitive Plausibility

If you tell a lie enough times, people will end up believing it. This is what has happened with Literalist Christianity. We are so familiar with the story of Jesus that we are unable to treat it in the same way as other similar stories. But look at it with an open mind and the Jesus story is obviously a myth. Are the gospels really eye-witness accounts of the life of a miraculous dying and resurrecting Godman? No. There is no more evidence for the existence of Jesus than there is for Moses, Joshua, David, Solomon and all the rest. All are Jewish literary creations. The Jesus story is a symbolic allegory based on ancient Pagan myths. It is just as much a parable as the many parables it contains. Looking for the real Jesus is as futile as looking for the real Good Samaritan.

Today there are some twenty thousand different Christian sects. Nearly all of them are Literalist and regard the New Testament, created by the Roman Church, as an authentic account of the life of Jesus. When asked why they are Christians, however, most people say it is because they experience a personal inner relationship with Jesus. The great irony is that this is an excellent reason to be a Gnostic Christian, not a Literalist Christian. The Gnostics saw Jesus as an inner spiritual figure, who represents the Christ within us all. When people experience a personal relationship with Jesus they are actually following in the tradition of the Gnostic Christians.

A spiritual experience of the inner Jesus isn't a good reason to be a Literal Christian, because it doesn't prove the existence of Jesus the man, any more than an experience of an inner Krishna or Osiris proves that these other Godmen really existed. The only valid reason to become a Literalist Christian, and stake the fate of your eternal soul on the gospel stories being historically accurate, is to seek out the evidence that Jesus really did resurrect from the dead. And there simply isn't any.

In our previous books, *The Jesus Mysteries* and *Jesus and the Lost Goddess*, we set out in much greater detail the evidence for the thesis we have explored in this chapter. Ever since we have received e-mails from readers every day. Many come from ex-Fundamentalists, thanking us for setting them free and opening their spiritual hori-

THE LAUGHING JESUS

zons. Others have expressed outrage at our revisionist history of Christianity. But is our thesis so outrageous? We think not. Rather it is the traditional theory of the origin of Christianity that is outrageous, compared to which ours is quite reasonable.

To a Christian policeman who e-mailed us stating that we could not possibly be right, we replied with the suggestion that we simply think in terms of competitive plausibility. This approach, we felt, should appeal to a policeman, schooled in weighing evidence. Our thesis is that Christianity emerged organically over time as a Gnostic synthesis of Paganism and Judaism. Literalist Christians believe that it all began when a virgin gave birth to the Son of God, who walked on water and came back from the dead. We suggested that if a witness in a court of law today claimed that such a story really happened, their case would be thrown out as nonsense. We did not receive a reply.

5

MUHAMMAD:
FROM MYSTIC TO MOBSTER

Woe to them who fake Scriptures
and say 'This is from God'
so that they might earn some profit thereby.
— The Qur'an[1]

In the beginning Allah created the light of Muhammad out of which he then created the world. Muhammad was a prophet from the beginning of time, even before Adam was made. When Muhammad was born in Mecca in 570 CE he was already circumcised and detached from the umbilical cord. At his birth the whole house filled with light and the stars bowed down as if they were about to fall to Earth. In Iran the fire-worshippers observed that their temple hearth, which had been lit for a thousand years, had turned ice-cold.

At the age of forty Muhammad went off to meditate in a cave on Mount Hira near Mecca. Here the angel Gabriel appeared to him with a written message from God and said 'Read'. But Muhammad was illiterate. Three times the angel seized Muhammad by the throat and ordered him to read, and three times Muhammad told Gabriel that he could not. Muhammad was so upset by Gabriel's visit that he tried to commit suicide. It was his favourite wife, Khadija, who finally convinced him that he was indeed God's chosen Prophet.

Muhammad began receiving more and more messages from God which eventually became the Holy Qur'an, and the Prophet established the one true religion of Islam, which superseded and completed the revelations of all previous prophets. With God personally directing him, Muhammad inspired an Islamic community of pious Muslims that grew in power and influence. In a few short years Muhammad became a great military leader, defeating the enemies of God and establishing an Islamic empire. 'Islam' means 'surrender', and through Muhammad, God calls on all humanity to surrender to his divine will and recognise his chosen Prophet.

At the end of his life Muhammad left Arabia at night on a flying horse. He stopped off at Jerusalem where you can still see his handprint and the hoofprint made by his horse miraculously preserved at the Dome of the Rock. In Jerusalem he met up with Abraham, Moses and Jesus, who acknowledged that Muhammad was the last of the prophets and that his new religion was not just a continuation of theirs but even better. Finally Muhammad ascended into Heaven where he now sits on the right hand of God and judges who deserves eternal life.

It's another great story, but is any of it true? Yes! At last, unlike Abraham, Moses, Solomon, Jesus, Peter and all the rest, Muhammad was indeed an historical figure. Unfortunately, when we tell you what the historical Muhammad was actually like, you may wish that he had never existed.

According to mystical Muslims called Sufis, Islam began with a small circle of Gnostics that formed around Muhammad, who was an inspired prophet channelling divine wisdom. But in a few years he became the most powerful man in Arabia, theologically, socially and militarily. Muhammad was a mystic who became a mobster.

Muhammad used his self-proclaimed status as God's messenger to the Arabs to unite previously warring local tribes into a powerful *umma*, or community. Members of the *umma* pledged to stop pillaging one another, which had been a common practise for centuries, and banded together to kick the hell out of all those who refused to sign up to Muhammad's Islamic alliance. The cult became an army and then an empire, with Muhammad as God's chosen military dictator. If the history of Christianity demonstrates how egalitarian Gnosticism can degenerate into an authoritarian Literalist religion in a few centuries, then the history of Islam shows that the same process can happen in a few decades.

The Gnostic Muhammad

Muhammad grew up among Jews and Christians whose influence on him was profound. But the Judaism and Christianity that Muhammad encountered in the Arabian Peninsula were not those that we are now familiar with. Many of the stories in the Qur'an about the Hebrew prophets and Jesus are quite unlike those we know from the Bible. So where do those stories come from? Muhammad was said to have been shocked when he learned that Judaism and Christianity were actually different faiths.[2] How could he confuse these two very different religious traditions?

The great scholar Adolf von Harnack provides the answer. What Muhammad actually encountered in Arabia was a form of Gnostic Judeo-Christianity, which the Prophet transformed into the religion we know as Islam.[3] Judeo-Christian Gnostic groups such as the Ebionites and Elchasiates flourished in the region in which Muhammad was born, and their influence on Islam is obvious.

These Gnostic sects were famous for the prominence they gave to the role of prophets and for seeking mystical visions out in the wilderness. So when Muhammad sought revelations in the wilderness he was following a well-established local tradition. And when he begins receiving messages from God, it is no surprise to find that they include many Gnostic motifs.

The most striking evidence of Gnostic influence on Muhammad is the Qur'an's treatment of Jesus' death. It states:

They did not kill him, and they did not crucify him, but one was made to appear to them like him.[4]

This idea is entirely heretical for Literalist Christians, but is fundamental to many Gnostic texts in which it is only Jesus' 'appearance' that is crucified. This seemingly strange idea is actually a common allegory encoding profound teachings about awakening to gnosis.

Another example of Gnostic influence on Muhammad is his decision to make Jerusalem the focus of worship for Muslims, although he later changed this to Mecca. Where did the idea of making a particular city the focus of worship come from? Not from Judaism. There is no evidence that Jews ever prayed towards Jerusalem. Nor does it derive from Literalist Christianity. Christians pray facing east, towards the rising sun. The Elchasiates Gnostics, however, did face Jerusalem when they prayed.[5]

Muhammad originally followed the Gnostics' egalitarian example in his treatment of women. There was a striking equality of the sexes in the early Muslim community. Women were amongst Muhammad's closest followers, they took part in public life, and even fought alongside men in battle. Muhammad forbade the killing of girl children, or regretting that they were not boys, and gave women legal rights of divorce and inheritance centuries before the West.[6] Sadly, all this egalitarian Gnosticism didn't last long. As Muhammad changed from mystic to mobster, his revelations from God began to take on a more authoritarian and patriarchal tone.

Channelling God

Muhammad's first 'revelation' happened in 610 CE and the last occurred just before his death in 632 CE. The contents of the Qur'an were thus revealed piecemeal over a period of two decades. But these revelations were not collated into a book in the lifetime of Muhammad. It is said that his followers, known as the Companions of the Prophet, recorded Muhammad's revelations on anything that came to hand, such as scraps of parchment and leather, stones and palm leaves, even camel ribs and shoulder blades. These fragments were neither numbered nor dated, but simply deposited in various receptacles without any regard to chronology or system.

All the scraps began to be compiled into the Qur'an under the direction of Muhammad's son-in-law Uthman around 660 CE. Some scholars have concluded, however, that no definitive version of the Qur'an existed until as late as the tenth century.[7] Also over this period other sayings and stories about Muhammad, called Hadiths, were collected to supplement the Qur'an. Most of the people who had supposedly recalled these sayings and stories had died in battle during Muhammad's lifetime, so they are at best second-hand accounts. Despite this, however, the Hadiths were declared to be 'authoritative'.

Both the Qur'an and Hadiths were chaotically thrown together over time, and so are full of the types of errors, omissions and interpolations found in all sacred scriptures. Muhammad's first revelation, for example, should be at the beginning of the Qur'an, but is actually found at the end.[8] What else might have happened is anyone's guess. Many scholars have commented on the fact that the text is often ambiguous about who is actually talking. Sometimes God seems to talk about himself in the third person, in other places as 'I', and in other places (sometimes in the same passage!) as 'we'. Many have ridiculed the Qur'an because God is even made to swear by himself![9]

The Qur'an really is a bit of mess. But, given how it was put together, we should not be surprised. Yet, surely, if the Qur'an is a divine book, wasn't it the Prophet's duty to compile it during his lifetime? After all, these messages are supposed to be revelations from God! Many Arabs criticised the Qur'an when it was first created because they argued that a genuine book from God would be revealed as one piece and would not be so repetitive.[10] These early critics of Islam are right. The Qur'an is extraordinarily repetitive, and often about the most unimportant things. So much so that one begins to wonder whether Allah has Alzheimer's.

The Qur'an makes some impressive claims about itself. It states categorically, 'This is the book wherein is no doubt'.[11] Yet even this statement itself is open to doubt. It can't be a revelation from God to Muhammad, because in Muhammad's lifetime there was no 'book', as the Qur'an had not been compiled. In fact the Qur'an makes no sense right from the start. Quite literally! It opens with the words 'ALIF LAM MIM', which don't mean anything.[12] Not even Muhammad himself understood their meaning. It is odd for God to begin his definitive Word with ambiguity, but this is typical of the hocus-pocus that accompanies the creation of so-called 'sacred' texts.

The Qur'an claims that God is absolute, does not include anyone in his government, and that no man's opinions or words form part of the Qur'an. Yet Muslim scholars acknowledge that at least fifty of the second caliph Umar's ideas were incorporated into the Qur'an. These include ordering women to wear veils, which was a custom copied from the Byzantine Christians, and other doctrines that have had a profound impact on Islam. Yet, despite these anomalies, the Qur'an declares itself to be free from inconsistencies. It asks rhetorically:

Why do they not ponder the Qur'an? If it had been from other than God surely they would have found in it much inconsistency.[13]

Anyone who actually ponders the Qur'an, however, soon discovers that it is so riddled with inconsistencies that all its major doctrines are self-contradictory. Proof, surely, that it was not written by God! These inconsistencies reflect Muhammad's journey from Gnostic to know-all. For example, the egalitarian Muhammad has God declare that Muslims must remember that no human being is God, so men and women should be just with one another. A few lines later, however, we get a completely different message from the authoritarian Muhammad:

Men have authority over women because God has made the one superior to the other . . . Good women are obedient . . . As for those from whom you fear disobedience, admonish them, forsake them in beds apart and beat them.[14]

As Muhammad changes he is forced to revise many of his 'revelations' to suit his new agenda. The Qur'an itself tells us that some of Muhammad's followers regarded his meddling with the revelations as nothing less than forgery. It says defensively:

And when we exchange a verse in the place of another verse—and God knows very well what He is sending down—they say 'Thou art a mere forger'.[15]

Luckily God provides Muhammad with an answer to the criticism that he is changing the nature of his revelations as he goes along. The argument is a familiar one used by religious Literalists through the centuries. God can do anything he wants, including contradicting himself, and you should just trust the Prophet blindly, because doubt is bad. The Qur'an affirms:

> Whatever verse We abrogate or cast into oblivion, We bring a better or the like of it. Knowest thou not that God is powerful over everything?[16]

But how can the Qur'an truly be the unchangeable and eternal word of God, if God Himself had to change certain verses during the lifetime of Muhammad? Surely God would get it right first time!

Islamic Gnostics interpret much of the Qur'an as myth encoding mystical teachings, and they are probably right to do so with Muhammad's early revelations. But as the new cult of Islam grew in power, Muhammad, like so many self-proclaimed prophets, lost the plot and started believing his own publicity. As time went by the purpose of Muhammad's divine revelations seem increasingly to be simply to aggrandise himself and justify his political ambitions. When these 'revelations' are placed in their historical context it becomes obvious what was really going on. Muhammad made self-serving decisions and then Allah would helpfully reveal a new revelation that endorsed these decisions.

Muhammad even uses his supposedly divine revelations to settle personal grudges. His paternal uncle Abu Lahab regarded Muhammad as an impostor and would follow him around interrupting his preaching and calling out to the crowd, 'Do not believe this impostor, he is a liar'. Abu Lahab's wife was equally hostile to Muhammad. Not surprisingly, according to Muhammad, God Himself couldn't abide Abu Lahab and his mischievous wife, and devised a grisly punishment for them. The Qur'an states:

> Perish the hands of Abu Lahab . . . he shall roast at a flaming fire and his wife, the carrier of the firewood, upon her neck a rope of palm-fibre.[17]

THE LAUGHING JESUS

Call us cynics if you like, but we can't help thinking it odd that God wastes his time abusing Muhammad's uncle when he could be announcing something useful such as the cure for leprosy.

The Godfather of Islam

However benign Muhammad's original intentions may have been, as his ambitions increased his agenda became more and more sectarian. Muhammad was a member of the Quresh tribe. He first sets about establishing the Quresh tribal deity called 'Allah' as the only God and the Quresh as God's favourite people. Even before Muhammad the Quresh were known as the 'people of Allah', but at this time Allah was merely one of 350 statues of the local gods of the Arabian Peninsula displayed within the shrine of the Ka'aba in Mecca. Muhammad changed all that. He established an Arabic dynasty ruled by the Quresh and endorsed by Allah the one true God.

Muhammad built his dynasty by making astute family alliances through marriage. The four caliphs who succeeded Muhammad were related to him by marriage and for centuries after Muhammad all caliphs came from the Quresh family. This was clearly Muhammad's intention, as his sayings make clear:

> The prerogative to rule shall remain vested in the Quresh, and whosoever is hostile to them, Allah shall destroy him.

> The right to rule shall belong to the Quresh even if only two men existed.[18]

Having exalted his own people and their tribal deity above other Arab tribes and their gods, Muhammad now sets about exalting the Arabs generally above all other peoples. Muhammad has God declare: 'You are the best nation ever brought forth'.[19] Despite the protestations of later Muslims that this verse of the Qur'an refers to the international community of Muslims, this cannot be true, because when Muhammad received this revelation there was no international community, just Arab Muslims.

Muhammad is above all an Arab nationalist promoting a specifically Arabic religion. The Qur'an says, 'By the Clear Book, behold, we have made it an Arabic Qur'an'.[20] It is for this reason that all Muslims to this day must learn Arabic in order to be blessed. Indeed, not only are the Arabs God's chosen people, to whom he sent his greatest Prophet, God has even chosen Arabic as the language to be spoken in Heaven. Muhammad states:

> Love the Arabs for three reasons, because I am an Arab, the holy Qur'an is in Arabic, and the tongue of the dwellers of paradise shall also be Arabic.[21]

The Prophet is explicit that 'Love of one's motherland is an integral part of faith'.[22] Are these truly divine revelations from the one God, or do they merely express the nationalistic sentiments one would expect from the prophet of an Arabic tribal deity called Allah?

Muhammad's nationalism gave Arabs a vision of themselves as something greater than just a bunch of separate tribes continually at war with one another. But, sadly, no sooner had the Arabs experienced the elation of transcending their narrow tribal identities into an integrated 'us' than the Islamic umma degenerated into the violent sectarianism of 'us versus them'. Like so many other nationalistic and religiously bigoted communities, Muhammad's Muslims were fundamentally held together by one thing. They were united against their enemies.

Over a period of twenty years Muhammad led eighty-two attacks against his neighbours in the Arabian Peninsula. That's one attack every six weeks! Other Arabs, Jews and Christians were ruthlessly plundered to build the wealth and power of Muhammad's umma. But this was no longer just the usual banditry that was customary for the time. It was now legitimised by Muhammad's revelations from God. It was God himself who now declared, 'Eat of what you have taken as booty'.[23] In a chapter of the Qur'an called 'The Spoils' it is God who prevents Muhammad from showing mercy to his captives by stating:

> It is not for any prophet to have prisoners until he make wide slaughter in the land.[24]

A conquered people's wealth, women and children were distributed amongst Muhammad and his companions. The Muslim policy of legitimising unlimited concubines, in addition to the four wives permitted by God, meant that the population growth of Muhammad's followers was exponential. Muhammad himself had either nine or twenty-seven wives, depending on which story you believe. This was possible because God had conveniently given Muhammad a special dispensation:

> Prophet, We have made lawful for you the wives to whom you have granted dowries and the slave-girls whom God has given you as booty. The daughters of your paternal and maternal uncles and of your paternal and maternal aunts who fled with you. And any believing women who gives herself to the Prophet and whom the Prophet wishes to take in marriage. This privilege is yours alone, being granted to no other believer.[25]

As the military power of Muhammad's *umma* grew, so did the ambitions of its leader, who now declared:

> Every Prophet is appointed for his own nation, but I have been appointed the Prophet for all nations.[26]

Convinced of his divinely ordained mission, Muhammad began to send armies to foreign lands with three simple instructions:

1. Invite people to join Islam.
2. If they do not accept they must surrender and pay tribute.
3. If they do not they must be attacked.

'Islam' may have originally meant mystical 'surrender' to the will of God, but now it came to mean simply 'surrender or die'. As Muslim territory expanded it became simply impractical to massacre all those who would not convert, and so the imposition of tribute money, which was simply a tax on unbelievers, became policy throughout the Arab empire. Muhammad had created a holy protection racket with himself as the divinely appointed Godfather. In the light of this it is perhaps not surprising that the word *mafia* is now thought by some scholars to be of Arabic origin.[27]

Muslims, Jews and Christians

In the early days of his mission the mystical Muhammad did not see himself in opposition to Jews and Christians. Quite the contrary. He portrayed himself as continuing their prophetic traditions and hoped that Jews and Christians would come to accept him as the Messenger of God. Muhammad didn't claim Islam to be a new religion, because he saw himself as simply bringing faith in the One God to the Arab people, who had never had a prophet before. He honoured Jesus, but not as the Son of God. For Muhammad Jesus was a precursor to himself, a prophet who had taught the same religion. The Qur'an states:

> He [Allah] has laid down for you the religion that He charged Noah with, and that We [Allah] have revealed to thee and that We charged Abraham, Moses and Jesus with.[28]

To begin with, Muhammad acknowledged Jewish claims of superiority, because they had a venerable prophetic tradition and already worshipped one God. The Qur'an has God proclaim:

> Children of Israel, remember My blessings wherewith I blessed you, and that I have exalted you above all beings.[29]

At this time the mystical Muhammad decrees that there should be 'no compulsion in matters of religion'.[30] But as he realizes that Islam is not going to be willingly embraced by Jews and Christians, Muhammad changes. Now he sets out to exalt Islam above all other faiths. The Qur'an boldly asserts:

> The true religion of God is Islam.[31]

> It is He [Allah] who has sent his Messenger [Muhammad] with the guidance and the religion of truth, that he may uplift it above every religion.[32]

Portraying Islam as a new religion gave Muhammad the opportunity to revise the stories told in the Judeo-Christian Bible to suit his own nationalistic agenda. The Biblical story of Abraham was in particular need of an overhaul. The tribe of the Quresh, to whom Muhammad belonged, claimed to be descendants of Abraham's son Ishmael. The Quresh believed that Abraham and Ishmael had come to Arabia in ancient times to rebuild the Ka'aba. Needless to say, the Bible makes no mention of any of this. What the Bible does say about Ishmael is entirely derogatory.

According to the Bible, Ishmael is Abraham's son, but not born in wedlock to his wife Sarah. Ishmael is the child of Abraham and Sarah's 'bondswoman' Hagar. Ishmael, to put it bluntly, is a bastard. The message of the Jewish story is that Arabs are descendants of the bastard son of a slave. According to the Bible, God prefers Abraham's legitimate son Isaac, who is the ancestor of the Jews, and tells Abraham to abandon Hagar and Ishmael in the desert to die. Obviously Muhammad could not stomach any of this.

Muhammad needed to incorporate the stories of the Bible into his teachings, because this gave them an aura of antiquity and religiosity, but he needed them to be different in important ways. So he changed them. Despite previously acknowledging the Bible as the Word of God, he now provides a completely different version of the story of Abraham. But it is not Muhammad who is changing things. Far from it. Muhammad is simply setting things straight. According to his revelations from God it is the Jews and Christians who have perverted the Word of God. Of course this completely contradicts another of his revelations that asserts 'No man can change the Word of God'.[33]

Through his revelations Muhammad did exactly what other religious extremists had done before him. He appropriates the mythical figures of the past for his own ends. He even goes so far as to claim that Abraham was not a Jew, but rather a Muslim. Indeed, it was Abraham who had first given the followers of Islam the name 'Muslims'.[34] Muhammad claims that it was not Isaac who was offered as a sacrifice to God, as it says in the Bible, but rather Ishmael.[35] And it was not the Jews' ancestor Isaac who was God's favourite, it was Muhammad's ancestor Ishmael. The essential message of Muhammad's version of events is this:

The two tribes that God chose as the best were the descendants of Ishmael and Isaac. God preferred the children of Ishmael. Then God created Muhammad in the chosen tribe of the Quresh [the descendants of Ishmael]. And then he chose his family as the best among the Quresh families and created Muhammad as the best of all men.[36]

According to the Bible, God made the Jews his chosen people because of Abraham's willingness to sacrifice his son Isaac. Muhammad's radical re-write undermines this claim completely and makes the Arabs God's preferred tribe. The Bible and the Qur'an are both supposedly the Word of God. So which one is telling the truth? The Jews had no doubts. The Bible was true and Muhammad was a false prophet. As far as they were concerned Muhammad couldn't be a genuine prophet, because the era of prophecy was over.

It is said that this rejection by the Jews was one of the greatest disappointments of Muhammad's life. From this time on, Muhammad's attitude to the Jews hardened. He now produced revelations from God that overturned earlier revelations. The Jews were no longer a blessed people. They were 'cursed' and 'shall not have a share in the Kingdom'.[37] The Qur'an's explanation for this change of heart is simple. The Jews had not accepted Muhammad as God's prophet.

Muhammad symbolised his rejection of the Jewish tradition by changing the direction of worship from Jerusalem to his home city of Mecca. Even some of Muhammad's followers were confused by this shift, but Muhammad produced a revelation in which God answered them, saying:

The fools among the people will say 'what has turned them from the direction they were facing in their prayers aforetime?' But to God belong the east and the west. He guides whomsoever He will to a straight path. We have seen you [Muhammad] turning your face about in the Heaven and now We surely turn you to a direction that shall satisfy you [Muhammad]. Turn your face towards the Holy Mosque [Ka'aba] and wherever you are, turn your faces towards it.[38]

This explanation doesn't make any sense. If both the East and the West belong equally to God, why change the direction? What these verses really show is that Muhammad had made the decision to change the direction of worship because he had been rejected by the Jews, and that his decision was later legitimised by a 'revelation' from God.

Mecca was now treated as so sacred that people were forbidden from defecating whilst facing in the direction of the city. All who did were infidels. The same was not true for once holy Jerusalem. A Hadith records one of Muhammad's companions as saying:

> People say that whenever you sit for answering the call of nature, you should not face Jerusalem. I told them, once I went up to the roof of our house and I saw God's Messenger answering the call of nature while sitting on two bricks facing Jerusalem.[39]

The transformation of the Muslims' attitude toward the Jews and Jerusalem could not be more explicit: 'I shit in your general direction'.

Holy War

As Muhammad becomes convinced that it is his divine mission to impose Islam on the world, his messages from God become more sectarian and violent:

> Oh ye who believe! The non-Muslim are unclean.[40]

> Surely the worst of beasts in God's sight are the unbelievers.[41]

> Humiliate the non-Muslims to such an extent that they surrender and pay tribute.[42]

> Oh ye who believe! Murder those of the disbelievers . . . and let them find harshness in you.[43]

Muhammad creates a divisive world in which Muslims are to be treated one way and unbelievers another. The Qur'an states: 'Muslims are hard against the unbelievers, but merciful to one another'.[44]

To be a Muslim is to be in 'God's party' and to be an unbeliever is to be against God. Indeed just to be friendly with an unbeliever is to be an evildoer. Even if that person is a close relative:

O believers, take not Jews and Christians as friends, they are friends of each other, whoso of you makes them his friends is one of them. God guides not the people of the evil-doers.[45]

O believers, do not treat your fathers and brothers as your friends, if they prefer unbelief to belief. Whosoever of you takes them for friends, they are evil-doers.[46]

Muslims are the people who do not love anyone who opposes God and his Messenger, not even if they were their father, or their sons, or their brothers or their clan.[47]

Consumed with religious mania Muhammad begins to claim that God wants Muslims to wage a *jihad*, or holy war, against all unbelievers:

O Prophet, urge on the believers to fight, if there be twenty of you, patient men, they will overcome two hundred. If there be a hundred of you, they will overcome a thousand unbelievers.[48]

Now Muhammad unleashes a savage policy of ethnic cleansing that eventually led to the expulsion of all Jews and Christians from the Arabian Peninsula. Muhammad declares:

O ye assembly of Jews . . . you should know that the earth belongs to God and His Messenger, and I wish that I should expel you from this land.[49]

I will expel the Jews and Christians from the Arabian Peninsula and will not leave any but Muslims.[50]

Muhammad's vengeance on the Jews for not accepting Islam was particularly brutal. The Jewish Banu Kainuka tribe had once entered into an alliance with Muhammad, but now fell into disfavour with the Prophet. After a long siege of their town by Muhammad's armies they surrendered. Muhammad wanted to execute all seven hundred of their soldiers. One of his companions, however, begged for them to be treated with mercy, so instead the tribe was banished from Arabia. The Jewish Banu Quraiza tribe were not so lucky. The angel Gabriel told Muhammad to destroy them entirely. Eight hundred Jewish men were slaughtered, their women became concubines, and their children slaves.[51]

The Banu Quraiza were taken out from their fortress and penned up in separate yards. During the night the Muslims, at the command of the Prophet, dug a long trench. As day broke Muhammad said his prayers to 'Allah the Merciful, the Compassionate' and took a seat by the pit to supervise the operation. The Jewish men were brought in groups of five or six with their hands tied behind their backs. They were ordered to lie down with their heads stretched out over the edge of the pit. Muhammad's companions Ali and Zubair then decapitated them with swords. By dusk the job was completed. Among the Jewish women who fell to the Muslims as spoils of war was an enchanting beauty of twenty-two called Rihana. Her husband, parents, friends and relations had just been massacred at the Prophet's command, but despite her grief Muhammad immediately proposed marriage to her. Rihana refused his offer, so the Prophet simply took her as another concubine.

Muhammad was now the leader of the most vicious gang in Arabia, and all those *kafirs*, or infidels, who dared opposed him met a grisly fate:

> The only reward of those who make war on Allah and His Messenger
> and strive after corruption in the land will be that they will be killed
> or crucified, or have their hands and feet on alternate sides cut off, or
> they will be expelled out of the land. Such will be their degradation in
> the world. And in the Hereafter theirs will be an awful doom.[52]

The ex-Muslim Anwar Shaikh, who as a young man was a religious zealot who killed non-Muslims, writes with passion against what he calls Muhammad's 'doctrine of extreme social conflict'.[53] He states bluntly:

The whole purpose of the Qur'an is to raise a *kafir*-hating community called the Muslims, who must be indoctrinated with the spirit of *jihad* to make them a dominant force, perpetually ready to glorify Allah and Muhammad by murdering, plundering and subjugating non-Muslims.[54]

Muhammad the Megalomaniac

Prophets are dangerous people because they profess to speak for God, which gives them a claim to absolute authority. Prophethood is a form of idolatry, because the prophet comes to represent God in the same way as a statue. Living prophets are far more dangerous than stone statues, however, because prophets are people with their own personal agendas. People with a puffed-up sense of their own significance, who really believe that they can tell others what God thinks. People who become inflated with their own delusions of grandeur and demand that they themselves be treated like God. People like Muhammad.

At the time of Muhammad there were several other prophets wandering around Arabia, such as Al-Aswad, the Veiled Prophet of Yemen; Taliha, who claimed to have the power of divination; and Musailima, who was said to perform miracles. But Muhammad makes it clear that he is above them all. Indeed he is the greatest prophet of all time. Greater than Moses and the other prophets of the Jews. Greater than Jesus. His revelations superseded all others before him and will never be superseded by anyone after him. He declares himself to be the last and greatest of the prophets. His sense of self-importance truly knows no bounds.

Islam is a personality cult created by Muhammad to eulogize Muhammad. According to Muhammad the way to salvation is to imitate Muhammad. Yet there is no suggestion that anyone could ever be equal with the Prophet himself. Muhammad expects his followers to follow, as the Qur'an makes plain:

O Believers, do not walk in front of the Prophet. Do not raise your voice above his.[55]

In the early days the mystical Muhammad makes it clear that he is not divine. He is not the Son of God, as Christians claim Jesus to be. But as the cult of Muhammad grows God gradually recedes further and further into the background and the Prophet takes centre stage. While still claiming to be God's slave, Muhammad actually becomes the master.

Despite the Qur'anic injunction that no one should be associated with Allah, praising Muhammad becomes an integral part of every Muslim's daily prayers. The basic Muslim confession is the *shahada*, which includes the name of Muhammad alongside that of Allah. The Qur'an is unequivocal that obedience to both is required:

> It is not for any believer, man or woman, when Allah and His Messenger have decreed a matter, to have the choice in the affair. Whosoever disobeys Allah and his Messenger has gone astray into clear error.[56]

As Muhammad's megalomania grows, the whole relationship between God and his Prophet is stood on its head with the statement:

> One may be negligent towards God but one must be respectful toward Muhammad.[57]

At the end of his life, we are told, Muhammad miraculously ascended to Heaven, where he now sits on God's right hand waiting to judge us all. With this myth the transition from humble prophet to divine super-being is completed. Muhammad finally usurps God's power altogether, because it is no longer God who holds the keys to Heaven. It is Muhammad.

The Qur'an may have previously taught that at the time of judgement 'no one shall be able to benefit someone else because the command shall belong to God'.[58] Now we are told that Muhammad can intercede on our behalf and that the Prophet's intercessions are *binding* on God. So it is Muhammad who will decide who is saved and who is dammed, because God must be governed by Muhammad's opinion.

And Muhammad's opinion is clear. It doesn't matter how much you believe in God, or how good you have been, if you reject Muhammad you're an infidel destined for eternal damnation. Although the Qur'an had clearly stated that 'God is the Master of the Day of Judgement', now Muhammad is more powerful than God, because God doesn't even have the power to save those who believe in him from Hell. The criteria for getting into Heaven is not subservience to God, but to Muhammad. The servant has become the master. The Prophet has become God.

Heaven and Hell

Fear is the basic tool of Literalist religion and there is no fear greater than the fear of death, except the fear of God's punishment after death. Like so many self-proclaimed prophets, Muhammad uses a crude carrot-and-stick technique to bring people into line, promising a wonderful afterlife if they believe and terrifying them with the horrors of Hell that await all unbelievers. The Qur'an asserts:

Whoever desires a religion other than Islam in the next world he shall be among the losers.[59]

The unbelievers of the People of the Book [Jews and Christians] and the idolaters shall be in the Fire of Hell, therein dwelling for ever.[60]

Surely those who disbelieve in Our signs—We [Allah] shall certainly roast them at a fire. As often as their skins are wholly burned, We shall give them in exchange other skins, that they may taste the punishment.[61]

Muhammad declares that anyone who has heard of Islam and not converted (which means about four-fifths of humanity as it is now constituted!) will be tortured for eternity in the most horrible ways imaginable:

As for the unbelievers, for them garments of fire shall be cut, and there shall be poured over their heads boiling water whereby whatsoever is in their abdomens and their skins shall be melted. For them await hooked iron rods. As often as they desire in their anguish to come forth from it, they shall be restored into it.[62]

The dweller of Hell is given to drink oozing pus, which he gulps and can scarce swallow. Death comes upon him from every side, yet he cannot die. And still before him lies harsh chastisement.[63]

In the light of this it is astonishing that all the chapters of the Qur'an except one commence with 'In the name of Allah, the Merciful, the Compassionate'! Yet Allah is compassionate to those who do what they are told and follow Muhammad. They will be admitted to paradise:

Whoso obeys God and his Messenger, He will admit him to the gardens [of paradise].[64]

Surely the pious shall be in bliss, upon couches gazing. You find in their faces shining bliss as they are offered to drink of wine sealed with musk.[65]

Surely for the God-fearing awaits a place of security, gardens and vineyards and maidens with swelling bosoms.[66]

Other sayings give details of the ever-young *houris*, or virgins, that will be available to all men in paradise:

A *houri* is a most beautiful young woman with a transparent body. The marrow of her bones is visible like the interior lines of pearls and rubies.[67]

A *houri* is a girl of tender age, having large rising breasts which are round, and not inclined to dangle.[68]

Every man who enters paradise will be given seventy-two of these *houris* and, no matter at what age he dies, in paradise he will be a thirty-year-old with the virility of a hundred men. For those of a different sexual persuasion there are also beautiful ever-young boys 'pretty like pearls' who wear silver bangles. On top of all this the inhabitants of paradise receive winged horses made out of rubies that will fly them wherever they want to go.[69]

And yet, for all this talk of rewards and punishments, Muhammad is actually a determinist. One saying states that forty days after a foetus is formed in its mother's womb 'God sends his Angel to it with instructions concerning four things, his livelihood, his death, his deeds and his fate'.[70] Other sayings explain:

> God has fixed the very portion of adultery which a man will indulge in, and which he must of necessity commit.[71]

> Whomsoever God leads astray, no guide has he, but whomsoever God guides, none shall lead him astray. Is not God all-mighty, all-vengeful?[72]

The Qur'an makes it quite clear that it is God who leads someone to Islam or away from it. Yet in the very same verse God holds unbelievers completely responsible for their own actions.[73] How can God appoint a Day of Judgement to try people for a destiny that he has allotted to them? Should it not be Muhammad's Allah who is tried for tormenting some people unjustly and favouring others undeservedly? It doesn't make sense. But, then, religion seldom does.

Muhammad's Legacy of Hate

Muhammad claimed he was bringing a new and better religion to humanity. But actually it was just the same old nonsense with a touch of Arabian spice. Just like the Tanakh and the New Testament, the Qur'an was put together by religious extremists to fulfil their sectarian agendas. And like these other 'sacred scriptures' the Qur'an continues to be a source of conflict and division today, especially in the so-called Holy Land.

Despite changing the direction of worship from Jerusalem to Mecca, Muhammad did not entirely renounce his claim upon Jerusalem. Although there is no evidence that Muhammad ever visited the city, a mythical story about his night flight to Jerusalem became incorporated into the Qur'an. This ensured that Jerusalem became a sacred place to Muslims, and hence gave them a divinely legitimised claim on the city. The result is that Jews, Christians and Muslims all now regard Jerusalem as their sacred city, which has led to centuries of diabolical suffering.

Inspired by Muhammad's teaching that the Day of Judgement will not come until the Muslims have destroyed the Jews, Islamic Fundamentalists are still butchering Jews.[74] And Jewish Fundamentalists, who want to appropriate Arab land to re-establish the mythical Kingdom of David, are murdering Muslims. And Christian Fundamentalists, who want to re-establish the Jews in Israel because it is a pre-requisite for the Second Coming of Christ, have armed the Jews to the teeth. Today Jerusalem is a stick of divine dynamite threatening to explode at any moment. And these religious Fundamentalists are convinced that it is all part of God's plan that it does explode!

The crisis has been exacerbated by the Muslim belief that, because the Jews had been cursed by God, they would never be allowed to return to Jerusalem and form a government of their own. When in fact the Jews did return to Israel and form their own government it struck at the very root of Islamic tradition. Who is right? Moses, who claimed that Israel is the land promised to the Jews by God, or Muhammad, who asserts that the Jews have been cursed by God and as a result cannot return to Jerusalem?[75]

There are some in the Muslim world who would rather see all the Jews in Israel driven into the sea than have their Holy Qur'an proved wrong. There are some in the Jewish and Christian world who want to see all Arabs driven from Israel in order to prove their beloved Bible right. There are many more throughout the whole world who want to see all these Literalists give up their dependence on the divisive 'sacred scriptures' that justify their appalling behaviour. Will this ever happen?

We believe it will. But the West is ahead of the game. Western scholars have been criticising the Judeo-Christian Bible for three centuries. The Muslim world has barely begun to analyse the Qur'an critically. The West is slowly pulling itself out of the morass of Literalist bigotry and establishing a new tradition that encourages individuality, not collective obedience to religious authority. A tradition that views doubt as better than blind belief.

Whilst the authority of the Qur'an remains unquestioned by the Muslim world, the secular liberal values of the West will be rejected as the work of the Devil, just as Muhammad would have wanted. The Qur'an is clear that salvation comes not through thinking for ourselves but by imitating the great dictator Muhammad. This is why Muslim Fundamentalists believe it is their duty to walk, talk, eat, drink, dress and think like Muhammad.[76] And make war on infidels just like Muhammad!

In the name of 'Allah the Compassionate' Muhammad has bequeathed the world a legacy of hatred. He has inculcated into his followers an 'us versus them' mentality, which has left pious Muslims perpetually at war with the rest of humanity. Semtex has replaced swords, but Islamic religious zeal and the suffering it causes remains the same. Now we have the chilling spectre of Osama Bin Laden living in a cave, like Muhammad, still urging young men to mass murder of infidels, like Muhammad, and still promising everlasting sex in Heaven as a reward for martyrdom. As the Muslim writer Irshad Manji puts it in her book *The Trouble with Islam*:

> Its like a perpetual license to ejaculate in exchange for a willingness to detonate.[77]

Why are these young men so eager to exchange their lives for empty promises? It is because they have been brainwashed into believing the Qur'an is an authoritative statement of God's opinions. And they are sure that Muhammad is in Heaven, sitting on God's right hand, waiting to judge how faithful they have been to his commandments. Of course Christian Literalists know this can't be true, because it is Jesus who is sitting on God's right hand. Perhaps it is because all these prophets are sitting on his hands that God is unable to do anything to stop the misery religion is causing in his world?

THE LAUGHING JESUS

6

THE DREAM OF AWAKENING

History is a dream from which I am trying to awake.
—JAMES JOYCE, *ULYSSES*

After many years studying the great religions of the world we have developed an almost allergic reaction to the downright gobbledegook contained in their supposedly sacred texts. Our studies have forced us to conclude that these books cannot possibly be the 'Word of God'. In fact, if we were God's lawyers we would advise suing for misrepresentation and defamation of character. But does this conclusion render these texts completely worthless? Of course not. After all, we accept that the words of Plato, Rumi and Shakespeare are just the words of men, but we consider them sublime for all that.

We are not saying for a moment that the Tanakh, New Testament and Qur'an don't contain moments of beauty, insight and wisdom. It is just that we cannot, and dare not, ignore the dreadful passages of intolerance, bigotry and hatred that they also contain. We can no longer go on pretending that religious terrorists are perverting the 'true' message of their sacred texts when the texts themselves create an us-versus-them world and incite their readers to divinely sanctioned violence.

The problem is that Literalist religions expect their followers to accept their sacred scriptures on an 'all-or-nothing' basis. Despite this, of course, most believers cherry-pick the passages they like and simply ignore the ones they don't. Don't get us wrong; we are grateful for this! If Jews, Christians and Muslims were to carry out what their scriptures demand in the average modern city there would be absolute anarchy. But how long will this era of tolerance last? For, in our reading of history, every culture has its equivalent of the Taliban waiting in the wings, dreaming of a return to absolute power and plotting their theocratic coup.

We must apply our God-given gift of discrimination to all scriptures and recognise they are so internally riven with illogicality and inconsistency that they have made us mad. For example, in the gospels Jesus says, 'He who is not against me is for me'. But he also says, 'He who is not for me is against me'. The first is egalitarian and inclusive. The second is narrow-minded and exclusive. They are mutually contradictory, so believing both makes Jesus a madman and ourselves schizophrenic.

We are not saying that there are not some inspiring passages in the New Testament. The commandment to love one's enemies is immensely profound. Does it make this teaching any less profound if Jesus didn't actually exist? Of course not. There was never a Hamlet, King Lear or Prospero, but we still love Shakespeare. His insights into the human condition will be relevant as long as there are human beings, as will those that someone put into the mouth of their hero Jesus.

During our lifetime the wisdom of the world has become available at the local bookstore and can be downloaded from the Internet. Surely it would now be absurd to continue confining ourselves to one tradition or to one sacred text. It's time to face up to the fact that nobody can be right about everything. The first half of Plato's *Timaeus*, for example, is a fascinating insight into the cosmology and mysticism of the Greek esoteric tradition. But the second half is quite frankly laughable. Anyone with a modicum of modern knowledge about human anatomy will realise that Plato is simply wrong. Likewise, the Bible may contain great wisdom but, unaccountably given its supposed omniscience, it has nothing to say about quantum physics. Any book is merely a product of its time and place.

There are so many excellent books out there that it is plain madness to remain fixated by one text. In our opinion, the *Upanishads*, the *Tao Te Ching* and the *Crest Jewel of Wisdom* are much better than the Bible. And if these are too Eastern for you, then look at the ancient philosophers such as Plato and Plotinus. Check out the sublime poetry of the Sufis, such as Rumi and Hafiz. Dip into the transcendental wisdom of the medieval Christian mystic Meister Eckhart. And if these are too old or too foreign, try Walt Whitman's ecstatic poetry or T. S. Eliot's *Four Quartets*, because these two authors are much more mystical than either Moses or Muhammad. But whatever you choose as your source of inspiration, remember it is only a book. And that includes the book you are reading right now!

The modern world offers us so many sources of inspiration to choose from that it has created what is often dismissed as a 'spiritual supermarket'. But what's wrong with supermarkets? When we were kids there were only religious corner shops offering a limited choice of dusty products that were well past their sell-by date. Now we can pick and choose the spirituality we prefer. We can say we like this, but we don't want that. Fantastic! Let's not crow about it. Let's celebrate it. It's a gigantic step forward from the days when the Church ran a monopoly on Truth.

Recovering from Religious Insanity

The world has moved on, but Literalist religion is stuck in the past. Unlike just about every other aspect of human culture, where new is sexy and old is outdated, in matters of religion old is holy and new is heretical. Muhammad expressed this backward-looking attitude perfectly when he announced:

> Beware of new things for every new thing is an innovation and every
> innovation is a mistake.[1]

The very nature of life is that things constantly change, but Literalists don't like change. Things were better in the good old days, when religion dominated our lives. We need to go back to how things were in Muhammad's time. We need to go back to the days of the early Church. We have fallen from a primordial paradise and are heading for the terrible punishment we deserve. The future we are offered is Armageddon, mass destruction, divine retribution, fire and brimstone. Are these really the images we want to be filling our children's heads with?

You can tell when a spiritual tradition has succumbed to Literalism because it stops changing. People repeat the same old creeds, perform the same old rituals and wear the same old costumes, although they no longer have any idea why. The Hasids began as a vibrant movement of Jewish mystics and free-thinkers in eighteenth-century Poland. But a few centuries later they have become a Literalist cult to be seen performing their devotions at the Wailing Wall in Jerusalem, still wearing eighteenth-century Polish dress designed for the Eastern European chill, despite the fact that they now live in the burning heat of the Middle East. Literalists cling to whatever gave them their identity in the past, no matter how mad it now may be.

Religion is obviously crazy. Yet, for some reason, there is a feeling that we should respectfully avoid criticising this craziness because it is a matter of 'faith'. Why? We don't feel compelled to show this sort of unquestioning deference in matters of politics, science or anything else. The time has come to announce that the emperor is wearing no clothes. Literalist religion deserves to be ridiculed, not respected. It is irrational, immoral and outmoded. And hysterically funny.

Religious Literalism is a bad idea poorly thought through. Christian Literalists, for example, proclaim their opposition to Paganism, yet celebrate Easter, which is named after the Pagan Goddess Eostre. And they don't celebrate this most important of festivals on a fixed date which marks the crucifixion of Jesus, but according to a Pagan lunar calendar. Even more absurdly, they mark this holy day by eating eggs, a symbol of the Pagan goddess. Why don't we have chocolate crucifixes? After all, Christianity is about eating the body of Christ. Although it might be a bit of a problem deciding which end to start!

Literalism is bonkers! If we told you that a friend of ours had been born of a virgin, could walk on water and had come back from the dead, who but the truly demented would believe us? Yet billions happily believe this based on a bizarre old book. If we were dealing with anything other than religious belief, such irrationality would be grounds for a diagnosis of mental illness.

Religious madness causes seemingly intelligent people to turn the truth inside out to fit their dogmas. Crown Prince Abdullah, a member of the despotic ruling aristocracy in Saudi Arabia and an Islamic Literalist, recently announced:

> Saudi Arabia has a constitution inspired by Allah and not drawn up by man. I do not believe that there is any Arab who believes that the Qur'an contains a single loophole which would permit an injustice to be done. If there is any truly democratic system in the world, it is the one now existing in Saudi Arabia.[2]

So democracy is not about the will of the people, but about following divine revelation and being ruled by a king! It is hard to know where to begin with someone who is willing to distort the meaning of words such as *democracy* to such an extent, in order to justify his religious prejudices and vested self-interest.

But it's not just mad Muslims who don't seem to recognise the obviousness of their own hypocrisy. The majority of American Christian Fundamentalists, who worship the 'Lord' and look forward to the 'Kingdom' of Heaven, are supporters of the 'Republican' party. Isn't republicanism about abolishing kings and lords? Irony, confusion and willful self-deception become so entangled it is difficult to see where one begins and the other ends.

Many Literalist leaders seem adept at fitting their faith to their personal self-interest. Fundamentalist figures in the U.S., for example, don't actually turn the other cheek, or love their enemies, or give all their money to the poor. They build big evangelical organisations with themselves at the top. They preach morality and approve those who bomb abortion clinics and wage war. They are exactly the sort of hypocrites that Jesus condemns in the gospels.

The irony is that the most extreme Fundamentalists are actually only one small step away from waking up. They are already completely convinced that everyone else's religion is utter nonsense. All they need to do now is realise that so is their own! But, for Fundamentalists, this small step is a giant leap into the unknown, requiring a genuine faith in the mystery of existence, which they have yet to find. Fundamentalists need to be certain they know the Truth, because the only alternative they see is terrifying. Fundamentalists are 'us' at our most lost. As the Christian Gnostic Theodotus put it many centuries ago:

> Those who are most asleep think they are most awake, being under the power of vivid and fixed visions, so that those who are most ignorant think they know most.[3]

Yet it is often because they have had a genuine experience of awakening from the illusion of separateness that people embrace Fundamentalism. Make no mistake about it, at Fundamentalist meetings people experience something special. They feel roused from the everyday numbness we call 'normality' and begin to feel alive again. They are having transpersonal experiences. But, then, so were people at the Nazi Nuremberg rallies. They also transcended their sense of being an isolated individual, but unfortunately became caught up in the greater limited identity of being a German. In the same way, religious Fundamentalists experience the relief of transcending their personal identity, but become embroiled in the larger limited identity of being a Christian, Muslim or whatever.

Many forward-thinking people are depressed by the rise of modern Fundamentalism, which threatens to take us back to the Dark Ages when religion ruled the world with an iron fist. But Fundamentalism is not to be feared, because it is nothing new. What is new is that so many of us now no longer see such bigotry as acceptable. What has changed is that throughout large parts of the Western world, especially Europe, new ways of thinking have steadily eroded the totalitarian regime that was Christendom. This has resulted in the demise of organised religion. But it has also revealed a last rump of believers who are desperately holding on to a medieval worldview whose day has long gone.

It is only because new ways of looking at the world have become so popular that we have felt the need to give a name to the old way of seeing things and call it 'Fundamentalism'. But creating a new name creates the erroneous impression that this was a christening when in fact it was a funeral. Fundamentalism is not proof of the power of religious Literalism, but rather of its weakness. Fundamentalism is religious Literalism in the throes of death, not the first flush of youth. Fundamentalists are fighting a defensive rear-guard battle against the modern world, because they know they are losing the war of ideas. The moment a set of beliefs is thought of as a 'tradition' that needs saving, it is already doomed.

When George W. Bush responded to the tragedy of 9/11 he used Biblical language to declare 'you are either with us or against us'. We feel that he is right, but not in the way he intended. The choice we face right now is to be with George Bush, Osama Bin Laden and all those religious Literalists who choose to perpetuate division through violence and hatred, or to wake up to oneness and choose love and forgiveness, as the Gnostics have taught for centuries. Are we for George and Osama or against them? How we make this choice will define the world we co-create in this new millennia.

The Heretical Heritage

Throughout history, Gnostics have presented the possibility of awakening to gnosis as an alternative to religious Literalism. Gnostics are always outspoken critics of the outdated status quo, which forever gets them into trouble. They are branded heretics and persecuted horribly. But through their courage the spiritual heart of religion has been kept beating through the ages. The great scientist and freethinker Albert Einstein writes:

> The religious geniuses of all ages have been distinguished by the kind of religious feeling which knows no dogma and no God conceived in

man's image; so that there can be no church whose central teachings are based on it. Hence it is precisely among the heretics of every age that we find men who were filled with this highest kind of religious feeling and were, in many cases, regarded by their contemporaries as atheists, sometimes also as saints. Looked at in this light men like Democritus, Francis of Assisi and Spinoza are closely akin to one another.[4]

Gnostics come from all sorts of different backgrounds but form one tradition of awakening. In the West this tradition has been called by many names, such as Pythagoreanism, Platonism, Mysticism, Esotericism, the Perennial Philosophy and a bewildering number of other things. We call this tradition 'Gnosticism', because it teaches the philosophy which leads to gnosis, or awakening. The different individuals who make up this tradition didn't all use this name, of course, but grouping them together as 'Gnostics', in this broad sense in which we use the word, enables us to treat this important movement in the evolution of ideas as one identifiable tradition.

Literalists teach blind adherence to their religion, but Gnostics are eclectics who seek out wisdom wherever it can be found. They emphasise that only by thinking in new ways will we become more conscious. It is no surprise, therefore, that in those periods of history in which Literalist religion has dominated we have become consumed by violence or simply stagnated. But for those brief moments when Gnosticism has flourished, we have enjoyed a flowering of culture and wisdom.

History repeats itself, albeit with subtle twists at every turn. One pattern discernible in the chaotic unfolding of events is that there are periods when humanity seems to wake up. Like a bright child we start asking some interesting questions. And, as in childhood, these intense bursts of enquiry are often accompanied by explosions of creativity. At such times anything seems possible and there appears to be no limits to the human imagination. The result is usually a spectacular blossoming of culture. And this should be no surprise, because what is culture but the measure of humanity's imagination?

Sadly, these eruptions of awakening are followed by long periods when humanity succumbs to the totalitarian grip of dogmatism and orthodoxy. Culture declines and usually goes into reverse. There is much talk about tradition and going back to basics. Few original works are created as the climate is simply too dangerous for them to appear. Culture becomes merely the repetition of forms of expressions declared safe by the monarch, or the mullahs, or the moral majority.

Although the average citizen does not have a clue as to what's really going on, it is shouted loudly from every synagogue, church or mosque that somebody somewhere is *absolutely certain*. They have the ear of the Almighty. They have all the answers in their big black book. Consequently no one else needs to worry their heads about these things. In fact, it's better if they don't think about things at all. And so, with nothing to think about, everybody slowly nods off.

That is until another meddling Gnostic philosopher pops up with childish questions such as 'Where do we come from?', 'Is there a God?' and 'Why is the emperor naked?' And thank goodness they do. There has to be someone to stand up to all those know-it-alls shouting into their megaphones, 'This is how it is. This is who you are. This is what you should do'! What we have found remarkable is that there have been so many prepared to take the appalling risks of confronting the men with the megaphones. And we should be eternally grateful to them, because they have sowed the seeds of all that is best about human culture.

Athens

One of the greatest explosions of culture happened in Classical Athens. For a brief moment in the middle of the fifth century BCE, there was an outburst of free inquiry, during which philosophers attacked the religion of Greece and ridiculed a Literalist interpretation of the works of Homer and Hesiod, which was the Greeks' Bible. Socrates and Plato taught the perennial Gnostic philosophy that all is one, and lambasted Homer and Hesiod, accusing them of attributing to the gods 'everything that is a shame and reproach among men, stealing and committing adultery and deceiving each other'.[5]

The Greeks were now thinking in startlingly new ways about the gods, creation and what it is to be human. The old ideas could not contain the outpouring of intellectual energy and broke apart. But look at the new ideas that were created: democracy, philosophy, science, education, literature, theatre, mathematics, architecture, sculpture, music, sport; the list goes on and on. The accomplishments of the Greeks are awe-inspiring and their civilisation formed the blueprint for our modern world. This vibrant, questioning culture produced incredible wonders and then utterly collapsed when it succumbed to religious dogmatism.

At the end of the fifth century the ousted Oligarchs resumed power and initiated a reactionary backlash. Tragically, but typically, the principal victims were the very people who had inspired the cultural renaissance in the first place. The brilliant and eccentric philosopher Anaxagoras, advisor of the great leader of Classical Athens, Pericles, was indicted for heresy and sent into exile. Xenophanes was indicted for impiety and banished from Athens. His crime? Expressing blasphemous sentiments such as 'If cattle and horses had hands they would draw the forms of their gods like horses and cattle',[6] and

No one knows or will ever know, the truth about the gods, for even if you did stumble on the truth, you would not know you had.[7]

Protagoras, the philosopher who famously made man 'the measure of all things', was indicted for heresy. His book was burnt in the street and he drowned whilst trying to escape his persecutors. Socrates, the most celebrated philosopher of them all, was condemned and executed. These are just some of the famous victims of the intellectual purge carried out by the Thirty Tyrants who now ruled Athens. Another fifteen hundred free-thinkers and philosophers also perished in the reign of terror. Athens had successfully cut off her own head. It was a horrible scenario, but one that history would repeat time and again.

Alexandria

The Athens experiment was ruthlessly crushed, but Gnosticism lived to inspire another great renaissance of wisdom and culture in

Hellenic Alexandria from the third century BCE. Here the spiritual wisdom of the world met and was synthesised into new dynamic forms by eclectic Gnostics. They merged Greek and Egyptian philosophy to create the *Hermetica*. Greek, Egyptian and Mesopotamian influences flowed together to create *The Chaldean Oracles*. Greek philosophy syncretised with Jewish mythology to create Christianity. Alchemy, Buddhism and every other spiritual tradition through to Zoroastrianism were openly practiced and discussed.

The great library of Alexandria was said to contain half a million scrolls, including works by writers such as Euclid, Archimedes and Ptolemy, who all worked at the library. It also contained the books of Aristarchus of Samos, who demonstrated that the Earth is one of the planets and orbits the sun. And Eratosthenes, who calculated the obliquity of the ecliptic and the diameter of the Earth with an error of less than 1 percent. And Hipparchus, who determined the precession of the equinoxes, the size of the sun, and calculated lunar eclipses. And Appolonius, who produced a study of conic sections fourteen hundred years before Kepler re-discovered this vital tool for calculating the orbits of the planets.

The scientist Carl Sagan argued that if human progress had not been interrupted by the Dark Ages, the medieval period of cathedral building might instead have witnessed the beginning of the Space Age. But this didn't happen. When Literalist Christianity became the religion of the Roman Empire the world went mad again. Free enquiry was officially terminated and the great library was put to the torch by rampaging bands of black-robed monks. Augustine constructed the first ever legal argument that the state had the right and duty to enforce religious orthodoxy on its subjects. Augustine's opponents denounced the 'unholy alliance' between Catholics and the Roman State, but they could now be legally suppressed with violence if necessary.[8]

Baghdad

With men like Augustine now firmly in control, the philosophers moved east, and the Muslim world was the beneficiary of this braindrain. In an astonishingly short period, beginning in the eighth century, the influx of Gnostic spirituality and science transformed Islamic culture into the greatest civilisation in the world. The philosopher-scientist Thabit ibn Qurra of Harran writes:

We are the heirs and propagators of Paganism. Who else have civilised the world and built cities if not the nobles and kings of Paganism? Who else have set in order the harbours and the rivers? And who else have taught the hidden wisdom? To whom else has the Deity revealed itself, given oracles, and told about the future, if not the famous men amongst the Pagans? The Pagans have made known all of this. They have discovered the art of healing the body, they have also made known the art of healing the soul; they have filled the earth with settled forms of government and with wisdom which is the highest good. Without Paganism the world would be empty and miserable.[9]

And he was right. Without Paganism the Western world really had become empty and miserable. But as the lights went out in Europe, they began to burn even more brightly in the East. Islamic culture was still young and anything seemed possible. The fruit of this open-mindedness, as always, was high culture.

In this period Baghdad saw a renaissance in which literary criticism, philosophy, poetry, mathematics, astronomy and medicine flourished as they once had in Athens and Alexandria. Baghdad had a thousand physicians, a free hospital, a regular postal service, and banks with branches as far afield as China.[10] The first university, called the House of Wisdom, was established here, where Greek texts on astronomy, navigation, geography, mathematics and medicine were translated into Arabic. Muslim scholars built on this foundation and went on to make more scientific discoveries during this period than in the whole of previously recorded history.[11]

Mystical sects, such as the Ismailis, used mathematics and science, just like their Pythagorean forebears, as a means of awakening the human mind to a sense of transcendent wonder. They attacked Literalist religion, arguing that no revelation could ever be definitive, since God was always greater than human thought.[12] Another sect called themselves the Faylasufs, from the Greek *philosophs*, which is also probably the root of the name 'Sufi' commonly given to Islamic mystics. Drawing their inspiration from the hundreds of Greek philosophical texts now available, the Faylasufs argued that human beings could transcend the apparent separateness of things and experience that all is one. They asserted that this philosophy was the original religion of humankind and all other religions were inadequate versions of the true teachings.

Yaqub ibn Ishaq al-Kindi taught that Muslims should seek truth wherever it was to be found, even from foreigners with a different religion. The teachings in the Qur'an were parables of abstract philosophical truths to make them accessible to the masses. Revealed religion was thus the poor man's philosophy. Abu Nasr al-Farabi went further and argued that philosophy was higher than revealed religion. He argued that religion was really just another means of controlling the masses and should be viewed as a branch of politics.

Muid ad-Din ibn al-Arabi urged Muslims to see all faiths as equally valid, and to be at home in a synagogue, mosque, temple or church, for as the Qur'an states, 'Wherever you turn there is the face of God'. Yahya Suhrawardi made it his life's work to trace Islam back to what he called the 'original oriental religion'. This wisdom, he claimed, had first been revealed in ancient Egypt and transmitted from there to the Greeks by Pythagoras and Plato. From the Greeks it had been passed through a succession of sages until it had reached his own master, Al Hallaj.

But by this time the Muslim world was sinking into orthodoxy. At the end of the tenth century Suhrawardi was executed for heresy and Al Hallaj was crucified by a mob possessed by religious zeal. Islam was now set on the same dismal trajectory that had previously been followed by Christianity. It cracked down on dissent and purged the very quality that had made it great: openness to new ideas. Now it deluded itself into thinking that only the Qur'an could provide everything needed to construct a just and orderly society. It was declared that 'the gates of independent thought are now closed' and it became a capital offence to criticise the prophet Muhammad.[13]

Islamic culture made a huge contribution to the human adventure before it fell asleep sometime in the Middle Ages. The fate of Islamic culture demonstrates once more the folly of basing a society on 'revelation'. Requiring people to obey antiquated laws that bear no relevance to current social problems condemns them to live at the same intellectual and cultural level as they did hundreds of years earlier. Modern Muslim women in Muhammad's homeland still have the same legal rights as a camel. And Fundamentalist men are still beheading their victims, despite proudly bearing their Kalashnikov rifles on their shoulders, because that's how Muhammad did it. And so the Islamic world remains lost somewhere in the medieval period, dreaming of past glories and snoring away under the soporific spell of Literalism.

Florence

As the Islamic world began to nod off, Europe began to awaken from its slumber. Just as the rise of Literalism in the West led to an explosion of Gnosticism in the East, so the degeneration into Literalism of the Islamic world initiated a renaissance of Gnosticism in the West. The Moors of Spain reintroduced the West to Neo-Platonism, Alchemy and a host of other long-lost traditions. Jewish Gnosticism re-surfaced in the form of Kabbalah and Christian Gnosticism re-appeared in the form of Catharism. All of these hidden streams eventually bubbled up in Florence.

In 1453 the Byzantine scholar Gemistus Pletho arrived in Florence and announced to his astonished listeners that the religious deception of Moses, Jesus and Mohammed was at an end. Philosophy was here to take its place. One of the members of Pletho's astonished audience was the wealthy banker Cosimo Medici, who sent his agents to seek out ancient philosophical works. Within a few years he had recovered the works of Plato, Plotinus, Iamblichus, Porphyry and other Greek philosophers, playwrights and historians, as well as esoteric texts like *The Chaldean Oracles*, *Hermetica* and *Picatrix*. No European had spoken Greek for centuries, but now Cosimo sponsored his protégé Marsilio Ficino to learn the language and translate his new acquisitions. He created a 'New Platonic Academy' in Florence based on the original Academy that had been closed by the Christian emperor Justinian in the sixth century.

In this tiny city the Western world suddenly regained some of its memory. When the works of the Pagan philosophers, that had been banished from Europe for a thousand years, came flooding back into Florence, they blew people's minds. Was it just accidental that so many geniuses were working in Florence in one brief period in the fifteenth century? Of course not. Leonardo da Vinci, Botticelli, Michelangelo, Raphael, Brunelleschi, Ficino and many others were all part of a Gnostic revolution which unleashed the natural creativity of all it touched.

Pico della Mirandola was the talented pupil of Ficino who, at only twenty-four years of age, was proficient in Greek, Latin, Hebrew and Arabic. In 1487 he invited scholars from all of Europe to come to Rome for a great debate. In nine hundred propositions, he claimed that Christianity, Islam, Judaism, Platonism, Hermeticism, Kabbalah and Alchemy were all parts of one philosophical tradition. Charged with youthful idealism, he rode around Rome posting his invitations. But all he actually succeeded in doing was alerting the Church authorities to what had been going on in Florence. The Pope put an end to any idea of a 'great debate' and Pico was forced to flee for his life.

Florence had done well to sustain its renaissance for thirty years, equalling, but unfortunately not exceeding, the Athenian Renaissance on which it modelled itself. But the forces of reaction were gathering in the wings. In 1492 the Roman Church, in league with the King of France, laid waste to the city. The 'New Learning', as the revived 'Gnostic' knowledge was called, had arisen at a fortuitous time, however. The invention of the printing press ensured that, try as it might, Rome was simply unable to stop the tide of books that spread these ideas throughout Europe.

Within a few years the Polish astronomer Copernicus published his theory that, contrary to appearances, it was actually the Earth that revolved around the sun. He acknowledged his debt to the Pythagoreans, saying that they had given him the courage to consider this idea seriously.[14] In the last years of the sixteenth century the Italian astronomer Galileo agreed with Copernicus and initiated the first major battle of modern times between religion and science.

In a superb illustration of the madness of Literalism, the Church condemned the theory that the Earth revolved around the sun because it contradicted two verses of the Bible. Against Copernicus and

Galileo's wealth of observations with the newly invented telescope, the Church cited as proof that Galileo was wrong *The Book of Joshua*, which claims that Joshua caused the sun to stand still.[15] If the Bible stated that Joshua caused the sun to stop moving, then clearly the Earth didn't go around the sun! On the basis of this absurd argument Galileo was led down into the dungeons, shown the instruments of torture by the Inquisition and advised to recant.

Galileo must have been aware of that other great philosopher-scientist, Giordano Bruno, who had met his end in this awful place. Bruno too had been a devotee of the New Learning, and raced around Europe arguing with theologians, writing books and founding little groups of esotericists. When he returned to Rome he was charged with heresy because he believed that the universe was infinite and that there might be other worlds out there apart from our own. Although he was imprisoned and tortured for eight years he refused to recant, so in 1600 he was led out into the *campo del fiore* and set alight. Galileo did recant and escaped being burnt alive. But he had still initiated a new way of thinking which created the modern world and which led to the demise of the totalitarian power of the Church.

A New Gnostic Renaissance

We are currently experiencing a new Gnostic renaissance. With the decline of the power of Literalist religion and the modern climate of free thought, Gnostic ideas are becoming discussed as never before. More and more people are realising that Gnostic teachings of awakening are to be found at the heart of all the spiritual traditions of the world, from Alchemy to Zen. They form a perennial wisdom that is our universal human inheritance. Only by recognising and valuing this inheritance can we avoid the nascent Gnostic renaissance we are witnessing today being crushed by the forces of reaction, as has happened in the past.

In Part 1 of this book we have focused on the nightmare of Literalist religion. In Part 2 we want to explore the Gnostic dream of waking up. To effect a genuine cure for the madness that is Literalist religion we need to clearly discriminate the living wisdom of gnosis from the religious calcifications that have been suffocating it for centuries. Then we can dispense with the dogmas that divide us and preserve the wisdom that unites us. We can throw out the bathwater and keep the baby!

Gnostic philosophy is not an intellectual theory about reality. It is a way of thinking designed to help you experience reality for yourself. The problem is that when Gnosticism calcifies into a dead tradition it degenerates into either dogmatic religion or esoteric mumbo-jumbo. It becomes either metaphysical religious assertions to be blindly believed or incomprehensible esoteric ramblings that lead us nowhere but round and round in the maze of arcane gobbledegook. In both cases it becomes divorced from the real experience of living and loses its power to transform and awaken us.

For Gnostic teachings to retain their transformative power, they must be continually brought to life by being re-invented to address the ever-changing experience of being alive. As Carl Jung writes:

All old truths want a new interpretation, so that they can live on in a new form. We need to take these thought-forms, that have become historically fixed, and melt them down again and pour them into the moulds of immediate experience.[16]

As things age they change. Today, for example, we can't hear the music of Beethoven as it was heard when he wrote it. Then it is was edgy, innovative and confronting. Now it is familiar, classical and conservative. In the same way, spiritual teachings, which in the past were the cutting-edge of consciousness, can seem safe and dated today. To be an authentic part of the Gnostic tradition we need to reject tradition! We need to be imaginative. We need to create a new language with which to discuss the old problems in a new way.

Whilst the simple message of awakening remains obscured by mystifying mumbo-jumbo, Gnosticism can seem to be an inaccessible, abstruse philosophy. But as an early Christian text boldly asserts, 'There is nothing about the Truth which is truly difficult'.[17] In our experience this is right. Gnostic philosophy is essentially simple and points to a natural state of awakening available to all of us. So, we are going to use modern language to wake us up by pointing to the simple Truth.

Gnostics who have lived at different times and in different cultures use different images to help us understand Gnostic teachings. But these diverse analogies often conflict and break down, which can confuse the simplicity of the essential Gnostic message. So, we are going to concentrate on one very powerful metaphor which is simple, clear, consistent and used by Gnostics throughout history. Life is like a dream and gnosis is like waking up.

Most people have had experiences of awakening, but have not had the necessary understanding to give their experiences a context, and have therefore ended up ignoring or forgetting them. Our hope is to give you an intellectual understanding of gnosis which can both help you taste the awakened state right now and give you a context for a continuing exploration of gnosis in your life. If you have been consciously on the journey of awakening for some time, we hope that the ideas we will explore may help clarify your understanding of gnosis, so that you can avoid getting caught up in unnecessarily complex 'spiritual' concepts and wake up more easily.

We don't want you to study our ideas and just agree with us. We certainly don't want you to adopt what we say on blind faith or because of the insidious authority of the written word. That is what leads to Literalism. We urge you to check out what we have to say against the only genuine authority, which is your own experience. We encourage you to take what works for you and leave the rest, albeit with the proviso that something may make more sense later. The Christian Gnostic Theodotus teaches:

All people, according to their stage of development, possess the gnosis in a way special to themselves.[18]

If this philosophy of gnosis resonates with you as deeply as it does with us, we want you to make it your own. And to pass it on in your own way to others, who will in turn make it their own. Only by transmitting the experience of gnosis from consciousness to consciousness, like the Olympic flame passed from torch to torch, can Gnostic philosophy be kept genuinely alive.

Although we gratefully acknowledge the inspiration of the great Gnostic masters who kept the flame of this tradition alive and passed it on to us, we aren't going to present Gnostic philosophy as they expressed in the past. But we are going to follow their example. Just as they inherited this tradition and reformulated it into a new language for new times, we want to offer an innovative approach to awakening that is designed to address the needs of human beings today. We have spent our lives exploring and writing books about all the Gnostic traditions of the world. This has put us in the position of being able to offer you the distilled essence of Gnosticism, as we have come to understand it, in a new way for new times. But, although the form may be new, the message remains essentially the same: wake up!

∞

PART II

The Baby

HIP-GNOSIS

We
(that indivisible divinity that operates in us)
have dreamed the world.
—JORGE LUIS BORGES, *OTHER INQUISITIONS*

Gnostic philosophy is extreme sports for the mind. It is for those who relish the rush of exhilaration as they free-fall into uncertainty. The buzz of alert concentration as they scale the mountain of imagination, seeking out a higher view. The thrill of anticipation as they wait to ride a swell of insight as it surges up from the depths. Always hoping for the big one. Gnostic philosophy isn't safely theoretical. It is live and dangerous. It is a profound exploration of the great mysteries of life and death. An heroic adventure to excite the soul. Some people dismiss all philosophy as abstract and irrelevant. But Gnostic philosophy can utterly transform our understanding of who we are and what it is to be alive. What could be more concrete and relevant than that?

At the heart of Gnostic philosophy is the outrageous claim that if we experience the state of gnosis we will recognise that life is a dream. This idea challenges our most fundamental assumptions about who we are and what life is. At first it may seem even madder than the maddest of Literalist claptrap. The Christian Gnostic Theodosius acknowledges:

> I know that the teachings of gnosis are a laughing-stock to most people. Some are startled by them, as when a light suddenly illuminates the darkness of a drinking party. But the truly blessed are those who rouse themselves from sleep and raise their eyes to the truth.

Is gnosis just another mad ancient theory? No. Gnosis isn't a theory at all. It's an experience. The Gnostics aren't trying to persuade us to adopt their opinion that life is a dream. They want to use philosophical ideas to wake us up, so we see for ourselves the true nature of reality. The Pagan Gnostic Plotinus teaches:

> The aim of philosophy is the same as someone who wishes to shake off the fantasies of a dream and bring to an awakened state the awareness which is creating them.

The job of the Gnostic philosopher is to 'wake people to the vision'. And this is what we want to do right now. But before we begin our journey of awakening it is important to clear up some common misunderstandings, which may prevent you grasping the essential simplicity of Gnostic teachings.

When we say that life is a dream we aren't dismissing the world as an irrelevant fantasy. The world is beautiful beyond words to describe. Gnosis isn't rejecting life as some sort of pernicious illusion. It isn't about denying the horrors and wonders of existence. It is simply seeing things as they are. And this is not an experience of detached indifference to life. It is appreciating how magical and mysterious existence really is. It is when we are unconsciously engrossed in the life-dream that it becomes a nightmare. But when we wake up we find ourselves in love with life in all its awesome, multifarious splendour.

When we say that gnosis is an experience of awakening, we don't mean it is the same as waking up from a dream in the morning, when the dream-world disappears and is replaced by this world. The experience of gnosis does not entail entering some supernatural state in which your everyday life no longer exists. It does not involve strange visions or paranormal abilities.

Gnosis is a natural state comparable to the experience of lucid dreaming. Lucid dreaming is the experience of dreaming, but consciously recognizing that you are dreaming. Gnosis is the experience of 'lucid living'. It is being conscious that life is a dream right now. When you dream lucidly the dream doesn't stop, but you are no longer unconsciously engrossed in the dream. In the same way, when you experience lucid living the life-dream doesn't stop, but you are no longer unconsciously engrossed in the life-dream.

Let us make this absolutely clear. We are not suggesting that the person you presently presume yourself to be is imagining the world. Quite the opposite. We are suggesting that the person you appear to be is part of the life-dream. When you dream lucidly you recognise that the person you appear to be in your dream isn't the real *you*, because you are the dreamer. In the same way, when you live lucidly you recognise that the person you appear to be right now is not the real *you*, because you are the life-dreamer which is dreaming itself to be everyone and everything.

Knowing Now

How can we check out the notion that life is a dream? Dreams exist only in the moment they are being dreamt. To discover if life is a dream, therefore, we need to investigate our experience of the present moment. This is the secret of waking up. Gnosticism is an investigation of the now. To experience gnosis you need to examine this moment closely and understand it in a remarkable new way.

Focus your attention on your experience of this moment. What is different about this present moment from every other moment you have experienced or will experience? There are, of course, an infinite number of things which make each moment unique, but there is something obviously different about the *now*. The present moment exists. The past has gone and the future is only a possibility, but the present is a reality you are actually experiencing. To understand existence you must pay attention to what exists and examine this moment.

The word *gnosis* is usually translated as 'knowledge', but it is better to think of it as a state of *knowing*. Gnosis is not information like the 'knowledge' you picked up at school. Gnosis is not a theory about life which you can learn. Gnosis is a state of awakening that arises when you examine the present moment and become conscious of what you are actually *knowing* right now.

Most of the things we claim to know are actually just opinions which we *believe*. To experience gnosis we need to differentiate *believing* from *knowing*. It is possible to doubt all our beliefs, but what we are *knowing* is self-evidently certain in the moment. We don't have to give up our opinions to experience gnosis. They may be useful, beautiful, valid opinions. But we do need to discriminate them from what we actually are *knowing* now.

Literalism is based on the belief that history can save us. The basic teaching of Literalist Christianity, for example, is that if you believe in the death and resurrection of Jesus you will go to Heaven when you die. But although it is possible to *believe* passionately that Jesus died and resurrected for our sins, as millions do, it is impossible to *know* this, because it is not happening right now. And all we actually know is the now. Gnosticism is rooted firmly in the reality of this present moment. It doesn't teach that history can save you. Rather, it suggests that history is the problem. History is a story we tell about the past to explain the present. The problem is that when we are busy believing that we know what is going on, we never really stand back from our opinions to look at realty with an open mind, so we become unconsciously engrossed in the life-dream and don't wake up.

Make no mistake about it, all the ideas about history that we have previously explored in this book have nothing to do with gnosis. They are just opinions about the past. Good, well-evidenced opinions, but opinions nevertheless. We can't know them to be true, because the past has gone. All we are left with are bits and pieces of evidence from which we can put together the best available theoretical understanding. But we are now leaving opinion behind.

The Mystery of Existence

What are you *knowing* right now? If you pay attention to your immediate experience of reality and ask yourself this question you will realise that most of what you think you know you really don't! Life is extremely mysterious. What is this moment? What is it to be alive? Completely focus on the now and you will feel a rush of excitement as you become conscious of the awesome mystery of existence. Step out of the world of your preconceptions and become conscious of reality for once. It is something most of us so rarely do it can be a liberating surprise.

We are usually so engrossed in the stories we tell about life that we don't notice something extremely important about our predicament. We don't know what is going on! We are so busy pretending that we know who we are and what life is that we somehow manage to ignore the shocking truth. We don't understand life at all. We are so lost in our concepts about life that we rarely give our open-minded attention to the mysterious experience of living here and now. We are eating the menu not the meal. No wonder we so often find life hard to swallow.

When we confront existence without our habitual assumptions we see our beliefs for what they are. Stories. Concepts. Words. And we see that the stories we tell about life are not life itself. Life is infinitely enigmatic. The word *reality* is not reality. We don't know what reality is. This radical not-knowing is the first step towards genuine *knowing*. This rejection of our theories about life in favour of becoming conscious of the mysterious experience of living in this moment is the prerequisite for gnosis.

Most people have experienced at least brief moments when they have found themselves catapulted into the mystery of the moment. Anything can trigger this. Often it is confronting death. Someone close to you dies, or you are diagnosed as seriously ill, and suddenly you are face-to-face with the fact that you really don't know what life is. Let alone what death is! Or it may be a moment of exquisite beauty which does it. You fall in love or give birth to a child, and suddenly you remember the miracle of existence. It may be a walk in the mountains or the feeling of the sun warming your back. Or it may happen for no obvious reason at all. Whatever the apparent cause, most of us have had moments of overwhelming wonder or overpowering terror in which we have suddenly become conscious of the awesome mystery of existence.

If, whilst reading these words, you have been able to put your opinions on one side and become conscious of the mystery of this moment, you will have already experienced a radical shift in consciousness. It will feel as if you previously existed in some sort of semi-conscious trance, in which you were so mesmerised by your ideas about life that you hardly noticed how miraculously strange it is to be alive. How mind-blowing it is that you exist at all. The mystery of existence will be so obvious it will seem astonishing that you are usually oblivious to it. You will realise how unconscious you normally are!

If you become conscious of the mystery of this moment you will begin to understand why the Gnostics compare life to a dream and gnosis to waking up. Because you will feel as if you have awoken from some sort of unconscious stupor. You will have begun to rouse yourself from the collective coma we mistake for 'real life' by becoming conscious of reality itself. You will understand why Plotinus teaches: 'It's as if we sleep through life and take the dream world on complete trust'.

Know Your Self

If you free yourself from the prison of your opinions and come into the mystery of the moment you will enter a state of profound and liberating doubt. Then you will be able to examine your immediate experience with fresh eyes to see if there is anything about which you can be genuinely certain. We can't do this for you. You must do this for yourself. But we can point out some things about the nature of the moment that you may have missed. And this may lead you to appreciate the moment in a radically new way. We can bring to your attention some things about which you are absolutely certain right now. And becoming conscious of these simple certainties is the state of gnosis, or *knowing*.

What are you *knowing* now? If you focus your attention on the mystery of the moment you will feel profoundly alive, because you will become acutely conscious of the fact *that you are*. You will recognise something about which you are completely sure. *You exist right now*. This is not an opinion. It is self-evidently true and beyond doubt. It is something you are *knowing* as your eyes pass across this page.

There is one thing which is always now. *You* are always now. But what is this 'you' which is always now? Gnosticism is an exploration of what you are in this moment. Above the famous Pagan Oracle of Delphi were written the words 'Know Your Self.' This is the perennial Gnostic challenge. The Christian master Silvanos urges us: 'Before everything know your self.' So what are you? The common sense reply is 'I am a person'. This is certainly what you *appear* to be, but the Gnostics suggest it is not what you really *are*.

In this moment you know that you exist. And you also know something else equally obvious and just as profound. You know you are *experiencing* something. If you were not experiencing anything you would be unconscious and you wouldn't know that you exist. So, you know you are *an experiencer of experiences*. You are awareness witnessing a flow of experiences we call 'life'.

In *The Gospel of Thomas* Jesus promises:

> I will reveal to you what no eye can see,
> what no ear can hear,
> what no hand can touch,
> what cannot be imagined by the mind.

What is it that you can't hear, touch, see or imagine? It is awareness which is witnessing the seeing, hearing, touching and imagining. The message of the Gnostics is that if you really come to know your self you will discover you are awareness.

What is awareness? You can't experience awareness with your

senses or imagination, because it is what is witnessing your sensations and imaginings. The Pagan Gnostic Porphyry teaches:

> What lesson have we learned from those who best understand the human condition? Surely, that you must not think of me as this person who can be touched and grasped by the senses, but my true self is remote from the body, without colour and without shape, not to be touched by human hands.

Plato teaches that to wake up we need to distinguish the ineffable, unchanging presence of awareness from our experiences which are always changing. Examine the reality of right now. What you are experiencing is never the same from one moment to the next. Awareness is the permanent background of the flux of experience which witnesses all the changes. It is the same now . . . and now . . . and now. It is a presence which is always present. The 'you' which is always now.

I and It

We would like to suggest that you have a dual nature. You *appear* to be a person, but you *are* awareness. What we are pointing out is actually obvious. You are both an object and a subject. Objectively you are a physical body. A *thing* in the world. But subjectively you are not a *thing* at all. You are awareness. Lucid living is recognising that you can see yourself in two entirely different ways in this present moment. You are both an 'I' and an 'it'. Focus on the reality of this moment and discriminate what you *are* from what you *appear* to be.

What you *appear* to be is constantly changing, but what you *are* is never-changing. Your body is in perpetual motion. Your thoughts are constantly coming and going. Over your lifetime the person you appear to be has been transformed almost beyond recognition. But don't you have the sense that the real 'you' is the same now as when you were eighteen or eight? What is this unchanging self? It is the witness of your ever-changing appearance: awareness.

We experience the knowledge of being awareness as the feeling 'I am'. If you examine your sense of 'I am' you will see that, although obvious, it is completely indefinable. There is nothing you can say about the 'I', except that it witnesses all the changing qualities of the person you appear to be. Most of us, however, habitually identify what we *are* with what we *appear* to be and believe 'I am a person'. As an experiment, let go of the idea 'I am a person' and discriminate the 'I' that you *are* from the person you *appear* to be.

When you dream at night you have two aspects to your identity. Your apparent nature is the person you appear to be in the dream. But your essential nature is awareness within which the dream is arising. Lucid living is being conscious that you also have two aspects to your identity right now. Your apparent nature is the person you appear to be, but your essential nature is awareness which is witnessing all you experience. Right now, just as when you are dreaming, you *are* awareness *appearing* to be a person.

When you are absorbed in a dream at night the experience can sometimes seem terrifyingly 'real', because you believe yourself to be your dream-persona wrestling with your dream-dramas, and you are unconscious of the fact that you are the dreamer. In the same way when you are engrossed in the experience of living, life seems very 'real', because you identify with your life-persona wrestling with your life-dramas, and you are unconscious of the fact that you are awareness.

If you become conscious of your essential nature as awareness, however, your appreciation of reality will be profoundly transformed. You will see that the person you appear to be is not your essential nature. It is what the ancient Gnostics call your *eidolon*. An 'image' or 'appearance'. It is your apparent nature within the life-dream. If you recognise this you will understand why Plotinus teaches:

> Those who identify the body with real being are like dreamers who mistake figments of their sleeping vision for reality.

Waking and Sleeping

It may help you to differentiate your essential nature from your apparent nature if you consider your everyday experience of waking and sleeping. When you go to sleep at night and wake in the morning you appear to be a body that is sometimes conscious and sometimes unconscious. That's how it looks to others from the objective it-perspective. But that's not how it is for you from the subjective I-perspective. What do you actually experience when you go to sleep?

When you sleep your body and the world disappear from aware-ness and you find yourself in a different world in which you may ap-pear to be a different person. This is a state of awareness we call 'dreaming'. And then the dream-world disappears and you don't expe-rience anything. This is a state of unconscious awareness we call 'deep sleep' in which you don't exist as a person at all. And then you wake up and the body you appear to be now and the world it inhabits reappear.

From the objective it-perspective you appear to be a body that is sometimes conscious. But from the subjective I-perspective you are awareness which is sometimes conscious of a body. From the it-perspective you appear to be a body within which consciousness comes and goes. But from the I-perspective it is the other way around. You are awareness within which the body comes and goes. And you experience this every day.

When you identify with your dream-persona in a dream at night you become engrossed in the dream. But if you become conscious that you are awareness imagining itself to be your dream-persona, you start to dream lucidly. In the same way, if you identify with the person you appear to be right now, you will remain lost in the life-dream. But if you become conscious of your essential nature as awareness, you will start to live lucidly. Then you will understand why Plotinus teaches:

> The true waking is not of the body, but from the body. Anything else
> is just a passage from sleep to sleep.

The Timeless Emptiness of Awareness

When you dream at night you appear to be your dream-persona which exists *within* your dream world. But if you dream lucidly you become conscious that you are the dreamer and your dream-world exists *within* awareness. In the same way, when you are engrossed in the life-dream you appear to be a person *within* the world. But if you live lucidly you become conscious that you are awareness and the world exists *within* you. If you adopt the I-perspective of your essential nature this will become obvious.

Everything you are conscious of exists as a flow of appearances within awareness. All that you see, hear, taste, smell and touch exists within awareness. The thoughts you are thinking right now exist within awareness. Your body exists within awareness. This book exists within awareness. The world exists within awareness. If it did not exist within awareness you would not be aware of it.

As a body you are an object which exists in the world, but as awareness you are an infinite emptiness which contains the world. Becoming conscious of your essential nature turns reality inside out. Quite literally! From the it-perspective awareness seems to exist inside the person you appear to be. But from the I-perspective awareness is an empty presence within which the whole life-dream is arising.

If you can get this you will also see something else equally astounding. Your essential nature 'is not at all in time or place, but is purely and simply in eternity', as Meister Eckhart puts it. As awareness you don't exist in time. Time exists in you. You are awareness witnessing the flow of appearances we call 'time'. Try it out. Be the timeless presence of awareness witnessing appearing to be a person in time.

If that seems far out, there's more. In *The Gospel of Thomas*, Jesus proclaims that if you understand the teachings of awakening you will 'not taste death'. But what does it mean? Will gnosis make you immortal? No. Gnosis is becoming conscious that you are already immortal and always have been. Awakening is the discovery of what the Christian Gnostics call your 'unbornness'.

If you become conscious of your essential nature as awareness you will see that you can't possibly die, because you were never born. You are awareness which witnessed the birth of the body and which will one day witness its death. But awareness doesn't age and die. It is a permanent presence within which the life-dream is arising. The body is mortal because it exists in time, and everything in time has a beginning and an end. But your essential nature as awareness does not exist in time. It is unborn and undying. A Christian text called *The Treaties on the Resurrection* asks, 'Are you—the real you— something that can decay?' Become conscious of your essential nature right now and answer this question for yourself.

One Awareness

If life is like a dream, isn't it a bit of a coincidence that we are all dreaming the same world into existence? How can we understand this? The Gnostic explanation is an astonishing insight into the nature of reality. Although we appear to be separate individuals within the life-dream, there is only one awareness dreaming the life-dream. Your essential nature is the same as everyone else's essential nature. We appear to be many, but essentially we are one.

This may sound outlandish, but it is the extraordinary message taught by Gnostics from all cultures. The original Christians call our shared essential nature 'the Christ within'. Buddhists call it our 'Buddha-Nature'. Hindus call it the 'Atman'. You call it 'I' and so does everyone else. And we all experience this 'I' as the utter certainty that we exist. It is our *being.* It is what we are.

From the perspective of the waking state it is easy to understand that in a dream at night everything and everyone in the dream is an expression of your deeper nature as the dreamer. In the same way, we want to suggest, there is one awareness dreaming itself to be everyone and everything right now. We are not saying that you as an individual person are dreaming the life-dream, because as a person you are part of the dream, as is everyone else. We are suggesting that the awareness which is conscious through each one of us is the same awareness experiencing the life-dream from different perspectives.

Check it out for yourself. If you examine your apparent nature as a person you will see that you are obviously different from everyone else. Your body and personality have distinctive characteristics. You inhabit a unique place in space and time. No one else is having exactly the experience of life that you are having. Now become conscious of being awareness. Is your essential nature different from anyone else's essential nature? No. You are a timeless presence witnessing the flow of time. And so is everyone else. As awareness we are indistinguishably one.

This is the paradox of our predicament. As awareness we are one. But what we are conscious of differs. We are one awareness experiencing different perspectives on the life-dream. Our diverse apparent natures and our shared essential nature are polar opposites. As persons within the life-dream we are many. As awareness we are one. The word *person* comes from the ancient Greek word for a mask. As diverse persons we are different masks being worn by the one awareness, which is 'unchangeable, indivisible, timeless being', as Plotinus puts it.

We think of ourselves as a some *one*. A discrete individual. But the person we appear to be is actually a complex group of ever-changing qualities. Examine the person you appear to be and you will see that your body is made up of myriad organs and limbs. Your personality is a composite of different character traits, memories, desires and fears. As a person you are a mutating matrix of coalescing characteristics. Yet, you *know* that the essential you which witnesses all of this is an indivisible unity. That's true, isn't it? What gives you this sense of being an individual is not your complex personal nature but your essential nature as the oneness of awareness.

You Are the Universe

On the surface you appear to be separate from everyone else. But if you stop looking at life superficially you will recognize that beneath the surface we are all connected like islands. If you plumb the depths of your identity you will discover that you are the life-dreamer. The source of the life-dream. This is why Simon Magus teaches that within each of us 'dwells the infinite power' which is 'the root of the universe'. And why *The Gospel of Philip* teaches:

> Whoever has not known himself has known nothing, but he who has known himself has, at the same time, already achieved gnosis of the depth of all things.

And why Meister Eckhart teaches 'Our true "I" is God'. And why Clement of Alexandria teaches:

> The greatest of all lessons is to know your self, because when you know your self you know God.

Most Gnostics have lived in cultures where the only vocabulary available to discuss these ideas has been a religious vocabulary, so they have used words like 'God' to point us to the one awareness which is dreaming the life-dream. We are frequently asked if we believe in God. Our answer is that we don't believe in anything but God! In reality, what else is there but the one life-dreamer dreaming the life-dream and experiencing it from infinitely various perspectives.

If you wake up from the dream of separateness you can know that all is one right now. Try it. Be awareness and you will see that you are not separate from anything or anyone. Everything you are experiencing exists within you as awareness. And awareness isn't separate from what it is witnessing, any more than an object is separate from the space it occupies. As the medieval mystic Jan Ruysbroeck teaches, 'We behold what we are and we are what we behold'.

A dream and the dreamer are conceptually two but in reality one, because you can't have a dream without a dreamer. In the same way, right now awareness and what it is experiencing are conceptually two but in reality one, because you can't have experiences without awareness. You are what you are experiencing. You are the life-dreamer and the life-dream. You are everyone and everything. As the Renaissance mystic Nicholas of Cusa paradoxically proclaims:

> The universe is in us in such a way that we are in it, so that everyone in the universe is the universe.

The Paradox of Our Predicament

Have you ever seen one of those amazing pictures which change depending on what you take to be the background and what you take to be the foreground? Look at it one way and it's a picture of a rabbit. Look at it another way and it's a duck. There's another famous example which appears to be a picture of an old hag, until you change your perception and suddenly it's a picture of a beautiful young woman. When you see the paradox of our predicament it's like that.

Look at your experience of the present moment from the it-perspective and you will see yourself as a body in the world. Look at it from the I-perspective and you will realise you are the emptiness of awareness and the world exists in you. Look at this moment from the it-perspective and you're a person confined by time. Look at this moment from the I-perspective and you're the eternal witness of the flow of experiences we call 'time'. Look at the moment from the it-perspective and you're a separate individual. Look at the moment from the I-perspective and all is one.

Lucid living is looking in 'two directions at once', as Plotinus puts it. It is simultaneously being conscious of both the I-perspective and the it-perspective. It is recognising that you are 'in the world but not of it', as the Christian Gnostics teach. It is appearing to be a separate person in the life-dream, whilst also knowing that essentially everything is an expression of our shared essential nature. It is both being the one and appearing to be someone. It is embracing the paradoxical nature of reality and realising, as Plotinus teaches, that 'you exist in a world which exists in you'.

When people first come across Gnostic philosophy they often experience an initial resistance to the idea of being impersonal awareness, because this feels cold and seems to devalue their humanity. This resistance displays an innate wisdom, because adopting the I-perspective *instead* of the it-perspective would feel cold and devalue our humanity. But lucid living isn't being the life-dreamer *instead* of a person in the life-dream. It is consciously being *both* the life-dreamer *and* a person in the life-dream. And this is not cold at all. Quite the opposite. It is an experience of all-embracing compassion we call 'big love'.

Big Love

Love is what we feel when we know we are one. We love someone when we feel so close that we connect beyond our apparent separateness. When we think we are just a person we love only those we embrace within our limited idea of who we are, such as our friends and family. We don't love those who threaten our personal identity and we are indifferent to everyone else. But when we discover we are one with all we find ourselves in love with all.

Gnosis is not an abstract intellectual understanding. It feels good. Indeed, nothing feels better. We taste a little of how good oneness feels when we arise from deep sleep and, for a few precious moments, bathe in the afterglow of unconscious oneness, subsumed in a warm feeling of complete well-being. Gnosis is being *conscious* of this wonderful oneness right now. And this is an experience of big love.

Big love has nothing to do with liking other people. It is an unconditional love of all, friends and enemies alike, because we know we are one with all. Big love has nothing to do with liking what is happening in the life-dream. It is an unconditional love of life, with all its joys and sorrows, because we know we are one with life. It is 'loving everything because everything is part of the whole', as the Christian Gnostic Basilides teaches.

As every parent knows, it is possible to love what we don't like. When a child behaves badly we may not like how they are acting, but this doesn't mean we stop loving them. We may need to reprimand or even punish the child, but we do this *because* we love them so much. In the same way, realising we are one with all doesn't mean we stop condemning those who are so lost in the illusion of separateness that they perpetrate all kinds of evil. But we are critical because we love them, not because we reject them as 'other'. We know there is no 'us and them'. There is just us. It is only this profound recognition of our essential unity which allows us to fulfil the profound Christian injunction to love our 'enemies'.

As awareness you are already unconditionally embracing everything with big love. You merely have to recognise this. Try it now. Be conscious of your essential nature which is one with all. Embrace everyone and everything with unconditional big love. Be the life-dreamer compassionately communing with yourself in all your many different disguises.

The Purpose of Life

If life is a dream what is its purpose? Why is the life-dreamer dreaming the life-dream? What does the life-dreamer want? Well, you are the life-dreamer, so you can find the answer by asking yourself what *you* want. You probably want many different things, but at the root of all your various desires is a fundamental impulse to feel good. Everyone wants to feel good. It's our undeniable basic urge. When we don't feel good we are propelled to change things so that we do. And when we do feel good we want it to get even better. We can't get enough of feeling good.

Follow back any of your desires far enough and at its root you will find the desire to feel good. You may want material prosperity. Why? Because you believe it will make you feel good. You may want to be successful. Why? Because you hope it will make you feel good. You may want to help others. Why? Because you have found making others feel good makes you feel good. Yet, if you ask yourself why you want to feel good, it's a silly question, because the answer is self-evident. *Good* is by definition what you want to feel.

Is there any more fundamental desire than the desire to enjoy living? Yes and no. If you imagine that your life is suddenly threatened, you will immediately realise just how much you want to live. Compared to this desire to *be*, all your other desires are inconsequential, because they all require you first to be alive! Yet it is not enough to simply *be*. Does the idea of being unconscious in a coma appeal? No. Because you want to consciously experience living. And it is not enough to simply experience *anything*. You don't want to feel bad. You want to experience feeling good.

How you interpret the fundamental desire 'I want to feel good' depends on who you think you are. Whilst you believe you are just a separate person, you will interpret the desire to feel good in a selfish way. But if you become conscious of our shared essential nature you will recognise that the fundamental life-impulse is the life-dreamer's universal desire for all to feel good. You will realise that you are the life-dreamer and you are dreaming the life-dream because you want to enjoy the experience of living in all your myriad forms.

As individuals within the life-dream we can play our part in fulfilling this fundamental life-impulse by waking up and living lucidly. When we are lost in the nightmare of separateness we become embroiled in a relentless quest to feel good as a separate individual, even if this means causing suffering to others. But when we become conscious of our shared essential nature we love living and are moved to help others wake up and enjoy life as well. We become compassionate participants in the epic adventure of our collective awakening.

8

NO REALITY WITHOUT POLARITY

How can all things be one,
yet each thing be separate?
—THE ODES OF ORPHEUS

What is going on right now? What is this bizarre business we call 'life'? It's extremely strange and infinitely mysterious. Perhaps it would be best to say no more than that. Except that we can't. We need a story to live by which explains our predicament, albeit in a way which can never do justice to the infinite mystery. We need narratives to help us navigate our lives, by telling us who we are and what life is all about. But the story we tell limits our experience of life, so we need to choose it very carefully.

Most of us just go along with whatever story happens to be in vogue in our culture. But Gnostics throughout history have offered an alternative story which opens up a deeper experience of the mystery of living. We want to offer you a new version of the Gnostic narrative, based on our previous investigation of the reality of the present moment. But, make no mistake about it, this is only a story. It isn't the truth. Its just the best falsehood we've found!

Our Gnostic narrative begins with the idea of polarity. You are experiencing something right now because the life-dreamer is dreaming the life-dream. Without the polarity of awareness and appearances there would be nothing. You know this is true from your experience of sleeping and waking. In the state of deep sleep there is only the oneness/nothingness of unconscious awareness. You become conscious when the polarity of awareness and appearances arises. As Carl Jung once said (in a great line that should be used on a rap record!): 'No reality without polarity'.

Polarity is paradoxical. The two poles of a polarity are irreconcilable opposites, yet indivisibly one because they can only exist together. What appears as either/or is essentially both/and. The primal polarity which forms the foundation of existence is the life-dreamer and the life-dream, which appear to be two but are essentially one. Existence is an essential oneness appearing as duality.

The life-dreamer is the oneness of unconscious awareness, which is the potential to experience everything. Its polar opposite is the infinitely various forms which comprise the life-dream. Awareness becomes conscious through these different forms. Consciousness is the relationship between awareness and a particular form it imagines itself to be in the life-dream. What awareness is conscious of through a particular form depends on the nature of the form. The life-dream is awareness experiencing an infinite spectrum of different states of consciousness through infinitely various forms.

The life-dream is awareness in the process of waking up from unconscious oneness to conscious oneness. What science calls 'evolution' is the life-dreamer progressively imagining ever more complex forms capable of greater consciousness. Through most forms the life-dreamer is relatively unconscious and identified with its apparent nature in the life-dream. But through the human form the life-dreamer can experience self-knowledge or gnosis, by becoming conscious of its essential nature as awareness.

Gnosis is the unconscious oneness of awareness dreaming itself to be an individual person who is consciously one with all. This is not some absolute state of awakening beyond which it is impossible to go. Consciousness arises within the duality of the life-dream, so we can always be relatively more or less conscious. Gnosis is being the life-dreamer appearing to be a person on a never-ending journey of becoming more conscious.

The bad news is we're never going to arrive, but the good news is *we're never going to arrive*. And this is very good news, because the more we wake up, the more we love living, so we don't want the adventure of becoming more conscious to have a conclusion. Gnosis is a way of travelling, not a destination. It is loving living. And this is not something we can achieve once and for all, because each moment is an opportunity to love living in a new way.

Re-emergence

The life-dream arises with polarity and is characterised by infinite polarities. One important polarity which defines existence is birth and death. Everything in the life-dream has a beginning and an ending. Our shared essential nature as awareness exists outside time, so it neither begins nor ends, but the person we appear to be exists in time and does have a beginning and an end. As awareness we are unborn and undying, but as a person we were born and will one day die.

What happens when our life-persona dies in the life-dream? Consciousness arises through our apparent nature, so will its death mean the end of our conscious experience as an individual? Do we continue to exist only as the oneness of unconscious awareness? Because that doesn't seem to be much of a comfort in the face of death!

Literalists promise believers a happy life after death as immortal individuals in Heaven. Gnostics are more concerned with achieving a happy life before death by awakening to oneness and big love. Gnosis is becoming conscious of what we are *knowing* right now, and we can't know now what will happen when we die, because we aren't dead yet! Death is by its nature a profound mystery, and one of the roles it plays in life is to remind us of the mystery which is actually ever-present in each moment.

Yet Gnostics throughout history speculate that the journey of awakening is not a process of one lifetime only, but of many lifetimes. Socrates reasons that life and death are a polarity that can exist only in relationship with each other. In the same way that day follows night and night follows day, death must follow life and life must follow death. An individual life doesn't go on forever, but life and death do go on forever. The ancient Gnostics call this process 'reincarnation' and we call it 're-emergence'.

What will happen when you die in the life-dream? Well, have you ever dreamt you died in a dream at night? If so you will know what happens. You wake up! The person you appeared to be in the dream disappears and you appear to be a different person. In the same way, the Gnostics teach, when your present persona dies in the life-dream you will find yourself appearing as a different persona in a different dream. Based on its past experience of being 'you', the life-dreamer will imagine 'you' again in a different way and in a different context.

Our conscious experience is punctuated by a period of withdrawal into the oneness of unconscious awareness every night in the state of deep sleep. Death is a deeper withdrawal into unconscious oneness from which we re-emerge as a different persona in the life-dream. Life and death is a cycle of becoming conscious, falling unconscious and becoming conscious once more.

Through the continuous cycle of life and death we gradually wake up. Each re-emergence, or re-birth, changes the objective perimeters within which our individual nature evolves. The new relationship between the part and the whole enables the part to become conscious in a new way. We become more conscious of our immortal essential nature through experiencing a recurring cycle of birth and death as a person in the life-dream.

Reincarnation, or re-emergence, is often interpreted literally as the idea that when we are re-born we come back *here.* But there is no *here* to come back to. There is no independently existing world that we can enter and leave. There is the unfolding of the life-dream within awareness. We should not assume the life-dream is limited to the experience of this world or even this cosmos, vast and various as it is. The totality of the life-dream should be conceived of as an infinite *imagnos* containing endless imagined worlds. Our cosmos is just one possibility within the endless imagnos. When the dream of appearing to be a person in this world ends, what arises is another perspective on the imagnos. But we should not assume this new dream will necessarily resemble the dream we are presently experiencing. The possibilities are endless.

Did we experience a life before this life? Just because we don't remember anything prior to our birth doesn't mean we didn't experience anything. After all, we don't remember being a baby, but this doesn't mean we never were a baby. Birth is the beginning of the process of re-emerging from unconscious awareness and becoming conscious again, so we shouldn't be surprised that when we are born we aren't conscious of our past lives, because we are hardly conscious at all.

The theory of re-emergence, like any theory, is only speculation. From the Gnostic perspective it is not that we can *know* what will happen when we die. It is rather that, because life is a dream, there is no reason to believe that the death of the body means the end of our individual experience. The body is a temporary part of the flow of appearances we are experiencing. It comes and goes within awareness every day when we rise in the morning and sleep at night. Why shouldn't a particular body leave awareness permanently when we die and a new one arise in its place?

As an experiment, stop thinking of yourself as a person with a past that began at birth and a future which will end at death. Try out a different possibility. See yourself as unborn and undying awareness witnessing a flow of experiences, which never began and will never end, within which you will always appear to be an individual part in relationship with the whole.

Enlivenment

Many spiritual traditions call waking up to our essential shared nature 'enlightenment'. By contrast we can refer to the state in which we are identified with our apparent nature as 'endarkenment'. But lucid living is neither enlightenment nor endarkenment. It is 'enlivenment'. It is really enjoying appearing to be a person in the life-dream, because we are *also* conscious of our essential nature and experiencing big love. Lucid living is understanding the fundamental polarity of existence and being all that we are.

Some spiritual traditions, however, teach that to wake up to oneness we have to eradicate our individuality. This common misunderstanding arises from either/or thinking and is resolved by adopting a both/and perspective. Endarkenment is being conscious of *only* one pole of our dual nature. The solution is not to identify with *only* the other pole instead. It is consciously embracing *both* our shared essential nature as awareness *and* our individual apparent nature as a person in the world.

Either/or spiritual traditions, however, teach that to wake up we need to extinguish our apparent nature in the void of awareness. But this isn't waking up. This is going to sleep! We do this every night when we merge with the oneness of unconscious awareness. Awakening is *consciously* experiencing our essential nature. And it is only when we appear to be a person in the life-dream that we are conscious, so it is only by having an apparent nature that it is possible to *also* become conscious of our essential nature as awareness.

According to either/or spiritual traditions, if we become enlightened we will never have to reincarnate again and can finally escape this horrible business of being human. But this pious distaste for life is not lucid living. When we dream lucidly we don't stop dreaming, we simply start dreaming consciously. In the same way, when we live lucidly we don't stop appearing to be an individual person in the world, we simply start living consciously.

It is fashionable in spiritual circles, however, to believe that to become 'enlightened' we must destroy our 'ego'. The word *ego* is used by different people to mean different things, which is a source of much confusion. If the word *ego* is used to signify the matrix of negative personal habits which keep us unconscious in the life-dream, then the ego is indeed something which stands in the way of our awakening. It is a psychic knot we need to untie. But often the word *ego* is used to signify our individuality generally. In this case the ego is not something to destroy, but something to emancipate from its illusionary isolation, so that we experience our individual identity as a part of the greater whole.

Awakening is not eradicating our personality and living a bland, boring existence as some sort of saintly zombie. Awakening is consciously being all that we are and having fun as a person in the life-dream, free from debilitating fear and isolation. Awakening doesn't diminish our individuality. It enhances and fulfills it. In this sense, lucid living is the celebration of the ego, not its destruction. But this celebration of our individuality is possible because we have transformed ourselves from an isolated self into an integrated self.

There is a feeling of dissatisfaction which motivates us to awaken. We feel there must be more to life than the anxiety and numbness we experience in the endarkened state. And there is. Much more. But because we presume we know what it is to be a person in the world, we think we must reject this and look elsewhere for what we are seeking. But actually our present experience of appearing to be a person contains everything we are looking for, if we can wake up and see it for what it is. And enjoy it for what it is. That's enlivenment.

In spiritual circles there is much talk of 'fully enlightened' sages who have achieved enlightenment, which is seen as the ultimate goal of existence. If 'enlightenment' is taken to mean ceasing to identify exclusively with our apparent nature, then it is something that we can achieve once and for all. It is possible to become conscious of our essential nature so profoundly that we never exclusively identify with our apparent nature again. But this is not the end of the story. It is just when it starts to get interesting, because we have finally discovered how to really love the experience of living. Enlightenment is the end of endarkenment and the beginning of enlivenment.

Loving Being Human

Lucid living is an experience of life-affirming *enlivenment*. It is not a life-denying refuge for holy escapists. It is not being a macho meditator who shuns the world. It is not the cessation of the life-dream longed for by kamikaze contemplatives who want to assassinate themselves. It is finally feeling safe enough to unconditionally participate in the human adventure. It is loving being human.

Either/or spiritual traditions, however, treat our humanity as a problem we need to overcome. To wake up, we are told, we must eradicate many of our natural human characteristics. We must stop desiring things to be different and acquiesce to the way things are. We must sever all personal attachments and be detached and aloof. We must become selfless saints who are never angry and fearful. We must become holy ascetics who deny ourselves the pleasures of the flesh. From the lucid both/and perspective none of this is true. Thank goodness! It's okay to be human. Let's think it through.

The Dilemma of Desire

To awaken, we are told, we need to extinguish all our desires. Most of us are so busy wanting things to be other than they are that we don't appreciate the miracle of the present moment. Our endless desires are a source of frustration and sometimes extreme suffering. Desire rarely leads to the satisfaction we crave, because when we get what we want, it seldom turns out to be what we wanted. And there is always more to be desired, which can makes us permanently discontent.

Should we, then, extinguish all our desires? No. That's impossible. And undesirable! Desire is a necessary part of existence. On a very basic level it is our desire to eat and excrete which maintains life. Desire is the fuel of transformation in the life-dream. Our desire to enjoy life and not to suffer is the carrot and stick which urges us to awaken to oneness and love.

The solution is to adopt the lucid both/and perspective, by being *both* awareness loving things as they are right now *and* also a person in the world desiring things to get better in the future. The present cannot be changed. It is a fact to be unconditionally accepted. But the future *will* inevitably change. And it is our desire for it to change for the better which will inspire us to act to make things better. Lucid living is embracing this moment as it is, including the desire for change. It is wanting life to be better because we love it so much.

Holy Indifference

To be able to love life as it is, we are told, we need to become indifferent to what happens in the life-dream. When we are lost in liking and disliking it is impossible to love living, because there is so much to dislike. The life-dream is characterised by polarity, which means there will always be experiences we like and others we dislike. Should we, therefore, just apathetically acquiesce with the way things are? Certainly not! As individuals in the life-dream we need to discriminate what is acceptable from what is unacceptable. We need to condemn the evil which makes us suffer and to nurture the goodness which brings us joy.

A Gnostic Christian text called *The Authoritative Teaching* states that 'the worst vices' are 'ignorance and indifference'. Ignorance is being unconscious that all is one. Indifference is retreating from life. Lucid living is the opposite of ignorance and indifference. It is consciously being the oneness of awareness passively embracing life as it is. And it is appearing to be a person actively seeking to transform the ugly, inappropriate and cruel into the beautiful, harmonious and kind.

The Bogeyman of Selfishness

Selfishness is another bogeyman we are told we must defeat if we are to wake up. And again this condemnation of a natural human tendency arises from either/or thinking, which requires us to choose between being *either* selfish *or* selfless. Lucid living is being *both*. Being *only* selfish causes immense suffering to others and ourselves, but this does not mean that satisfaction comes from some sort of ascetic selflessness. Those who attempt to deny their own desires end up as distorted as those who are driven by them, because both approaches to life arise from a misunderstanding of the human predicament.

If we suppress our own desire to feel good as an individual (which is actually impossible!) we would be defeating the very purpose of the life-dream, which is to enjoy living. Yet our essential identity also expresses itself as all the other individuals who share the life-dream with us, and to deny their desire to feel good would also be to defeat the very purpose of the life-dream. The solution is to further both our personal and our collective enjoyment of existence, because they are intrinsically the same.

Lucid living is recognising that the way to feel good individually is to be conscious of everyone else's desire to feel good as well as our own, and to do our best to make them feel good as well, rather than simply grabbing our own enjoyment at the expense of others. Lucid living is seeking personal happiness which enhances rather than hinders the happiness of others. And because we are all one, helping others to feel good makes us feel good. The best way to be selfish is *also* to be selfless.

Personal Attachments

Another natural part of being human which is often demonised is attachment. We are urged to relinquish our attachments to people and to things because they are the cause of suffering. But would we really want to be unattached to those we love? Would we really want to befriend, marry or parent someone who was utterly unattached to us? Would we want to be indifferent to the things we cherish or the life-projects we pursue? Surely not! And the good news is we don't have to. The problem is not being attached. It is being *only* attached. We don't have to get rid of our attachments. Rather we need to realise that our essential nature is not attached and never will be. Lucid living is not denying our human attachments and personal relationships. It is living with temporary attachments as a person in the life-dream, whilst knowing that essentially we are awareness which is not attached to anything.

Negative Emotions

Awakening is often portrayed as some super-human state in which we are always compassionate and never feel normal human emotions such as anger. But anger is not always a bad thing, because it can be an appropriate reaction to a bad situation. The problem is not being angry. It is being *only* angry. When we are lost in separateness it is easy to become consumed by destructive anger. But anger is only an expression of our separateness if we are angry *instead* of being compassionate. Anger, impatience and frustration can sometimes be positive expressions of big love. Every parent knows that it is possible to be angry with a child whilst still loving them. Anger can be 'tough love'.

Fear is another natural human experience which is much maligned. But fear is not *just* a negative emotion. It can sometimes play a positive role in our life, much like pain. Pain warns us to change because the body is not happy about something. In the same way, fear is our imagination warning us that something could happen in the future that we really don't want to happen, which can sometimes help us avoid the undesirable.

When we identify only with our separate self, fear and pain can be utterly debilitating. Fear and pain are by definition unpleasant experiences, because they are designed to impel us to change our situation. But sometimes we can't alleviate the pain or avoid the event we fear. The solution is to also be conscious of our essential nature and embrace fear and pain with unconditional acceptance. This doesn't make the fear or pain magically disappear, but it does mean we *also* experience the courage to face fear and the endurance to withstand pain.

The Pleasures of the Flesh

Many spiritual traditions have a particularly unhealthy attitude towards 'the pleasures of the flesh' because, we are told, 'the price of pleasure is pain'. But that's a bargain! Surely 'the honey is worth the sting', as Rumi enthuses. Do we really want to forgo pleasure to avoid pain? Lucid living is a both/and alternative. It isn't denying ourselves the pleasures of life. It is enjoying pleasure but not getting lost in pleasure. It is also staying awake so that we can continue to love life when the pleasure passes, as it inevitably will.

Sex is a pleasure continuously libelled by pious killjoys, probably because it is so much fun and these people don't like fun! Once again the problem is either/or thinking. We are given the choice of *either* wholesome love *or* sordid lust. But from the lucid perspective we can embrace both. When we *just* lust after someone as an object of our desire we don't acknowledge them as a subject who also has needs and desires. But lucid living is being able to lust whilst also loving. It is enjoying the fact that we are both sensitive subjects and desirable objects.

To experience lucid living you don't have to become puritanically clean-living and treat your body like a temple. Sometimes it's fun to treat your body like a nightclub! You don't have to abstain from the pleasures of the flesh. Quite the opposite. Lucid living is enjoying all the pleasures and poignancy the life-dream presents us with. It is the secret of appreciating both the delights and the dramas of appearing to be a person. So why not wake up and love being human? Go on. You know you want to.

THE LAUGHING JESUS

I understand your wounds that have not healed.
They exist because God and love
have yet to become real enough
to allow you to forgive the dream.
—Hafiz, Sufi Gnostic

If you can stand back far enough from your cultural conditioning, the Literalist Christian message looks absurd and grotesque. You were born in sin and deserve to be punished. So God sent his own son, Jesus, to planet Earth to suffer horribly on the cross to pay for your sins. Jesus died for you and then resurrected and went to Heaven. And, if you believe that this really happened, you will also go to Heaven when you die, where you will have a very nice time forever. But if you don't believe that the resurrection really happened, when you die you will go to Hell and be subjected to really horrible tortures for all eternity. By a God of love!

It's a gruesome doctrine and inherently flawed. Surely, for any compassionate person, the existence of Hell must make the enjoyment of Heaven impossible. How could anyone with an ounce of kindness enjoy Heaven knowing that others languished in Hell, simply for not believing in an historical event for which there is no evidence anyway! It seems somewhat harsh. If there really is a God running this post-mortem apartheid, then he's a monster and we need to indict him for crimes against humanity.

We are extremely glad to tell you, however, that this grim Literalist version of the Christian message has nothing to do with the teachings of the original Gnostic Christians. They did not teach that believing in the historical death and resurrection of Jesus would save us from Hell when we die. That would be impossible because, according to the Gnostics, we are already dead and living in Hell right now!

We are the dead and we don't know it. It's a spooky thought which sounds as though it has come straight out of a Hollywood blockbuster like *The Sixth Sense*. But look around you and you'll see what the Gnostics mean. Most of us wander around like semi-conscious shades, tormented by endless fears and anxieties. Listen to us moaning about our worries and woes, like weary banshees longing for rest. Look into the dull and fretful eyes of someone on their way to work in the morning rush hour and you'll see the face of the living dead.

For the Gnostics Heaven and Hell are not places we go when the body dies. They are two ways of experiencing the life-dream. When we are identified with our separate life-persona we are 'dead' to our essential nature, and life becomes a nightmare of fear and suffering. We have 'fallen asleep in Hell', as Plotinus puts it. We need to 'wake up from heavy sleep and take off the garments of Hell', as *The Secret Book of John* urges.

Heaven and Hell are here and now. Whilst we are identified with the separate self the life-dream inevitably becomes a nightmare, but the moment we wake up to oneness Hell is transformed into Heaven. Heaven is the experience of big love. It is not somewhere we go when we die. It is a state of loving life which arises when we wake up and live lucidly. Life is 'a joy to those who have rediscovered who they really are by waking up', as *The Gospel of Truth* teaches. Whilst we are engrossed in the dramas of the life-dream we can't see how wonderful life is. But when we wake up and live lucidly we find that we are already in Heaven. In *The Gospel of Thomas* Jesus is asked by his disciples, 'When will Heaven come?' He replies, 'It won't come by waiting for it, because Heaven is spread out upon the earth but people don't see it'.

Waking the Dead

The essential message of Christianity is that whilst we identify with the separate self we are dead and we need to come to life or resurrect. In the Greek used by the original Christians the word usually translated 'resurrect' also means 'awaken'. The resurrection represents waking up and experiencing gnosis. The resurrection is not something which happened in the past to Jesus. That's just a story. Neither is it something which may happen to you after you die. That's just a fantasy. The resurrection is something you must experience for yourself in this present moment by becoming conscious of your essential nature as awareness. A Christian text called *The Treatise on the Resurrection* (which could equally be called *The Treatise on Awakening*) announces:

> The world is an illusion. The resurrection/awakening is the revelation of reality.

This text teaches that when Jesus resurrected he 'swallowed the visible by means of the invisible and showed us the way to our immortality'. To resurrect is to become conscious of being the emptiness of invisible awareness which contains the world, and which exists unborn and undying beyond time. This is why the Gnostics teach that Christianity is about being 'saved' by resurrecting to 'eternal life'. The Greek word which is usually translated 'saved' means to be 'preserved' or become 'permanent'. Gnosis is being 'saved' because it is the discovery that our essential nature is the eternal presence of awareness.

According to Tertullian the Gnostics teach that 'Those without gnosis are the dead'. Resurrecting is awakening to gnosis. It is the discovery of what Paul calls the 'Christ', who represents our shared essential nature as the oneness of awareness. As a Gnostic teacher he sees his job as 'working until the Christ arises in you'. He urges:

> Wake up sleeper.
> Rise from the dead.
> Let the Christ enlighten you.

This is the authentic message of Christianity. Whilst we are unconsciously identified with our separate persona in the life-dream we are the dead Christ, lost in the nightmare of separateness and suffering in Hell. But when we awaken to our shared essential nature as the Christ we resurrect from the dead and we partake in eternal life. Resurrecting from the dead transforms the life-dream from the Hell of separation to the Heaven of big love. In Christian mythology Jesus is portrayed as resurrecting in the body, because big love is a *feeling* we experience *in the body*. Resurrecting from the dead is coming to life as a person. To resurrect is to become *enlivened*. It is loving being in the world through knowing our essential nature which is not of the world. Paul teaches:

> When anyone is united with the Christ there is a new world. The old disappears and a new order begins.

Suffering

In some versions of the Gnostic Jesus myth, it is not the 'real' Jesus who is crucified, but only his *eidolon*, or image. The 'real' Jesus is represented as laughing whilst his apparent nature suffers. The wonderful figure of the laughing Jesus is the Western equivalent of the laughing Buddha. Both represent the discovery of joy and the transcendence of suffering through ceasing to identify with the separate self. But what is so powerful about the symbol of the laughing Jesus is that Jesus isn't represented as *just* transcending suffering. His apparent nature is *also* suffering terribly on the cross. The laughing Jesus symbolises the state of lucid living in which we are able to love life even when we are suffering.

Suffering is unavoidable because life is predicated on suffering. Every life-form exists by killing and consuming other life-forms. Life is possible only because the cosmos is continually consuming itself. To be a person in the life-dream is inevitably to suffer. As separate individuals we are insignificant specks in a huge and hostile universe. Each one of us is just another vulnerable body amongst billions of bodies waiting to die. No wonder we so often feel fearful, insecure and alone.

Suffering is by definition undesirable. To *like* suffering would be impossible and perverse, but to embrace suffering with loving acceptance as an inevitable part of the dream of awakening is perfectly possible. Suffering is unavoidable, but *just* suffering can be avoided. Lucid living is the paradoxical state of appearing to be a person in the life-dream who sometimes suffers, yet knowing ourselves to be awareness which exists beyond all polarities, including joy and suffering.

Lucid living doesn't mean we never suffer, because we still have an apparent nature which sometimes experiences physical pain and psychological anguish. But when we experience lucid living we don't *only* suffer. If we are conscious of *both* our essential nature *and* our apparent nature, we can suffer as a person when life is tough, whilst also embracing our suffering with unconditional loving acceptance as awareness. As Jesus teaches in the *Acts of John*, we can learn to suffer and not to suffer.

Waking up is an experience of big love. A love so big that it mitigates the horrors of life. From the it-perspective of our apparent nature within the life-dream, suffering, illness and death can be truly terrible experiences. But the experience of big love enables us to embrace both the happiness and the heartbreak of life. It does not diminish the anguish of grief and tragedy, but adds to these experiences a bittersweet poignancy. The experience of big love assuages our suffering and enables us to bear the unbearable.

When we are lost in the illusion of separateness we see our experiences as *either* good *or* bad. Lucid living is adopting a both/and perspective and recognising that every experience is *both* good *and* bad. Even the most wonderful experience entails the suffering inherent in impermanence, because we know that, since everything changes, feeling good must pass. And even the worst experience can act as a catalyst for our awakening. Indeed, as those who have suffered much often testify, it is sometimes the most difficult of experiences which most powerfully wakes us up from the numbness we call 'normality'.

Everything in the life-dream exists in polarity and is *both* good *and* bad. There is nothing so good that it does not have a bad side and nothing so bad that it does not have something good in it. Science has given us the ability to almost eliminate some horrendous diseases, but it has also given us Hiroshima and Nagasaki. World War II entailed untold cruelty, yet it led to peace in Europe. The Holocaust was designed to exterminate the Jewish race, but it inadvertently led to the establishment of a Jewish homeland in Israel for the first time in two thousand years. This was good for the Jews but bad for the Palestinians who already lived there. Everything has a good side and a bad side.

This present moment is full of both joy and suffering. Right now a mother is cuddling her beautiful newborn baby. Two young lovers are telling each other of their feelings for the first time. Someone is reaching out to comfort a stranger in distress. But also in this present moment a mother is watching her baby starve to death. Two young lovers have discovered the heartbreak of betrayal. Someone is walking past a stranger crying out for comfort with detached indifference.

Lucid living is embracing all of this with big love, which takes great courage. Loving isn't *just* a good feeling, it *also* entails suffering willingly. When we love others we share in their anguish as well as their joy. It is the suffering inherent in big love which stops many of us waking up. We feel it is simply too painful to wake up and love, so we choose to be numb and withdrawn. But it is only too difficult whilst we remain identified with the separate self. It is too much to expect an isolated individual to open their heart to all the suffering of the world. But the more we awaken to oneness, the more big love becomes not only possible but natural. When we live lucidly we find ourselves loving all and suffering willingly with all. This is the state of gnosis symbolised by the sublime figure of the laughing Jesus.

Death Is Safe

Jesus laughs in the face of death. He would prefer that this 'cup' of death pass him by, but when he realises he is destined to die he accepts it unconditionally. Jesus is able to embrace death because he has already metaphorically 'died' by ceasing to identify with his apparent nature. The Gnostic secret of being able to face death is simple. Don't wait. Die now! Plato describes the 'true philosopher' as someone who 'makes dying his way of life'. Paul writes, 'I die daily'. Valentinus teaches, 'We choose to die so that we can annihilate death completely'. The Islamic Gnostic Abd al-Kader explains:

> There are two types of death. One which is inevitable and common to all, and one which is voluntary and experienced by the few. It is the second death which Muhammad prescribed saying 'Die before you die'. Those who die this voluntary death are resurrected.

When we identify exclusively with our physical body, we are consciously or unconsciously in a constant state of anxiety, because decay and death is what inevitably lies ahead for this walking-talking skin-bag. But when we wake up we realise we need not fear the death of the body any more than we need fear dying in a dream. The more lucid we become the less we fear death, which makes living a lot more enjoyable!

When we awaken to the way things actually are, we realise that death is safe. Fearing and resisting death is like a young child fearing and resisting sleep, because it doesn't understand that renewal comes only through dissolution. Worrying about the death of our apparent nature is like worrying about what will happen to our reflection when we stop looking in the mirror. The Gnostic Pagan Epictetus teaches:

> It is your fear of death that terrifies you. You can think about a thing in many ways. Scrutinize your idea of death. Is it true? Is it helpful? Don't fear death. Rather, fear your fear of death.

Death seems terrifying to the degree that we are identified with our mortal nature. Most of us fear death because we are extremely attached to our present persona in the life-dream and don't want it to end. But death is the discovery that we are really not attached to our present life-persona, any more than to a persona in a dream at night. We feel attached whilst we are dreaming, but not when we wake up. In the same way that we don't mourn the passing of a dream when we rise in the morning, when we die we will not mourn the passing of the person we appear to be in the life-dream right now.

Plato teaches that 'the best life is spent preparing for death', because death is the climax of life. Death is not a meaningless end to a meaningless existence. It is the destination which gives life its meaning. Death is the supreme opportunity to come to life. We wake up when we let go of our conceptual stories about life and enter the mystery of the moment. Such moments of awakening often occur when we encounter the unfamiliar, because our stories can't cope with the unfamiliar. Death is the ultimate unfamiliar experience. When the identification with our apparent nature is dramatically prevented by death, it allows us to become conscious of our shared essential nature as the emptiness of awareness. Death is an opportunity to consciously merge with what the Christian Gnostics call 'the dazzling darkness' and Tibetan Buddhists call 'the clear light of the void'.

Our experience of the present moment is either hellish or heavenly, depending on whether we're lost in the illusion of separateness or awake to our essential nature. In one way, the moment of death will be just another present moment. It will be hellish or heavenly depending on how awake we are. In this present moment it is possible to experience lucid living, so why should it not be possible to experience lucid dying and embrace the end of this dream with appreciation, excitement and big love. On his deathbed, the Gnostic poet Allen Ginsberg declared, 'I thought I would be terrified, but actually I feel exhilarated'.

Pronoia

The laughing Jesus represents a state of awakening in which we realise that life is good and death is safe. We call this becoming 'pronoid'. If paranoia is the irrational fear that life is out to get you, then pronoia is the reasonable faith that life is on your side. And everyone is out to help you, whether they know it or not! 'Pronoia' is 'faith' by a funkier new name. The word *faith* has become so contaminated by Literalist religion that it is almost unusable. Faith has come to mean blind belief in irrational dogmas. Being pronoid has nothing to do with faith in this sense. It is a profound trust in the fundamental goodness of existence, which arises when we awaken to oneness.

Whilst we believe ourselves to be no more than separate individuals we are just vulnerable specks in a vast accidental universe. But if we wake up we become pronoid, because it becomes obvious that we don't need to fear life any more than we need to fear a dream. What we are experiencing is a manifestation of our own essential nature as the life-dreamer, so how can we ever really be victims of life? And, because everything is an expression of our own essential nature, all we experience is showing us something about who we are, so life is replete with meaning, like a dream.

Being pronoid is not indulging in some feel-good fantasy. It is not retreating into some optimistic la-la land. It is not adopting a fixed smile in the face of all adversity. It is not being perpetually positive by refusing to acknowledge the negative. Quite the opposite. Being pronoid is embracing the inherent polarity of existence. But it is experiencing life as a love affair of complementary opposites, rather than a clash of contradictory contraries. A dance rather than a war. A duet rather than a duel.

The life-dream arises with polarity. *What* we experience is *relatively* good or bad. But *that* we are experiencing anything at all is *absolutely* good. Being pronoid is acknowledging that life is sometimes bad, whilst remembering it is always *also* good. And when we understand that every moment is both good and bad, we can choose to seek out the good. As the Scottish comedian Billy Connolly puts it, 'There is no such thing as bad weather, just the wrong clothing'. There is no such thing as a solely bad experience, only the wrong attitude. When we are lost in separateness things are either good or bad, but as we wake up we recognise that all experiences are *both* good *and* bad, depending on how we look at them. Is this moment good or bad? It is both. It is always both. So even when it is very bad it is also partly good and vice versa. Is that good or bad? It depends on how you look at it.

Being pronoid is seeing things as they really are. It is acknowledging that suffering is bad, but *also* understanding that suffering is not *just* bad. Suffering makes us more compassionate, because only by suffering ourselves can we understand the suffering of others. It is often only when we face the worst tragedies that we finally get around to communicating how much we love each other. Indeed, because every experience in the life-dream is part of the process of awakening to oneness, all our bad experiences are ultimately good. As Rumi writes:

> If God demanded:
> 'Rumi praise everything
> that has led you into my embrace',
> I would have to honour
> each and every experience of my life.

Walt Whitman succinctly captures the essence of pronoia when he pronounces:

> What is called 'good' is perfect,
> and what is called 'bad' is just as perfect.

Such bold pronoid statements often evoke the outraged reaction: 'Life is perfect?! You've got to be joking!? Tell that to the mother whose child is dying of cancer! Tell that to an African who hasn't eaten for weeks! Tell that to any one of us as we confront the suffering and misery that every life entails!' From the lucid perspective, this response is to be applauded, because we must refuse to trade world-weary pessimism for naïve optimism. The lucid reply is 'Yes. You're right. Life isn't perfect. But can you see it is *also* perfect?'

When we identify exclusively with our life-persona it is easy to get caught in a 'vicious circle'. We feel separate and vulnerable, so we become frightened of life, which makes us withdraw into numb normality, then we feel more separate, so we become more frightened and anaesthetise ourselves further. But when we experience lucid living we set in motion a 'virtuous circle'. We begin to experience that all is one, so we feel more pronoid about life, which makes us engage more wholeheartedly with the process of awakening, and this means we awaken further to the essential unity of all things, so we become more pronoid and engage more wholeheartedly with the process of awakening. And living wholeheartedly is twice as good as living half-heartedly!

The irony is that the more we identify exclusively with our apparent nature as a person, the more scared of life we become. But the more we know that we are really not a person, the more we can unreservedly engage with the dramas of appearing to be a person in the world, because being pronoid gives us the confidence to commit to the life process, no matter how daunting. It makes us secure enough to surf the ups and downs of the adventure of awakening, because we appreciate that adventure can't always be easy.

Being pronoid isn't always feeling good. It is feeling okay about sometimes feeling bad. Being pronoid doesn't mean we never get confused. It is understanding that being confused is sometimes for the best. Being pronoid doesn't mean we never make mistakes. It is accepting that we learn only by making mistakes. Being pronoid doesn't mean always having an easy time of life. It is trusting that our problems are part of a curriculum of awakening.

How would your everyday experience change if you allowed yourself to live a pronoid life? If you approached your life-dramas as adventures on a journey of discovery, in which you are continually being offered the opportunities you need to wake up and become more conscious of all that you are? If you saw that your ordinary life is as charged with significance and meaning as a dream? If you lived with the knowledge that life is good and death is safe?

Enjoying the Show

Does the possibility of lucid living seem too paradoxical to be practical? It really isn't. You enter a comparable state every time you go to see a movie. You identify with the hero of the adventure, but you also know you are safely in the auditorium. And it is this both/and perspective which enables you to enjoy the story. Even the scary bits. If you were to completely identify with the hero of the movie, an exciting adventure would be transformed into a terrifying ordeal. You would really believe that the baddies are going to get you and that you are going to suffer and die. This is an analogy for what happens when we live our lives identified with the body. Lucid living is realising it's okay. We aren't really characters in the movie. We're safely watching the show.

But lucid living isn't the equivalent of sitting in the cinema pinching ourselves so we don't mistake the movie for reality. If we did this we would stay conscious that we are only watching coloured lights projected on a white screen, but this would ruin our enjoyment of the experience. A movie is worth seeing because we don't just remain conscious of being in the auditorium. We only enjoy the illusion when we are taken in.

Many spiritual traditions urge us to do the psychological equivalent of pinching ourselves to make sure we don't mistake the movie for reality. This can be a helpful short-term strategy to prevent us continually identifying with our apparent nature. But there's something wrong with this as a long-term approach to life. It's rather rude. There's this spectacular show laid on gratis and it's not being appreciated.

Lucid living is adopting the paradoxical perspective we adopt when we enjoy watching a movie. We sit there in the auditorium and completely abandon ourselves to the movie, hoping we will be entertained, excited, transformed, made to think and feel. But we know that we are not in the movie. We don't have to sit there repeating to ourselves 'I'm not in the movie . . . I'm not in the movie . . .' We are so sure of it that we don't have to think about it. It's obvious.

To enjoy a movie we need to *both* enter into the fantasy *and* know we are essentially safe. We let ourselves be in the movie, but we know we are not of it. And that's the secret of enjoying the show. Lucid living is adopting a similarly paradoxical perspective on the life-dream, which enables us to unreservedly enter into the dramas of life, even when it's sometimes a white-knuckle ride. Lucid living is recognising that we actually want the conflicts and dilemmas of life, because this is what transforms us. This is what makes us really *feel*. This is what we enjoy. Who wants to see a movie which starts with everyone happy, continues with everything working out and ends with all being well? We want life to be more than a superficial light comedy. We *also* want drama. We want life to be exactly what it is. A cathartic feel-good masterpiece of such depth and poignancy that it defies description.

THE WAY TO AWAKEN

Your vision will become clear
only when you look into your own heart.
Who looks outside dreams.
Who looks inside awakes.
— CARL JUNG, *Letters*, Volume I

We are living in sin and we need to repent. It is preached endlessly by Literalist priests and TV evangelists. And do you know what? They're right! We *are* living in sin and we *do* need to repent. It's just that Literalists misunderstand the meaning of the words *sin* and *repentance*. For Literalists we are sinners because we have broken the rules. We didn't do as we were told by Big Daddy and he's pissed with us. So the only way to avoid being severely punished is to feel really guilty, say we are very sorry and promise not to be bad again. But this has nothing to do with what the original Gnostic Christians meant by 'sin' and 'repentance'.

The Greek word *hamartia*, usually translated 'sin', comes from archery and simply means 'to miss the point'. The Greek word *metanoia*, usually translated 'repentance', means 'to change perspective'. So sinning isn't disobeying some set of divine regulations. It is simply missing the point. And repentance isn't giving yourself a hard time or toadying up to some judgemental God. It is simply seeing things from a different perspective.

In the Gospels Jesus teaches that 'the beginning of salvation is repentance'. The first step in the process of waking up is to recognise that you're missing the point and to change perspective. But what is the point of life? Ask a child and the answer is simply: 'To have fun'. We are dreaming the life-dream because we want to love living. This is not something that we want for the future. We want to love living right now. We want to love this moment. This is the fundamental life-impulse at the root of all our desires. This is what we *really* want. This is the point and purpose of life.

It is easy to tell when we're missing the point and need to change perspective. When we become so engrossed in the dramas of the life-dream that we forget we want to love living right now, we're missing the point. When we're so sure we know what's going on that we don't notice the mystery of existence, we're missing the point. When we're so numb we don't notice the miracle of the moment, we're missing the point. A conclusive sign is when we begin to lose our sense of humour. When this happens we've definitely fallen asleep at the wheel and gone off the road!

We miss the point when we are so lost in the it-perspective of our life-persona that we are unconscious of the I-perspective of our essential nature. Lucid living is being conscious of both. So to wake up and live lucidly we simply have to also adopt the I-perspective, by consciously being awareness embracing all that is right now. And when we do this we find ourselves in love with the moment, which is the whole point of living.

Witnessing

Be awareness witnessing your experience of appearing to be a person right now. This doesn't mean not thinking about the past and future.

It means simply observing whatever thoughts and sensations happen to be occurring in this moment. Witnessing isn't thinking of yourself as a detached little man watching the world from inside your head. Quite the opposite. It is 'disengaging' from your apparent nature as a body, as Plotinus puts it, and recognizing that you are the spacious emptiness of awareness within which the life-dream is arising. Witnessing is transcending your separate self by being awareness which contains the world.

Witnessing is the simplest possible perspective on the reality of this present moment. It is being conscious of the primal polarity of experiencer and experiences. It is being awareness observing the life-dream unfolding as a metamorphosing oneness. It is passively watching everything spontaneously happen. Try it for yourself right now. Be spacious awareness witnessing the experience of appearing to be a person reading these words.

This state of witnessing is not gnosis. It is preparation for gnosis. Gnosis is knowing that you are one with all. This is possible once you have reduced this moment to the primal polarity of experiencer and experiences, because then you can see that awareness is one with what it is witnessing. There are no experiences separate from the experiencer. As Meister Eckhart teaches, 'The seer and the seen are one'. You *are* all you experience. You are one with everyone and everything.

Oneness

To awaken to oneness you need to let go of the idea of yourself as a separate, autonomous individual with free will. Most people find this extremely difficult, so it may help to consider the evidence. In what way are you a 'free' individual? Did you ask to be born? Did you choose to be a man or a woman? Did you choose to be a human being at all? Did you choose your parents or your nationality? Did you choose to become a teenager by switching on the hormones that would change your body and fuel your desires? There are ten thousand chemical processes that every cell in your body must perform every second to keep you alive, but are you a chemist? Do you think that one day someone with a clipboard will sidle up to you and ask when and how you would like to die? Of course not. Your death, like your life, will just happen.

There is one area in your life, however, where you do seem to have individual free choice. You can choose how you act. But even here, if you examine the evidence, you will see that things are not what they seem. An action is volitional when you consciously intend to act. All your volitional actions arise from your intentions. And intentions are thoughts. But do you choose what you think? If you watch your thoughts for a while you will soon see that you don't. Your thoughts come and go of themselves. You aren't in control of them. This becomes particularly obvious if you try to stop thinking, because you will find that you can't! Thoughts arise whether you like it or not. So if you're not the 'thinker' of your thoughts, then you aren't the 'doer' of your intentional actions either.

You are not a separate individual with free will, because everything is happening as an integral part of the ever-changing life-dream, including 'your' thoughts and actions Your thoughts are coming and going, but there is no individual 'thinker'. Your eyes are passing across this page right now, but there is no individual 'doer' of this action. In reality there is no separate 'you' to be free or otherwise. There is only the life-dreamer dreaming the life-dream. All 'your' individual actions are actually the actions of the life-dreamer or God or Christ or whatever name we use to represent the source of all. This is why Paul declares:

The life I now live is not my life, but the life which the Christ lives in me.

And why Abd al-Kader teaches:

The mystics are not themselves but exist in God. Their actions are God's actions. Their words are God's words uttered by their tongues. Their sight is God seeing through their eyes.

When you dream at night your dream-persona appears to be an individual who chooses to do this and not that. But if you were to dream lucidly you would realise that really you are the dreamer who is the unconscious source of everything that happens in the dream. In the same way, lucid living is recognising that your essential nature is the source of everything that happens in the life-dream. As awareness you are passively 'doing' everything.

The Importance of Choice

When people first come across the idea that all is happening as one, including their thoughts and actions, they sometimes find it deeply offensive, because it seems to deny their ability to choose how they act, which is one of the defining characteristics of our humanity. In spiritual circles this resistance is often condemned as ignorance arising from identification with the ego, but actually it is a sign of innate wisdom. Because lucid living is not *just* being awareness witnessing the metamorphosing oneness. It is *also* recognising the importance of appearing to be a person who can choose this not that.

Right now you can choose to carry on reading, or tear this page to shreds, or throw the book at someone. As individuals within the life-dream our experience of choice is a fact that can't be denied. Indeed, we rarely acknowledge the overwhelming extent of the choices available to us in every moment. But when we do it is utterly exhilarating! So what is this experience of choice and are we right to value it so highly?

Everything is arising spontaneously, like a dream, from unconscious awareness. But awareness becomes conscious of the life-dream through us as individuals. And when awareness is conscious of something through an individual it has the opportunity to consciously decide how to react. This is the experience we call 'choice'. Through you as an individual the life-dreamer becomes conscious of the intention to act before the action itself happens and can, therefore, choose to act or refrain from acting.

As an individual you are an integral part of the life-dream, not a separate autonomous agent. It is not the individual 'you' that chooses what you do. It is the life-dreamer conscious through your life-persona which makes all 'your' decisions. This doesn't devalue your experience of choice. Quite the opposite. It makes it even more important. The intuition that the experience of choice is of immense importance is right, because it is through your individual life-persona that the life-dreamer can consciously shape the life-dream, by choosing to make things better. The more conscious you become as an individual, the more choices the life-dreamer has through you.

It is increasingly fashionable to believe that we 'create our own reality' and in a way this is true. As the life-dreamer we are creating all of reality. But we are not doing this consciously as individual personas in the life-dream. Waking up is the recognition that as individuals we are not really doing anything. We are part of what is happening. However, there is still a sense in which we are all co-creating reality as individuals, because as we become more conscious the life-dreamer is able to make better choices through us and that changes reality. Lucid living is *both* being the life-dreamer *unconsciously* dreaming the life-dream *and* appearing to be a person playing our part in *consciously* co-creating reality.

Transcendence and Transformation

The life-dreamer progressively wakes up by becoming more conscious through each one of us as an individual. Whilst we are relatively unconscious individuals we are so embroiled with the dramas of the life-dream that it is hard to wake up. And if we do manage to wake up for a while, we fall asleep again very quickly. To deepen and sustain the awakened state we need to become more conscious, so that we can transform those aspects of our apparent nature which trap us in separateness. Then we will be able to transcend our personal self more easily and become conscious of our essential nature. The process of awakening often begins with years of personal transformation, before someone is ready to even understand what it really means to wake up to our shared essential nature.

Personal transformation and impersonal witnessing are two complementary aspects of the way to awaken, which the Pagan Gnostics call the active life and the contemplative life, and Paul calls the *psychic* and *pneumatic* initiations. Many spiritual traditions, however, emphasise only one of these two aspects of the journey of awakening. For those who practise only witnessing oneness, personal transformation seems a shallow distraction. And on its own it is. Constantly struggling to make oneself a better person can be like rearranging the furniture in a prison cell. It is easy to get so caught up in wrestling with our neuroses that we don't recognise that every moment is an opportunity to let go of the past and wake up now.

For those who practise only personal transformation, witnessing oneness seems abstract and impersonal. And on its own it is. The teaching that our essential nature is the life-dreamer or God is condemned as dangerous because it can lead to inflation. And this is right. If someone believes their personal self is God, this is gross inflation and the opposite of awakening.

But we don't have to get caught in this either/or dichotomy. We need to *both* transform *and* transcend. The process of waking up requires us to embrace all the different polarities inherent in the life-dream. There is a time to emphasise personal transformation and a time to concentrate on witnessing. There is a time to push and a time to be passive. A time to be disciplined and a time to play. A time to give to others and a time to care for ourselves. How do we get the both/and balance right? It's like learning to ride a bike. The balance is not something you find once and for all, it is something you have to find in each moment as the road you're travelling changes. You know you've got it right when you don't fall off!

Personal Transformation

How do we transform our personal nature so that we can more easily wake up to our essential nature? The Pagan Gnostics called the process of personal transformation *catharmos*, meaning 'purification', because it is a process of purifying ourselves of those character traits which keep us an unconscious, isolated, selfish individual. It is examining our 'shadow', or 'bad', side. The Pagan philosopher Epictetus advises:

> Do you want to be good? Then first understand that you're bad. The beginning of philosophy is making conscious your own weakness and failings.

Personal transformation is the process of becoming conscious of the bad habits that keep us asleep and replacing them with good habits that help us wake up. We need to notice when we habitually act selfishly and routinely go numb. It is easy to go unconscious and just roll on automatic in the same familiar ruts. The only way we can escape our unconscious patterns of thought and behaviour is by recognising these patterns and choosing to change them. *The Gospel of Philip* explains:

> As long as the root of evil is hidden, it is strong. But if it becomes known it dissolves. If you ignore it, it takes root in you and brings forth its fruit in the heart. It takes you captive so that you do the things you don't want to do and don't do the things you want to do. It exerts this power because you haven't recognised it.

Personal transformation requires us to be honest with ourselves about our faults and foibles. But we don't need to get bogged down in guilt and self-recrimination. As Homer Simpson wisely puts it: 'Don't keep blaming yourself. Just blame yourself once and move on'. Temporary shame can transform us into better, more conscious, human beings. But lingering guilt just cripples us and saps our confidence in our ability to evolve.

We need to transform our negative personal characteristics into positive attributes, rather than eradicate them. When we identify with the separate self we distort what are actually qualities into foibles. An assertive person becomes dominant. A humble person becomes subservient. A confident person becomes arrogant. A brave person becomes aggressive. An inspiring person becomes manipulative. But, as we transform ourselves from an isolated self into an integrated self, our foibles become our qualities. Then, as the American spiritual teacher Ram Dass quips, 'our neuroses become our *style*'!

Check it out for yourself. Examine your personality and become aware of a foible you would like to transform. Then ask yourself, 'What is the quality that is being distorted here? How can I transform this weakness into a strength?' Your foibles are part of what makes you a particular individual and it will probably take perseverance to change them into your style, so don't become disheartened if you find yourself constantly getting caught up in the same old neuroses. It's like that for all of us. It's the human predicament. And don't be surprised if overcoming one problem creates another. Life is a journey of transforming problems into other problems. That's how things evolve.

Being Love and Loving Being

In *The Gospel of Matthew* Jesus replaces the endless religious laws and regulations of Jewish Literalism with just two simple commandments, and even then he remarks that 'the second is much like the first'. The first commandment is to 'love God with all your heart'. The second commandment is to 'love others as your self'. These two commandments succinctly capture the two aspects of the Gnostic way of awakening. We need to become one in love with our shared essential nature which is the source of all. And we need to transform our apparent nature into a conscious and compassionate individual, who recognises that everyone is an expression of the oneness of awareness, so that we, quite literally, love others as our self.

Lucid living is unconditionally loving everyone and everything. Do you love unconditionally? Take a look at the options below and see which best reflect your own attitude:

- I love life when I like what is happening.
- I love life as it is and try to change things for the better.

- I love others if they are loveable.
- I love others regardless which may help them become more loveable.

- I will love myself when I become a better person.
- I love myself anyway and this might make me a better person.

Most of us love conditionally. How can we learn to love unconditionally? In the same way that we learn to do anything, by practising.

People invest huge amounts of their lifetime learning to do all sorts of wonderful things, such as playing a musical instrument, becoming adept at a sport and mastering a profession. If we recognise that what we *really* want is to love, then we will invest even more of our valuable attention in learning to love. Let's do it!

Loving This Moment

Experiment with loving this moment right now. Appreciate what a miracle life is. Recognise how extraordinary it is to be alive in this wonderful world. Love the fact that you exist. The word *present* is used to signify both 'now' and a 'gift'. Become conscious of what a precious gift the present is. You've got one chance to appreciate the unique qualities of each moment of your life and then it is gone.

It is only possible to unconditionally love each moment if you accept that there will always be things you like and dislike about every situation. If there is anything about this moment you find unacceptable, accept your lack of acceptance and love the moment anyway. Find the good in what appears bad. This is easy because the fact that this moment exists at all is absolutely good. What you experience is good and bad, but that you are experiencing anything at all is unconditionally good.

Loving life is like a romantic relationship. When we first fall in love with someone, our beloved is an enigmatic source of delightful surprises and the relationship is full of magic. But over time we lose sight of the mysterious being we fell in love with and start relating to a fixed idea of who our beloved is. And what happens? We fall out of love. The magic stops. The good feeling goes. It is the same with life. When we think we know what life is, it goes dead on us. We stop loving life and settle for getting on with it. The way to prevent life becoming mundane is to remember what a mystery the moment is. This will keep your love affair with life alive.

Loving a Friend

Now experiment with loving others. The secret to loving others is to change the way you see yourself, because what you experience yourself to be you also experience others to be. If you see yourself as an isolated selfish individual you will see others as isolated selfish individuals, and then you will find them extremely difficult to love. But if you see yourself as the life-dreamer appearing as a particular person, you will also see others as expressions of our shared essential nature and come into love with them. And the more you recognise you are everyone, the more you will try to see things from everyone's point of view. The more you will feel that deep sense of communion we physically embody when we embrace one another.

Socrates suggests that the way to learn to love is to start by loving those we are close to and then expand this to loving all. Bring to mind someone you find easy to love. Explore the feelings and thoughts which arise with this love. See how their joy is your joy and their anguish is your anguish, because you are so close you intuitively see through the veil of separateness. Now ask yourself, 'Is this love conditional or unconditional?' Whilst we are identified with the separate self our love inevitably comes with strings attached, because we seek to serve the interests of the isolated individual we presume ourselves to be. We claim to love someone, yet if they stop loving us we stop loving them. We think we are loyal, but if someone is not loyal to us we are not loyal to them. How would it feel to love without conditions?

Loving a Stranger

Now bring to mind someone towards whom you feel indifferent and also embrace them with love. You will not feel the same bonds of attachment that come with personal love, but hold them in universal compassion by recognising that they are also an expression of our shared essential nature. The fact that you really don't know this person, or may not like them if you did, is irrelevant. Loving has nothing to do with knowing someone or liking them. Love this stranger unconditionally simply because they exist as another persona in the life-dream we are collectively dreaming.

Loving Your Enemies

If you are okay with loving a stranger, try something more ambitious and experiment with unconditionally loving an 'enemy', as Jesus encourages us to do in this glorious passage from *The Gospel of Matthew:*

> You have heard the saying 'You shall love your neighbour and hate your enemy'. But I say to you, love your enemies and pray for those who persecute you. Then you will become children of your Father in Heaven. For he makes the sun shine on the evil and the good alike. And sends the rains to unjust men as well as just men.
>
> You have heard the saying 'An eye for an eye and a tooth for a tooth'. But I say to you, don't resist evil with evil. If someone strikes you on your right cheek, turn the other one to him as well. And if someone wants to sue you for your coat, let him also have your cloak. And if someone forces you to walk a mile with him, walk with him for two miles. And don't ignore someone who wants to borrow from you, but if you are asked for something give it away.

With this unconditional generosity of spirit, bring to mind someone you find difficult to love and hold them in compassionate awareness. See beyond their unlikeable personality to their essential nature which is indivisible from your own. Recognise that they have a life-story which has led them to be the way they are. See them as part of 'us' so trapped in separateness that they are capable of acting in ways you find offensive. Realise that if they could awaken they would instantly be transformed. Reach out with understanding and forgiveness, because those who are so lost they cause others to suffer are those who are most in need of love.

Loving Yourself

If you can love your enemies, although you don't like them, you may even be able to love those aspects of yourself you don't like. For many of us this is the most difficult challenge. We are so self-critical we cripple ourselves with self-loathing, which actually makes it harder to change. Try a different approach. Be patient and tolerant with yourself. Accept that you are sometimes lost in separateness. We're all waking up, which means we're all asleep to different degrees. It's not easy being a person. Cut yourself some slack! Love yourself anyway.

Genuine self-love is possible only through self-knowledge. If you become conscious of your essential nature you will be able to unconditionally love your apparent nature, with all its faults and foibles. Try it out. Transcend your personal nature altogether and hold both the good and the bad aspects of yourself within compassionate awareness.

Your personal self is like an immature child. Sometimes selfish and prone to tantrums, wanting what it can't have and what isn't good for it anyway, easily lost and quick to complain. And yet, exquisitely beautiful, nevertheless. Lovingly parent yourself. Bad parents constantly criticise and love conditionally. Good parents criticise when necessary, but always love unconditionally whatever the child may say or do. Love yourself unconditionally. This is not an indulgence. It is the ground from which you can compassionately criticise those parts of yourself that need to change.

Living in Love

When we awaken to oneness and experience big love we naturally express this love in our lives. We feel motivated to do all we can to relieve our collective suffering and further our communal well-being. Mohandas Gandhi put it beautifully when he wrote:

> When a person loses himself into God, he immediately finds himself in the service of all that lives. It becomes his delight and recreation. He is a new person never weary in the service of God's creation.

How we affect others depends on whether we are relatively more asleep or more awake than those around us. What we really have to give each other is our state of being. What we say and do is secondary. We change others inadvertently all the time just by being different from them. When that difference is that we love unconditionally, we can be the catalyst for others to awaken. When we love we can be of genuine help to others, because what everyone really wants and needs is love, whether they know it or not. We can't make people accept our love. That is not up to us. But if we stay loving despite rejection, they have the chance to enter into love with us should they wish to take it. How would your life change if you decided to live in love with all?

The Game of Life

When we are born we don't come with an instruction manual, so we don't know the purpose of life. The purpose would seem to be to work out the purpose! As children it becomes obvious that the point is to enjoy ourselves and love living. But as we become adults we realise this isn't easy, because some aspects of life aren't very enjoyable. We then start living our lives as if the purpose is to change our situation so that it becomes more enjoyable. But we end up so caught up in trying to improve our life that we forget to appreciate it as it is. So who's right? Kids or adults? They're both right. The purpose is *both* to appreciate *and* to improve.

Life is like a game. When we play a game we have two different but complementary goals. The real reason we play is to have fun. But within the game we are presented with a particular goal which we must seek to fulfil, and a failure to engage seriously enough with this goal can undermine the enjoyment of playing. The process of the game involves overcoming the obstacles that prevent us achieving this goal. Whilst our successes and failures may temporarily affect how much we enjoy the game, we can still enjoy playing, even when the game is not going our way. Because if the game was always easy there would be no game.

The game of life also has two complementary goals. The primary purpose is to enjoy playing. We are the life-dreamer dreaming the life-dream to enjoy the experience, which we can do by awakening to oneness and big love. But as a person within the life-dream the goal is to overcome the obstacles which prevent us enjoying life, by alleviating suffering, our own and others, so that we can collectively love living. Because life is a game we can only win together.

Life is a game of awakening and the way we win is remarkably simple. We live our ordinary life, just as we have always done, but we choose to live *consciously*. We recognize that even the most seemingly trivial events are opportunities to enjoy the moment and love others. We embrace the stranger who serves us at the local shop with big love, because we no longer see them as just a cashier, we know they are also the mystery made manifest. And when we love others we may help them wake up and become more loving. In this way we can send out ripples of kindness wherever we go.

We wake up by approaching our everyday existence as an ongoing spiritual practise. Not in some overly serious way, but like a game we enjoy playing. Yet it does also have a serious aspect. Life will naturally present us with the challenges we need to become more conscious, some of which can be hard to face, and the best way to avoid being pushed is to keep moving.

We tend to think that it is when we feel bad that we need to wake up and when we feel good everything is fine as it is. But actually it is often when we are enjoying life that we become most unconscious. When life is bad we are impelled to do something about it and we may take a step forward on our journey of awakening. But when we feel good it is tempting to settle into a comfortable unconsciousness. We need to pay attention to waking up all of the time, not just when we are pushed into it because we feel bad.

Once we understand that the game of life is about waking up and that what we really want is to love this moment, we will cease distracting ourselves with the relentless quest for transitory satisfaction, through accumulating material possessions, acquiring social status and attaining personal power. We will stop numbing the pain of separateness with TV and trivia. Instead we will give our precious attention to the process of awakening. We will stop seeing lucid living as an attractive idea and make it a reality. We will stop procrastinating and go for it.

Most of us choose to be asleep, but if you want to wake up you can. Yet awakening is a possibility, not an imperative. It is not something you have been commanded to do by some outside authority that you must obey. It is something you can do if you want. It's up to you. And the secret of waking up is simple. If you want to wake up more than you don't want to wake up, you will wake up.

Your life is an opportunity to become a unique individual consciously participating in co-creating this amazing dream we call 'life'. It's not easy being you, but no one could do it better. What would happen if you stopped holding back and realised the potential of the particular person you happen to be? Because for us to fulfil the fundamental life-impulse by collectively awakening to our shared essential nature, represented mythologically by the coming of the Christ, each one of us needs to wake up and make our distinctive contribution to the evolving life-dream. The Jewish mystic Rabbi Nachman of Bratzlaw urges:

> Every one should know and remember that his state is unique in the world, and that no one ever lived who is exactly the same as he; for had there ever been anyone the same as he, there would have been no need for him to have existed. In reality each person is a new thing in the world, and he should make his individuality complete, for the coming of the Messiah is delayed through it not being complete.

Shortly before he died the playwright George Bernard Shaw was asked by a reporter, 'If you could live your life over and be any person from history, who would you be?' Shaw replied, 'I would choose to be the man George Bernard Shaw could have been, but never was'. What would happen if you decided to become the person *you* could be right now and audaciously play *your* role in the unfolding story of life? Wouldn't it be fun to find out?

11

SPIRITUALITY WITHOUT RELIGION

Unthinking respect for authority is the greatest enemy of truth.
— ALBERT EINSTEIN

We live in extraordinary times. The West is presently experiencing an unparalleled Gnostic renaissance. There has never been such freedom of thought and expression. In recent years this has led to an explosion of alternative forms of spirituality. Many of these new forms of spirituality are still Literalist in different ways. Sometimes we have merely replaced unsubstantiated old superstitions with equally unsubstantiated new superstitions. But this should not blind us to the genuine awakening which is presently occurring. Religion is in decline, but spirituality is thriving. The recent growth of conservative Fundamentalism is merely a desperate reaction to the presence in the marketplace of so many new competing brands of spirituality, which has destroyed the monopoly of the old religious cults.

Slowly but surely we are throwing off the dead weight of Literalism and freeing spirituality from the authoritarian structures which have smothered it for centuries. This is giving birth to a new phenomenon. Spirituality without religion. We suggest this historically unique development points the way forward for spirituality. To create a form of spirituality which can really help us to collectively awaken in the twenty-first century we need to free Gnosticism from religion altogether and align it with science. After all, the word *scientist* is just the Latin version of the Greek word 'Gnostic', both of which mean 'knower'.

Since we have stopped blindly believing what was written in dubious old religious books and adopted the scientific approach of paying close attention to our actual experience of the world, our understanding of the human predicament has increased incredibly. It has been the great triumphs of science which have undermined our old religious certainties. An alliance between Gnosticism and science would create a formidable force for awakening and help us finally reject Literalist religion once and all. It can help us conceive of a secular form of spirituality which, like authentic science, is both openminded and discriminating, which bases itself on our actual experience of life, not external authority, and which presents awakening as entirely natural.

What, then, would be the future for religion? Religion, like everything in polarity, is both good and bad. So we simply need to keep the good and discard the bad. Religion has many attractive aspects, such as its many beautiful rituals, which it would be a great shame to lose entirely. We suggest keeping religious traditions alive as a form of cultural nostalgia, as we do folk music and traditional dress. This is already happening with festivals such as Christmas, which is enjoyed by millions of non-believers. We can also honour our sacred scriptures for the role they have played in human history, whilst also recognizing that they are archaic curiosities with limited relevance to our modern world. There is no reason to abandon the positive aspects of religion, because religion is only a problem if it traps us in the past and stops us evolving further.

Gnostic Science and Literalist Science

Science and Gnosticism may seem unlikely allies, because science is commonly believed to be the opposite of Gnosticism. It is assumed that science proposes a Materialist philosophy, which teaches that matter is all that exists. But nothing could be further from the truth. None of the great physicists who have shaped our modern scientific understanding of the world—such as Newton, Einstein, Heisenberg, Schrödinger, De Broglie, Jeans, Planck, Pauli and Eddington—were Materialists. Quite the opposite. They were self-professed mystics or Gnostics.

Scientific research has found that it simply doesn't work to conceive of the universe as a giant machine made of matter. On the contrary, science has discovered that the best way to understand the universe is as a giant thought arising within awareness. Sir James Jeans, who made important contributions to the dynamical theory of gases, the mathematical theory of electromagnetism, the evolution of gaseous stars, the nature of the nebulae and so on, writes:

> Today there is a wide measure of agreement which, on the physical side of science approaches almost to unanimity, that the stream of knowledge is heading towards a non-mechanical reality: the universe begins to look more like a great thought than like a great machine. Mind no longer appears as an accidental intruder into the realm of matter; we are beginning to suspect that we ought rather to hail it as the creator and governor of the realm of matter—not, of course, our individual minds, but the mind in which the atoms out of which our individual minds have grown exist as thoughts.

Sir Arthur Eddington, who made important contributions to the theoretical physics of stellar systems and was a leading exponent of relativity, announces:

> The idea of a universal Mind or Logos would be, I think, a fairly plausible inference from the present state of scientific theory.

> I assert that the nature of all reality is spiritual, not material nor a dualism of matter and spirit. The hypothesis that its nature can be, to

any degree, material does not enter into my reckoning, because as we now understand matter, the putting together of the adjective 'material' and the noun 'nature' does not make sense.

The Nobel Prize winner Erwin Schrödinger, whose work became the heart of modern quantum mechanics, claims:

> The overall number of minds is just one. I venture to call it indestructible since it has a peculiar timetable, namely mind is always now.

> We do not belong to this material world that science constructs for us. We are not in it; we are outside. We are only spectators. The reason why we believe that we are in it, that we belong to the picture, is that our bodies are in the picture.

The great scientists reject Materialism because it is a flawed philosophy. It is a soulless vision of an outside with no inside. It just doesn't make sense. Of course, more exists than we can sense and measure. This idea we are considering right now, for instance, has neither weight nor place nor any tangible qualities. As Eddington quips:

> If those who hold that there must be a physical basis for everything hold that these mystical views are nonsense, we may ask: What, then, is the physical basis of nonsense?

Science describes the world in terms of mathematics, but numbers have no material existence. Scientific 'laws' are formulas which, although they inform physical reality, have no physical existence themselves. You can search the physical universe forever, but you will never find a single 'law of nature'. They are not *things* within the physical world. They are the information which shapes the physical world.

The scientist Rupert Sheldrake has suggested we stop thinking of science as revealing the 'laws of nature', which is an analogy taken from the Christian idea of a creator God who decrees the laws which govern the universe. We should think instead of science as revealing the 'habits of nature'. When we discover the so-called 'laws of nature' which underlie physical reality, we are exploring the primal habits of awareness which define the nature of the life-dream.

Materialists claim that, because matter is all that exists, consciousness is a sort of side effect of the brain. But the fact is, even if someone knows what every neuron in your brain is doing, that won't give them access to a single one of your thoughts. This is because thoughts don't exist in the world. They are not *things*. They are not made of matter. This leaves Materialists with a fundamental duality between mind and matter they can neither explain nor avoid. And this completely undermines their claim that matter is all that exists.

Gnosticism, however, is able to resolve the duality of mind and matter very easily. If we take awareness, rather than matter, as the ground of reality, everything exists as an experience within awareness. Some of our experiences are private thoughts and feelings. Others are sensual experiences of our shared world. There is fundamental polarity here, but like all polarities it is an expression of an underlying unity. Our mental and sensual experiences are qualitatively different, but they are both *experiences* which exist in awareness. And awareness is only conceptually different from what it is aware of, so this polarity also resolves to an essential unity.

Science is commonly assumed to give us a down-to-earth understanding of the world. But science has actually undermined our common-sense view of reality, and replaced it with an extremely weird and wonderful account of the universe. Common sense tells us that the things around us, such as this book you are holding, are solid objects. Science has discovered that 'solid objects' are actually mostly empty space and mysterious quantum particles. Ideas don't come much stranger than that!

Scientists and Gnostics both suggest that our common-sense ideas are not adequate and suggest radically different ways of seeing things, which at first seem extraordinarily bizarre. When Galileo suggested that the Earth goes around the sun it was ridiculed. Yet, although this idea is more difficult to understand than the notion that the sun goes around the Earth, it actually gives us a simpler and more elegant understanding of the cosmos. In the same way, although the Gnostic idea that the world exists in awareness can be difficult to understand

and contrary to common sense, it actually gives us a much simpler and more elegant understanding of reality.

The insights of science harmonize with the insights of Gnosticism. Gnostics say that time and space are a sort of illusion. Science has found this to be true, because if we could move at the speed of light, these fundamental dimensions would cease to exist. Just as Gnostics teach that from the I-perspective of awareness there is oneness and eternity, science has found that from light's point of view there is no space and no time. Physics has wrestled with the paradox that light sometimes appears to be made up of particles and sometimes to be a wave. This is comparable to the Gnostic observation that from the it-perspective each individual is a discrete 'particle' of consciousness, but from the I-perspective individuals are like waves on one ocean of awareness.

Science and Gnosticism are natural allies. They are commonly misunderstood as enemies because science has degenerated into Literalist science, which preaches crass Materialism. Science has become an authoritarian tradition, with its own dogmas, high priests, career structures and vested interests. Scientific Literalists, like religious Literalists, claim their opinions to be the absolute Truth. But, as we have seen, the great scientists were not dogmatic Materialists. They were not dogmatic at all. What made them able to change our understanding of the world was that they were capable of questioning received opinion and thinking in radically new ways. A very Gnostic trait.

Literalist scientists would have us believe that science has now advanced so far that we've pretty much understood the cosmos. A few more advances and all the mysteries will be solved. For Gnostic scientists this is simply crazy. Existence is an absolute mystery and our scientific understanding of it remains primitive. The Nobel Prize winner Wolfgang Heisenberg, who was a founding father of quantum physics, writes:

I for one no longer understand what we mean when we say we have understood nature.

Nobel Prize winner Albert Einstein, perhaps the most respected scientific thinker of all time, concurs:

The human mind is not capable of grasping the universe. We are like a little child entering a huge library. The walls are covered to the ceilings with books in many different tongues. The child knows that someone must have written these books. It does not know who or how. It does not understand the languages in which they are written. But the child notes a definite plan in the arrangement of the books. A mysterious order which it does not comprehend, but only dimly suspects.

The way forward, we want to suggest, is to follow the example of the great scientists, by rejecting religious and scientific Literalism, and embracing Gnostic spirituality and authentic science, which complement each other perfectly. Science requires a rigorous examination of our shared objective experience in time. Gnosticism requires a rigorous examination of our subjective experience of the present moment. Science is the investigation of reality from the it-perspective. Gnosticism is the exploration of reality from the I-perspective. Science is the study of the nature of the life-dream. Gnosticism is the art of waking up.

According to Einstein science should be motivated by the state of awakening he calls 'the cosmic religious feeling':

> The most important function of science is to awaken the cosmic religious feeling and keep it alive. It is very difficult to explain this feeling to anyone who is entirely without it. The individual feels the nothingness of human desires and aims, and the sublimity and marvelous order which reveal themselves both in nature and in the world of thought. He looks upon individual existence as a sort of prison and wants to experience the universe as a single significant whole.

> I maintain that the cosmic religious feeling is the strongest and noblest motive for scientific research. A contemporary has said, not unjustly, that in this materialistic age of ours the serious scientific workers are the only profoundly religious people.

The Nobel Prize winner Wolfgang Pauli, a physicist whose brilliance exceeded even that of Einstein, asserts:

I consider the ambition of overcoming opposites, including also a synthesis embracing both rational understanding and the mystical experience of unity, to be the mythos spoken or unspoken of our present day and age.

Certainty Divides Us and Doubt Unites Us

To create a secular spirituality for the twenty-first century we need to adopt the basic premise of authentic science, that all our theories about life are hypotheses, not facts. There is no absolute conceptual knowledge. There are just stories we tell to make sense of our experience and no story is expansive enough to capture the limitless grandeur of existence.

This does not mean we need to adopt the 'relativist' theory that all stories are equal. Just because all descriptions of reality are inadequate doesn't make them all equally inadequate. Some stories are clearly better than others. To say you are presently reading a book doesn't begin to capture the whole truth of this moment, which is infinitely rich and so ultimately indescribable. Yet to say you are reading a book is clearly more true than to say you are eating an elephant. None of the stories we tell to help us navigate life are the Truth, but some come closer to being true stories than others.

If we recognise this we can all at least agree about one thing. Life is a mystery and our understanding of it is necessarily always provisional and partial. Nothing is certain. Everyone is giving it their best guess. If we acknowledge this, then we can play with ideas, not fight about them. We can share our insights and intuitions with each other to see which stand up to scrutiny, look prettiest and work best, from a starting point of universal agreement.

The Gnostic story is just one possible story. But, unlike other stories, it doesn't claim to be the absolute Truth, because it teaches that Truth can't be captured by concepts. Gnosticism does claim, however, to reveal something extremely important about reality ignored by those stories which leave us unconscious in the life-dream. It is a way of thinking which points beyond concepts to an experiential *knowing* of our shared essential nature. But Gnostic philosophy is still expressed in concepts and so remains only an attempt to articulate the art of awakening, not an absolute dogma. From the Gnostic perspective we need to engage in an ongoing quest to create new ways of thinking which reveal more of reality.

We need narratives to live by. Without them we would be like amnesiacs or newborn children, unable to negotiate our lives. Unfortunately most of us are so wrapped up in our stories we mistake them for certain knowledge. We treat our stories, which are at best relatively true, as the absolute Truth. We are so convinced we know all the answers, we don't notice the great ever-present question. As *The Gospel of Philip* cautions:

> Concepts are very deceptive because they turn the heart aside from the real to the unreal.

When we see our ideas are ideas, we can use concepts to navigate our lives as individuals within the life-dream, whilst simultaneously always being conscious that life is an absolute mystery. Not a relative mystery that we could one day solve, such as whether there is life on Mars, but a mystery by its very nature. Our ideas may be relatively better or worse, but the mystery remains. It is when we forget the absolute mystery of existence that we become lost in our narratives and fall asleep in the life-dream. It is by seeing our narratives for what they are and staying conscious of the mystery that we wake up.

Gnosticism encourages us to doubt the conceptual certainty which keeps us unconsciously engrossed in the life-dream. Literalists condemn doubt as a great sin, but doubt is a pre-requisite for awakening. Literalists long for constant confirmation of their prejudices, but Gnostics are adroit at doubt. And if we embrace radical doubt we can all meet as equals before the mystery of existence. Because it is when we are sure we know what is going on that we end up fighting over our opinions. Certainty divides us and doubt unites us. (Although we're not sure about that!)

Free-thinking

Scientists have transformed our understanding of the world, because they dared to question the dogmas of religion and think in original ways. They used the power of rational thought to expose the irrationality of religious superstition, and to create better ways of understanding reality. Twenty-first-century spirituality also needs to reject external authority and encourage rational free-thinking, because it is only by thinking for ourselves that we become more conscious and start to wake up.

It is hard to wake up because most people around us are asleep. We are constantly subjected to the mass media, which projects a banal view of life, which keeps us lost in the life-dream. It is astonishing that, despite programmes exploring everything from interior design to serial killers, no one in the media seems to ever mention the obvious and perturbing fact that life is a breathtaking mystery. It's as if we have entered into a conspiracy of self-deception so that we avoid facing how truly perplexing our predicament is. The only way to wake up from this collective coma is to stop listening to others and become independent free-thinkers.

Most of us go along with the way of thinking that happens to be in vogue. And the joke is that we don't notice that the point of view we so proudly call our own is actually just an ad hoc assortment of second-hand opinions, inculcated during growing up or adopted like the latest fad to help us fit in with our social set. To wake up we need to question our social conditioning and transform ourselves from an unconscious member of the herd into a conscious individual.

In spiritual circles today, however, it has become fashionable to undervalue thinking. A dichotomy is often created between the head and heart in which the head is the bad guy who leads us astray and the heart is the good guy who leads us back home. What is actually meant by the 'heart' is usually left conveniently vague, but the underlying assumption is that feeling or intuition is good and thinking or rationality is bad.

This is often justified with reference to the Gnostic teaching that the Truth cannot be expressed with words or comprehended by the intellect. Yet most Gnostics were actually rational philosophers who criticised Literalist religion precisely because it of its irrationality. Gnostics teach that gnosis is not an intellectual opinion, it is an experience of *knowing* directly in the immediacy of the moment, but this does not stop them from valuing the intellect as a wonderful tool to help us transform ourselves and the world.

Religion has always championed irrational 'faith'. Tertullian famously announced of Christianity 'It is true because it is absurd. I believe it because it is impossible'. Do we really want to tolerate this sort of nonsense in the twenty-first century? When modern spiritual traditions reject rationality they are simply continuing a ruse used by ecclesiastical authorities for centuries to persuade us to blindly believe, not consciously question. This is not the way forward. Because when we stop being rational we don't wake up. We just become stupid.

Like everything in the life-dream, thought has a good aspect and a bad aspect. Thinking is just talking to ourselves. Like all talking, sometimes this is just meaningless drivel, but sometimes it can help us wake up. Our ability to think rationally is a great blessing, without which we would never become more conscious, because it can expose the craziness of our assumptions about life and open up new, liberating possibilities. Being rational is simply insisting that opinions be justified with valid reasons. It is being reasonable. Rationality is our bullshit detector, which enables us to discriminate unsubstantiated prejudice from genuine insight.

But being rational doesn't stop us from also being intuitive. Intuition is our faculty to have profound realisations we can't justify with reasons. Intuition is knowing something is right, but not knowing why it is right. It is being conscious of the conclusion, but not of the process that got us there. Intuitions are messages from our deep unconscious self that burst through into consciousness as new and startling insights. Our intuitions are the cutting-edge of our understanding, which we are still in the process of making conscious.

It is important, however, that we distinguish genuine intuitions from groundless assumptions, cultural conditioning and wishful thinking. The authenticity of an intuition needs to be tested by making conscious the reasons it is right through rational thought. Most of the great scientists have said that their groundbreaking insights came in the form of intuitions, which they later were able to justify rationally.

The idea that we have to choose between *either* intuition *or* rationality is spurious, because they *both* play an important role in the process of becoming a conscious individual. Einstein, one of the greatest intuitives and rational free-thinkers of all time, advises, 'The important thing is not to stop questioning', because if we keep asking penetrating questions, profound answers will emerge from the depths of our being in response.

The Big Boss

Science is a rigorous study of our actual experience of living. Twenty-first-century scientific spirituality, likewise, needs to teach that the only absolute authority is our own actual experience. This means freeing ourselves from the supposed authority of sacred texts, holy prophets and even God. The Literalist God is the ultimate external authority figure. He is the big boss of the cosmos who tells us what to do and punishes us if we fail. This conception of God will never help us wake up. If we are to use the dangerous word 'God' at all, we need to use it, like the ancient Gnostics, to signify the oneness of awareness within which the life-dream is arising.

We need to reject Literalist images of God, which are a legacy from our primitive past. Yahweh and Allah, for example, are just tribal deities whose function was to give a particular people some form of social cohesion. We need to follow the example of the early Christians, who replaced the pompous monster Yahweh with the Gnostic conception of God as the mysterious source of all. The Christian Gnostic Cerdo teaches:

> The God proclaimed by the law and the prophets is not the God of Jesus Christ. The God of the Old Testament is known, but the God of Jesus Christ is the Unknowable.

Our traditional images of God are tired and outdated. He is a great king who demands to be worshipped. The ultimate aristocrat who will shower his favour arbitrarily on someone one day and order their execution the next. A fickle lord who will listen to the prayers of his favourites, by providing them with a parking space here and good luck in a sporting event there, whilst completely ignoring the prayers of those millions dying from AIDS or starvation. If absolute power corrupts absolutely, it is no wonder that the Literalist God is as corrupt as any feudal baron.

The Literalist God is an old-fashioned Victorian father who is ready to punish his children brutally to discipline them. He expects blind obedience and rarely offers explanations for his seemingly arbitrary judgements. He likes rules and hates free-thinking. He wants us to shut up and do as we are told. And our reward for compliance will be enrollment in the afterlife kindergarten of Heaven. Surely we have now left behind such infantile conceptions. The time has come to grow up.

The Literalist God is a big person with a whole load of opinions. But his opinions turn out to be suspiciously like the opinions of the particular prophets that relay them to the rest of us. And each prophet produces a different set of opinions that purport to be divine. This has left us arguing endlessly over what God's opinions really are. But there are some areas of broad agreement. God is a misogynist. And he isn't keen on sex. Especially not for pleasure. And definitely not between members of the same sex, because that is obviously just for pleasure.

God has opinions about everything, but they vary depending upon which Literalist religion you subscribe to. He doesn't like men trimming the hair around their temples. He likes women to cover their heads or preferably the whole of their bodies. He likes big beards. He doesn't like pork or shellfish. He likes fish on Friday. Do we really want a God with such peculiar fashion sense and arbitrary dietary preferences?

According to myths such as *Genesis*, God is the creator of the cosmos. But science has presented us with all the evidence we need to reject the idea that God created the world in seven days some six thousand years ago. Many people still cling to this silly idea, but their attempts to explain away the findings of science are getting ever more desperate. Is it really credible that God deliberately hid dinosaur bones so that when we dug them up and concluded that giant reptiles walked the Earth millions of years ago, our blind faith in the veracity of the Bible would be put to the test? Such a God would be pathologically insane!

The cosmos is simply too absurd to be a conscious plan of a wise being. Look at how haphazard its history is. How many false starts there have been in the creative process. If there is a creator God, he clearly doesn't know what he is doing. Yet the cosmos is also too ordered and organised not to be seen as arising from some form of intelligence. And the fact that intelligence comes out of the cosmos proves that intelligence must exist implicitly within the source of the cosmos. The Gnostic conception of God as the life-dreamer solves these conundrums. The life-dream is not some formulated conscious plan. The life-dream is arising from *unconscious* awareness, which is becoming *conscious* of its nature through the process of evolution.

The idea of an omnipotent and omniscient God can seem comforting, but it's actually profoundly disturbing and creates many contradictions which have disturbed theologians for centuries. The most obvious is the problem of evil. The Literalist God is meant to be both all-good and all-powerful. But how can he be both? Either God is all-good and wants to eliminate evil but isn't powerful enough to do so, or he is all-powerful but chooses not to eliminate evil, which makes it hard to see him as good. How could an omnipotent super-being allow all the horrendous suffering in the world? Why wouldn't an all-compassionate deity intervene to rescue us from the horrors of the world? Literalist theologians have come up with many ingenious responses, but all have failed because the problem is inherent in their very concept of God.

This is not a problem, however, if we adopt the Gnostic concept of God as the life-dreamer who is becoming conscious *through* creation. Evil is not something God consciously creates, showing himself not to be good. Nor something he allows, showing himself to be callous. Evil is the inevitable price of the polarity which is necessary for there to be conscious experience at all. God did not allow such atrocities as the Holocaust. God *is* the holocaust. The victims and the perpetrators. There is only God. The one awareness in the process of waking up from the nightmare of separateness to the wonder of oneness.

The idea of God makes sense only if we adopt the Gnostic

perspective and understand God as representing our essential shared nature. The 'I-in-all' is a God we can seek to serve. Because when we experience lucid living, we want this universal 'I' to enjoy life in all its many forms and will do all we can to allow this to happen. We become willing servants of God.

We are not saying we should never adopt a personal image of God, because this can be a powerful way of relating to our essential nature whilst we are struggling to awaken from identification with the separate self. Although the Gnostic God represents our own essential nature, and you can't get any closer than that, until we really understand what this means, this impersonal conception of God can seem remote and abstract. As individuals within the life-dream we are persons, and the easiest way for us to relate to the source of all is to imagine it as a big person. This allows us to have a loving relationship with the life-dreamer as the 'Beloved', to use a Sufi term, who is both the object of our devotion and our own true self. A sentiment Rumi captures succinctly when he writes:

> I am a lover of the universal and the universal lover. I am you in love with yourself.

Relating to our own personal God as a friend, parent or lover can be a wonderful and moving experience. Twenty-first-century spirituality can reject the Literalist God whilst embracing devotion to a personal God-image. To presume otherwise is like saying it wouldn't have room for art and imagination. And there's room for prayer too. But from the Gnostic perspective, prayer is not petitioning the favour of the king of the cosmos. It is a way of communicating and communing with our own deeper nature. It is consciously feeding back to the source our desires and aspirations, which may affect our future experience because the life-dream is extremely reactive to conscious intentions.

Relating to a personal God becomes a problem only if we make an idol of our God-image. We need to make sure we never claim that our image of God is the one and only image of God. We need to make sure we don't claim to have access to God's divine opinions. We need to make sure that our image of God doesn't obscure the mystery of existence which it represents. Because then we will become Literalists. And Literalists can be very dangerous people. As the Sufi poetess Rabia of Basra writes:

> *Since no one really knows anything about God,*
> *those who think they do are just troublemakers.*

Love or Law

If we can abandon God as an external authority figure, we can also let go of the idea that sacred scriptures contain his infallible opinions about how we should live our lives. When we let old books define our modern morality we end up stuck in the primitive ethics of the past. The time has come to grow up and realise that there is no outside authority that can tell us how we should behave. Twenty-first-century spirituality needs to help us learn to make independent moral judgements by becoming more conscious and more loving.

A common defence of Literalist religion is that without sacred scriptures we would be savages, because they provide the ethical glue that holds society together. Well, we've now examined what these books actually teach. The Bible justifies genocide, rape and pillage. So does the Qur'an. Is this really the sort of morality we want in the modern age? If we have to have some sort of violent mythical text to teach us right from wrong, how about going for *The Lord of the Rings*? It's more ethical than the Bible or the Qur'an. And more plausible!

Literalists claim that religious laws are divinely inspired, but these laws are not divine. They are human and reflect the values of the age in which they were created. Do we really still want to follow Jewish law that demands the death sentence for those who work on a Saturday and condones selling children into slavery? No, of course we don't. Neither do we want to follow Islamic law that condemns the corrupt to be partially beheaded, then crucified, and condones men beating their wives so long as they don't break any bones. We're more humane now. Thank goodness!

Far from providing the ethical glue which holds us together, Literalism pulls us apart. In the Gospels Jesus urges us to forgive those who wrong us, but this doesn't stop Literalist Christians demanding that transgressors of the law be punished severely, not forgiven. It is the Religious Right which champions retributive justice, from hitting naughty children to the death penalty for adults. For Literalists violence is the solution, but for Gnostics it is the problem. Retributive justice is just hurting ourselves again. We suffer *both* as the victim *and* as the perpetrator. 'An eye for an eye' is the justice of separateness. 'Love others as yourself' is the justice of oneness.

Not only is the Literalist sense of what constitutes 'justice' abhorrent, it is deeply disturbing that this justice is often delivered by judges who are clearly too gullible to execute their office. In the U.S. especially, many judges are Literalist Christians who are ready to blindly believe that someone was born of a virgin, changed water into wine, fed five thousand people from bits of bread and a few fishes and came back from the dead. Can we really feel safe that anyone with such scant regard for evidence is able to discern fact from fiction in a court of law, when someone's life may be hanging in the balance? It's a worrying thought!

From the Gnostic perspective we have become obsessed with laws and punishments because we have forgotten to love. Paul explains that 'love is the whole of the law'. We need laws when we don't love. People resort to law only when human efforts to be fair and just have broken down. And when they do it is usually only the lawyers who benefit. No wonder the Christian Gnostics portrayed their superhero Jesus as constantly criticising lawyers! The dispute between Literalists and Gnostics is between lawyers and lovers.

Literalists are dedicated to upholding the moral law, but Gnostics are devoted to embodying love. Literalists presume that human nature is basically bad and needs coercing into shape. Gnostics know that, like everything in polarity, human nature is good and bad. When we are lost in separateness we can be terribly selfish, but when we wake up to oneness we can be wonderfully kind. From the Gnostic perspective we need to wake ourselves up, not tie ourselves up with *should*s and *shouldn't*s, because when we know our essential nature we become spontaneously good.

Twenty-first-century spirituality needs to teach that external coercion won't make us good. We need to realise our natural goodness from the inside. We need to obey 'the law inscribed on the heart', as Valentinus puts it. We need to understand that we naturally act well when we live with the understanding that we are all one. We need to see that when we ask what is the right thing to do, the answer is always to act from love. Let's stop debating what is and isn't acceptable behaviour and go right to the heart of matter. Let's start debating what it is to really love and how we can create a culture of compassion.

The Pernicious Problem of Perfect People

If we are willing to dismiss the absolute authority of the Literalist God and sacred scripture, we can also reject the absolute authority of God's representatives on Earth: prophets, avatars, holy saints and enlightened masters. Twenty-first-century spirituality needs to free itself from the myth of perfect people, so that each of us can become empowered to trust our own experience, rather than any external authority.

In Western culture the ultimate perfect person is Jesus. Recognising that Jesus is a mythical, not historical, figure frees us from this external authority figure. The Zen Buddhists have a phrase: 'If you see the Buddha on the road kill him'. In the West we need to adapt this to: 'If you see Jesus on the road kill him'. It sounds a bit drastic, but its meaning is profound. If you think that the Buddha or Christ is someone other than yourself, you have completely missed the point, because the Buddha or Christ represents your own essential nature.

There have been many remarkable individuals throughout history whose profound insights into the mysteries of life and death can help us on our own journey of awakening. But they lived in a particular culture which informed and limited their perspective on the life-dream, so there will inevitably be aspects of their teachings which are outdated. If we understand this we will abandon the absurd notion that we have to accept everything such people say, and feel free to discriminate what speaks to us in their teachings from what does not.

The idea that some perfect person really does have all the answers can be very alluring. Many of us are desperately searching for someone who isn't searching for anything. In spiritual circles there is much talk of masters who are 'fully enlightened'. Yet there have been endless exposés and scandals demonstrating the all-too-human nature of these supposed super-beings. The time has come to recognise that no one is so wise they can't become a fool for a moment. And no one is so foolish they can't surprise us with their wisdom. We're in this together. Remembering and forgetting. Numbing out and waking up. Always evolving but never arriving.

Just as some people have a genius for music and others for sport, some people have a genius for penetrating the mysteries of life and death, and helping others to do likewise. But they are still ordinary men and women, often wrestling with the same addictions, moodiness and other personal problems as the rest of us. They are guides not gods. If we put them on a pedestal it just makes it more difficult for us to really understand the genuine wisdom they have to impart.

We don't treat our scientists, artists, politicians or plumbers as infallible. But when it comes to spirituality this reasonable approach goes out the window and we expect those with a talent for spiritual insight to somehow be perfect. And if they fail to live up to our unreasonable expectations we see them as irrevocably flawed, even when much of their wisdom may still be of great value.

We are easily awed by those who are more awake than we are, because to be in the presence of someone who is experiencing an expanded state of consciousness can expand our own state of consciousness. This is what the Pagan Gnostics called *paradosis*, or 'transmission'. In India they call this *darshan*. There is nothing particularly mysterious about this. (Or no more mysterious than everything else!) We experience this sort of transmission all the time. Being around happy people can make us happy. Being around depressed people can make us depressed. And being around awake people can wake us up. This can be an extremely valuable experience, but it doesn't make someone an absolute authority on everything.

The problem is that many teachers on the spiritual circuit encourage us to see them as infallible authority figures. Such teachers often have immense charisma, which makes them extremely attractive. But charisma, like all magic, can be white or black. Some teachers use their charisma to enchant their students into awakening to the wonder of their own true nature. But other teachers use their charisma to mesmerise their students into becoming obsequious devotees.

The test of a teacher is simple. Look at their students. A teacher can be trusted if they have helped their students wake up and move on. But they should not be trusted if they have made their students into dependent sycophants regurgitating the words of the master, but never thinking for themselves. Because many teachers are actually in the business of imprisoning their students within a personality cult, not setting them free to become their own masters. Their real agenda is to become a spiritual celebrity and enlarge their fan club.

Authentic teachers are self-confessed phoneys. That doesn't mean they are hypocrites. In fact it means they are much less likely to be hypocritical, because they are conscious of *both* how wise they are becoming *and* how foolish they remain. Someone is for real when they feel a fraud. This is why Pythagoras refused to be called 'wise' and called himself only a 'lover of wisdom' or 'philosopher'. And why in the gospels Jesus does not allow his disciples to call him 'good'.

The life-dream arises with polarity, so everyone within it is *both* wise *and* foolish. As individuals we exist somewhere on a continuum between the ignorance of unconscious identification with our life-persona and the unattainable ideal of absolute awakening. To be a person is to be in the *process* of waking up and evolving further. And how awake we are varies from moment to moment, because everything in the life-dream is in constant flux.

Let us be absolutely clear, the authors of this book are not making any claims to being exceptional in any way. We are certainly not saintly, as our friends and family will readily testify. Sometimes we can be wonderfully wise, compassionate and vital. But sometimes we can be stubbornly stupid, selfish and numb. Does that sound familiar? Of course it does! It's the human predicament. So let's just see it like it is and get on with it.

12

THE BIG IDEA

*Love is the answer
and you know that for sure.*
— 'MIND GAMES', JOHN LENNON

The good news is we are all one. The bad news is only a small minority of us realises this. Most of us are asleep in the nightmare of separateness. And the misguided conviction that we are separate from each other is the cause of untold suffering. It is the root cause of all our individual troubles. And it is the root cause of our present world crisis created by 9/11 and its aftermath. For Gnostics the only solution is to wake up to oneness and reject Literalism. Because Literalism is, above all, the mistake of taking ourselves literally as separate individuals.

The tragicomedy of our predicament is that we think we are separate but in reality we are one. Throughout history we have torn ourselves apart with terrible tribal wars. Yet the labels we have used to define our tribal identities are so fluid they make no sense. Take the inhabitants of a few small islands off the edge of Europe who now call themselves 'British'. Until recently these people proudly dominated the world with a vast 'British' Empire. But actually the only Britons left in Britain are the Welsh (many of whom want independence from Britain!), because the original Britons were pushed into Wales by the Romans two thousand years ago.

The 'real' identities of the other peoples inhabiting these small islands are just as confused. The Irish were originally Scots who sailed across the sea and settled in Ireland. These Scots were themselves originally Picts, who came from what would one day be called England. But England only came to be called England after it was conquered by the Angles, who came from Germany. As did the Saxons, who then conquered the Angles. They were then conquered by Danes and Vikings, who came from Scandinavia, and the whole lot were then conquered by the Normans from France, who themselves were originally Vikings or Norsemen. It's all very confusing!

When these mongrels arrived in the New World they re-branded themselves as Americans. They weren't really Americans, of course, as this name applies to the indigenous people of the Americas, who themselves are thought to have come from Siberia. The indigenous Americans were pretty much wiped out by the European invaders. Modern 'Americans' are actually a people whose ancestors come from every corner of the world. Modern America is so spectacularly diverse in origin that it really is fitting that it is called the US!

All of the labels we use to define our race and nationality are mere conceptual constructions. Geneticists have demonstrated that we are all Africans under the skin, so let's embrace each other as brothers and sisters. Let's start seeing ourselves as the inhabitants of one world, not separate countries defined by arbitrary lines on a map.

But while bogus national identities might be easy to throw off, as evidenced by the speed at which they can be traded for others, religious identities are often more entrenched and harder to discard. All the stories we tell to define our separateness are dangerously divisive, but none more than religious ideologies that pretend to represent the absolute Truth. Religious Literalism creates a divinely sanctioned gulf between believers and infidels which has driven believers throughout history to commit the most horrendous crimes against humanity to please their God.

In Western culture we no longer tolerate discrimination against people on the basis of their gender, race or sexuality. Discrimination is still rife, of course, but we at least condemn it and have made it illegal, which is a huge step forward. So why should we continue to tolerate religious bigotry? The bizarre idea that God prefers some people over others is medieval. Surely the time has come to consign this 'faithism' to the compost heap of history, along with nationalism, racism, sexism and all the other 'isms' which keep us trapped in the nightmare of separateness.

Science has demonstrated that the elements that make our bodies formed in the hearts of stars that burnt and exploded in supernovas billions of years ago. We are quite literally stardust. We have arisen from the cosmos and so are truly 'cosmopolitans'. We are one human family and the universe is our mother. When we finally recognise that we are kindred we might finally begin to treat each other with kindness.

Us Versus Them

As long as we live in the 'us versus them' world created by the illusion of separateness, we will continue to squabble and fight. We will continue to project the evil within ourselves onto 'them'. It will always be the other side that is untrustworthy, duplicitous, criminal and inhumane, whilst we are good, honest, legal and loving. It will always be the other guy who is a terrorist, whilst 'we' are the freedom fighters. At a press conference following 9/11 President Bush stated:

> How do I respond when I see that in some Islamic countries there is a vitriolic hatred for America? I'll tell you how I respond. I'm amazed. I just can't believe it because I know how good we are.

He's right, of course. But only half-right. America *is* a good country. And in many ways it is leading humanity into a new and better world. But America, like every country and every person, has its shadow side. As long as it refuses to acknowledge this, it will continue to project its own 'evil' onto the 'other'. In an 'us versus them' world there must always be an evil 'them'. Just look at how, when the 'evil empire' of Soviet Russia fell, a new 'axis of evil' was created within a few years to fill the void.

But life can never be reduced to a simple morality tale of the triumph of the good guys over the bad guys, no matter how much Hollywood may want to portray it that way. In reality there are no good guys and bad guys, because we are all a mixture of good and bad. As long as we delude ourselves that evil is 'out there' and can be fought 'out there', we will never find the solution. The only answer is to recognise that the 'evil' is in ourselves. Until we truly absorb the implication of the teaching 'let he who is without sin throw the first stone' we are forever doomed to hurl stones at each other.

From the Gnostic perspective, the first step to healing the present world crisis would be for us to be big enough to understand our enemy's point of view. As Jesus says in the Gospels, we need to stop pointing out the speck of dust in our opponent's eye and acknowledge the great plank of wood in our own. We need to seek out and humbly acknowledge everything we have done to divide 'them' from 'us'. We have to make amends for our own failings, whilst forgiving our adversaries. We have to trust even where trust has been betrayed. And love even where love has been rejected. We need to refuse to play the game of winners and losers, and make it clear that we can only win together.

Following the atrocity of 9/11 a wave of sympathy for America swept the world, and was just as quickly squandered. It could all have been so different. Imagine if the American president had addressed the world in the authentic spirit of the original Christians:

> The American people are hurt and shocked by these terrible attacks on our country. But as a culture rooted in the Christian tradition, it is in such dark times that we must draw on our deepest wisdom, which teaches us to have faith in the power of love and forgiveness. In the New Testament Jesus teaches that we should forgive those who wrong us and turn the other cheek. He declares 'You have heard it said "an

eye for an eye" but I say "love your enemies" '. Only love can heal hate. Suffering is redeemed only when it motivates us to make things better. Therefore, even though our hearts are breaking and filled with anger, we will not take revenge. Instead we will try to forgive those who have hurt us so badly. We invite all of you who consider us to be your enemy to come and talk with us. Let us sit around a table and settle once and for all the differences between us. Help us to prove beyond doubt that we are not the enemy of anyone. If we have been guilty of causing suffering and pain, tell us what we can do to make things right. We will continue to nurture our dream. A dream that one day little Muslim boys and girls will be able to join hands with little Jewish boys and girls, and little Christian boys and girls, as sisters and brothers. Come and help us make that dream a reality.

What would have happened if the president of America had responded in this way? The world would have changed forever. We would have turned a monumental corner in the evolution of consciousness. It would have signalled a completely new way of conducting politics. But, sadly, this did not happen. When the Buddhist celebrity Richard Gere even suggested the possibility of love and forgiveness at a public meeting in New York, he was booed and heckled. Having been badly stung by a hornet, America's response was to follow the hornet back to its nest and beat it with a big stick. Suffering further stings only caused a now enraged America to beat the hornet's nest harder. Another great opportunity to change the world was lost.

The Politics of Love

Life is a dream we are co-creating together as we become more conscious. We can choose a future of hate and division or of love and oneness. Gnostics keep alive the utopian dream of Heaven on Earth. They nurture the hope of creating a world in which we can enjoy the delights of living in all our many forms. The Gnostic aspiration is universal enlivenment. This is the great ambition that motivates the life-dream.

At present we are caught up in the illusion of being separate from each other, which means the life-dream keeps degenerating into a nightmare. But the more we become conscious of our essential unity, the more we will change division and discord into compassion and co-operation. We will come to understand, as the Dalai Lama puts it:

> Our highest duty as human beings is to search out a means whereby all beings may be freed from all kinds of unsatisfactory experience and suffering.

Einstein expresses the Gnostic perspective perfectly when he writes:

> A human being is a part of the whole, called by us the 'universe', a part limited in time and space. He experiences himself, his thoughts and feelings, as something separated from the rest—a kind of optical delusion of his consciousness. This delusion is a kind of prison for us, restricting us to our personal desires and to affection for a few persons nearest to us. Our task must be to free ourselves from this prison by widening our circle of compassion to embrace all living creatures and the whole of nature in its beauty.

Identifying exclusively with our separate persona leads to selfishness, blame and greed. Identifying with our shared essential nature leads to kindness, forgiveness and generosity. Awakening to the oneness of awareness transforms the person we appear to be into an embodiment of love. And the more we can live from love, the more we can genuinely contribute to the great ambition of universal enlivenment.

From the lucid perspective we are creating all our problems ourselves by failing to recognise that life is an expression of our own deeper shared nature. If we can simply realise that we are one, we will naturally cease to treat each other and the world around us as separate from ourselves. We will cease solving our differences by killing each other. We will stop destroying our natural environment. We will no longer use others as means for our personal satisfaction. We will start practising the politics of love.

Politics tends to revolve around the polarity of liberty and equality.

Traditionally the right emphasises liberty and the left emphasises equality. Yet there is a third principle in the famous revolutionary slogan 'liberty, equality and *fraternity*'. Fraternity, or kindness, is the missing element which the politicians of love needs to emphasise. Because only when we love will we set ourselves free and treat each other as equals.

Currently we are the blind led by the blind. It is no good blaming the politicians. We get the politicians we deserve. At present we choose leaders who offer short-term benefits to satisfy our immediate personal desires, often at tremendous cost to other people, the environment and the future. But we need to choose leaders with the vision to guide us towards a truly compassionate world. There is so much ignorance and self-interest to overcome, this may appear an impossible task. The world is run by the rich for their own benefit and changing this seems a Herculean challenge. But vested self-interest can overthrow itself given the right ideas. Each one of us needs to overcome our vested self-interest to awaken. And those with power and wealth are just as capable of awakening to big love as anyone else.

In the gospels Jesus teaches that it is easier for a camel to pass through the eye of a needle than for a rich man to experience Heaven. This is not a moral judgement of the wealthy, it is just stating a fact. Heaven is the state of big love which arises when we awaken. It is impossible to truly experience Heaven whilst we are so lost in separateness that we are able to enjoy vast wealth whilst others starve in poverty. In our present culture we regard being disproportionately rich as a great blessing, but perhaps we need to see it as a curse.

What would happen if we started to regard the indulgent super-rich as displaying anti-social behaviour and in need of some sort of community rehabilitation? If we recognised that the powerful businessmen of today are just the latest version of what were once feudal lords and barons? If we replaced the familiar 'rich list', which eulogises those who have amassed the most wealth, with a kindness list, which eulogises those who had done the most good? What would happen if society changed its attitude so that great *giving* was admirable and excessive *having* was abhorrent. We need to make compassion fashionable!

Today we judge the success and failure of our culture by its economic achievements. What would happen if we replaced our economic index with a happiness index. If we judged how well we are doing not by how rich we are but by how much we enjoy living? What would happen if we chose to create a culture of kindness in which we feel good, not a culture of cash in which we feel ever more stressed?

All that is required to makes things better is for each of us to wake up and live in love. Because if we truly love each other we will do all we can to alleviate each other's suffering. Anything we do only from economic or ideological self-interest will ultimately rebound on us, because what comes solely from a sense of separateness will trap us further in separateness. Anything we do from the knowledge of our essential unity, however, will help in some way to overcome our sense of separateness and wake us up to oneness and love.

In his song 'Mind Games' John Lennon wrote 'Love is the answer and you know that for sure'. What a wonderfully audacious assertion. Somewhere deep inside, all of us do *know that for sure*. Love is the solution to all of humanity's problems. Nothing else will do. No clever theories. No political revolutions. No diplomatic compromises. Only love. Because love is how it feels to recognise our essential unity. How can we heal the divisions between us? Only by knowing we are one and living in love.

The Big Idea

To create a new and better world we need to think in new and better ways. As Einstein puts it:

> The problems of today cannot be solved with the same mind-set that created them in the first place.

There is much talk of looking for a big idea that can offer us new hope in a climate of increasing hopelessness. We want to suggest that the Gnostics have been proposing such a big idea for centuries. *All is one.* Life is one awareness becoming conscious of itself in infinitely various forms, and to consciously recognise this is an experience of all-embracing love. This is a very big idea indeed. It takes our most common-sense assumptions about life and turns them inside out. It utterly changes how we perceive the world and ourselves. And it is more than an idea. It is something we can know to be true for ourselves in this moment.

Right now the big idea that we are all one is understood only by a few mystics and misfits on the fringes of society. But it is only a matter of time before it breaks out of the mystical ghetto in which it has been kept alive throughout the ages. Life is a dream of awakening, so sooner or later the Gnostic big idea will take off in mainstream culture, as we hesitantly, falteringly, sporadically, but inexorably, wake up.

We tend to envisage the future as a bigger, better version of the present. We have begun to explore outer space, so we imagine a future of giant spaceships and alien encounters. We have created extraordinary new technologies, so we imagine a future of super-computers and artificial intelligence. This may turn out to be true, but just as our ancestors could not have predicted the transformations in human culture we have experienced, so it is most likely the real changes that lie ahead will be unexpected.

We suggest that the great surprise that lies ahead for humanity is waking up to oneness and love. One day the barriers of separateness that divide us will come down, as suddenly and effortlessly as the Berlin Wall. This may sound idealistic and that's because it is. Gnostics are idealists in both the philosophical and the utopian sense of the word. We need to be visionaries to see where we are trying to get to. Ideals are stars to chart our course by.

We also need to be pragmatic, of course, because on its own idealism is ineffectual. But pragmatism on its own isn't being 'realistic', as is so often claimed. It is being small-minded and missing reality completely. We mustn't get caught in the either/or logic that demands we choose between the two. We must be *both* idealistic *and* pragmatic. We must clarify our vision of a better world and what practical steps we need to take to get there.

One of the things that stops idealists creating real change is that they tend to search for absolute solutions to problems. But the life-dream arises from polarity, so every solution can only be partial and brings with it new and often unforeseen problems. Yet it is only by engaging with this process that we evolve. Of course we will fail to realise the Gnostic utopian vision. If we don't fail we aren't taking on big enough challenges. But we can keep on trying. And fail again. But fail better.

There is always further to go. There is always the need for more understanding, more unity, more love. But this should not blind us to how far we have come. The modern world, despite all its terrible faults, is more just, compassionate and full of fun than any other form of human civilisation before it. Areas of the world, such as Europe, which have has been divided by war since the dawn of history, have recently forged what promises to be a lasting peace. Relatively poor human beings in affluent countries are enjoying a standard of living which kings could not have dreamed of in the not-so-distant past. A growing percentage of the world is now run by some form of democratic consensus, not authoritarian might. We even have a fledgling world parliament beginning to develop in the guise of the United Nations.

In significant areas of the modern world racism is now abhorred, although not long ago it was regarded as a virtue to be encouraged. Sexism, likewise, is gradually, but in historical terms extremely speedily, being eradicated. We've even embarked on cross-species compassion and started to argue about animal rights. We may not have been able to prevent the invasion of Iraq in 2003, but thousands of people all over the world protested to prevent it, which has never happened before. At any other time in history the idea of people in Europe, America, Asia and Africa caring about Iraqis would have been ridiculous.

We have been able to make these astonishing advances by becoming more conscious of our human failings, but this has given us a very negative collective self-image. Today many of us see human beings as warlike, aggressive, selfish, exploitative parasites, who infect the earth like a disease. This is admirable because it shows a willingness to face the unpalatable aspects of human nature, which is necessary if we are to change. But it is also a one-sided appraisal of human beings, which leads to cynicism and apathy. And this saps our faith in our ability to evolve.

We need to follow the lead of social groups who have consciously turned around their negative self-image. The black community defiantly proclaimed itself 'black and proud'. The gay community dared to be 'gay and proud'. Now we need to be collectively 'human and proud'. Because we're actually doing okay. We have come a long way in a short time and show no sign of stopping. Most human beings are astonishingly kind and compassionate. The level of co-operation we take for granted is extraordinary. We should be proud as well as penitent. It is true that we are still horribly asleep in separateness and selfishness, but we are also waking up to oneness and love. Make no mistake about it.

There are certainly mountains to climb, but there is no reason to feel disheartened. Look at the past and you'll see the huge mountains we have already climbed. If we could do that, we can do this. If we are conscious of just how far we have come, we can feel empowered to face the challenges ahead. Because there are still so many problems to overcome and now on a potentially more devastating scale.

To progress further we need to understand history, not just as the tale of power-hungry politicians but as the evolution of consciousness. And we need to have confidence in this process. Only a few decades ago slavery was seen as acceptable by otherwise kind and decent men and women, yet it is now unthinkable that we would legalise slavery today. In the same way, the horrors that we treat as acceptable today will seem unthinkable tomorrow. All it takes is for us to become more conscious.

We need to have confidence in our creative ability to make things better. For centuries we presumed it was impossible for human beings to fly, but once we started paying the possibility attention we soon found ourselves flying around in jumbo jets and travelling to the moon. If we want to wake up and make the life-dream better so we collectively enjoy it more, all we have to do is give this our conscious attention.

Those of us who have begun to wake up to oneness are clearly a minority right now, but this should inspire rather than depress us. To be on the cutting-edge of anything is, by definition, to be in a minority. The problem is that the advocates of oneness and love tend to whisper politely, rather than shout defiantly like the promoters of division. But the time has come to really live what we *know* and be ambassadors for oneness. It is admirable to be humbly reticent, but that doesn't change anything. The philosopher Bertrand Russell captured the predicament perfectly when he quipped:

> The trouble with the world is that the stupid are cocksure and the intelligent are full of doubt.

Appalled by the evangelical pushiness of those promoting Literalist religion, those with a Gnostic perspective often choose to keep their awakening a private matter. And there is great wisdom in this, because we won't awaken others by thrusting the Gnostic big idea into people's faces, but only by embodying big love in our own lives. Yet, the choice is not between aggressive evangelism or silent reticence. We can both respect the autonomy of others and be willing to uncompromisingly live and speak what we know.

We are currently facing an unparalleled opportunity to take a significant stride forward on our journey of awakening. But we are also facing the possibility of a reactionary backlash which could set our awakening back decades. For unconscious people to prosper all that is needed is for conscious people to do nothing. It is up to each of us to choose to be part of the solution, not part of the problem. To prioritize compassion. To live lucidly. We have written this book as our contribution towards our collective awakening. It is a manifesto for a new reality. Will you wake up and join the party?

Only Heretics Get the Joke

Watching the daily dose of confusion and conflict we call the TV news, life doesn't seem much like a party. It is as if we are gathered around a pile of rubbish in a huge and beautiful garden complaining about the mess. There is a mess and we should make sure we clean it up. But let's not forget to turn around and appreciate the garden. It is exquisite. Unless we remember to enjoy life, just as it is, we are missing the point. Let's *both* appreciate *and* improve. Let's remember to value each mysterious passing moment. Because being alive is magical.

Let's respect ourselves and admire each other. We are amazing. *You* are amazing. You are the mystery of existence made manifest. You are the universal mind which is imagining this magnificent cosmos. And you are a unique human being with the opportunity to contribute your verse to the glorious song of life. There is no one in this world who is greater than you and none lesser. You are a marvel. There are no words adequate to describe all you are.

Let's stop being so sober and celebrate our existence. Let's stop being so frightened of life and adopt a pronoid perspective. Let's live lightheartedly and revel in the humour of our predicament. Because life is a black comedy so ironic that most of us miss the gags. 'God is a comedian playing to an audience too terrified to laugh', as Voltaire quips. So, let's lighten up and enjoy the show. Then we'll understand why the Gnostic Jesus laughs. Because life is funny. But only heretics get the joke.

If we want to fulfil the primal life-impulse to love living, we need to laugh more and worry less. We need to heed the Pagan Gnostic Lucian when he advises:

> The best way to live is to be in the present moment and get along as best you can, trying to see the funny side of things.

As his 'spiritual practise' the Gnostic genius and alcoholic Alan Watts would wake up each morning and stand naked in front of a mirror for ten minutes laughing. If you can learn to laugh at yourself you'll have a lifetime of amusement. And when you don't take yourself so seriously, it is easier to be good-humoured with others. We are one human family. So, let's learn to play nicely.

A
Philosophical
Workout

Waking up, like anything else, takes practise. A powerful way to engage with life as a journey of awakening is to create a regime of philosophical exercises, which you practise on a regular basis, in the same way that you might a physical fitness programme. Here are a number of simple exercises, based on the Gnostic teachings of lucid living we have explored in this book, which you might like to include in your philosophical workout. Pick those exercises you find attractive to devise a regime to suit your own unique needs. The ancients called their universities in which they studied philosophy 'gymnasiums'. With these exercises you can create your own philosophy gym in which you can build up the mental muscles you need to stay awake.

Awakening Now

This is a simple exercise incorporating all the major teachings of lucid living, which you can practise anywhere and anytime. Indeed you can do it all the time. Waking up is really one movement in consciousness, but in this exercise we have broken it down into stages to make it easier to remember and practise. Don't worry if you find some stages easier than others. And remember that waking up is always a relative experience, so don't expect to enter a deep state of gnosis immediately. But don't rule this out either. Anything is possible. Just experiment with the exercise and see what happens:

- **Wake up:** The first step to awakening is to recognise that you are asleep and that you want to wake up.

- **Witness:** The second step is to change perspective by disengaging from your life-persona and consciously being awareness witnessing all you are experiencing.

- **Be one loving all:** The third step is to embrace everything within compassionate awareness and be one with all in big love.

- **Appreciate and improve:** Stay conscious of being the oneness of awareness unconditionally appreciating life as it is. Now also pay attention to your experience of appearing to be a person. How can you act from love to transform yourself and the world to improve our collective experience of the life-dream?

Communion and Compassion

This is another very simple technique you can practise at any time to keep you conscious:

- Focus on your breath.

- As you breathe in commune with all that is by consciously being awareness that is one with everything and everyone.

- As you breathe out embrace everything and everyone with unconditional compassion.

Sitting

In many spiritual traditions this practise is known as 'meditation' or 'silent prayer', but these terms come with so many connotations that we prefer to call the practise simply 'sitting'. Sitting is a way of making it easier to enter the state of witnessing, by being quiet and still so that there are less distractions to keep you engrossed in the life-dream. Sitting is an excellent way of making a regular reality check. Long, intensive periods of practise are very helpful to deepen your experience of gnosis. But little and often is also good, because it will help you maintain a more awakened state on an ongoing basis:

- Sit comfortably in a quiet environment in which you won't be disturbed. Ideally you want to be relaxed and alert, rather than stressed or dull. It can be helpful to limit your sensual experience by closing your eyes, although this can lead to drowsiness. If you choose to sit with your eyes open, it is best to keep your eyes focused on one place, such as a candle, a white wall or a spot on the ground.

- Witness whatever you are feeling, hearing, seeing and smelling. Recognise that all your sensations exist within awareness.

- Now witness your thoughts coming and going. Recognise that the individual 'you' is not the thinker and watch your thoughts arising spontaneously of themselves. Awareness is like a spacious blue sky and your thoughts are like clouds rising and falling above the horizon of consciousness.

- Identify with the mysterious source of your thoughts. Be awareness witnessing whatever arises.

- You will find that the more you simply witness, the more calm your body and mind become, and the easier it is to be conscious of being awareness. To begin with, however, you may find yourself continually becoming lost in your thoughts and forgetting to witness. If this happens patiently begin the practise again.

- When you have reduced your experience of the moment to awareness witnessing a flow of appearances, recognise that awareness is one with all that it witnesses.

Whilst you are sitting all sorts of fascinating experiences may arise. Some spiritual traditions advise that we ignore these as distractions, but we suggest adopting a both/and approach. Enjoy investigating whatever happens while you are sitting, but don't become so enamoured with the experience that you stop witnessing. As you become deeply relaxed the sensation of breathing may become intensely pleasurable and you may become conscious of how beautiful it is just to *be*. Appreciate the experience but recognise that it is arising because you are witnessing. If you have your eyes closed you may find that visions arise in the imagination. Appreciate them but don't get lost in them. You may find they are telling you something. Note any insights that arise but don't stop witnessing.

Whilst sitting it is possible to enter a deep state of introspection in which the world begins to disappear from consciousness altogether. Sometimes this is accompanied by a blissful feeling of complete well-being, and an experience of light and vibrating sound. This is happening because you are *consciously* entering the state you normally experience *unconsciously* as 'deep sleep'. You are exploring the edge where conscious awareness and unconscious awareness meet.

Because of the inactivity of sitting, you may feel yourself drifting off if you become lost in your thoughts and dreams. You may experience your head nodding forward suddenly as you find yourself falling asleep for a moment. This is not a sign of failure. It is actually an extremely interesting state which can teach you a great deal. Watch yourself becoming sucked into your thoughts and be conscious of the psychological effort it takes to pull yourself back into the state of witnessing. Practising this whilst sitting will make it easier to stay awake in your everyday life, because what causes you to become lost in the life-dream is the same psychological inertia and what can wake you up is the same psychological effort. Being awake is effortless, but the process of waking up requires a determined effort.

The Ladder to the Source

Awakening to oneness requires a radical shift of perspective. If you're finding that difficult, it may be easier to get there step-by-step, by working your way back through the polarities that make up your experience, like climbing a ladder back to awareness, the source of all. Take this exercise extremely slowly to make sure you really get it:

- If you examine your experience of appearing to be a person, you will recognise that you are experiencing *feelings* of being a body and *perceptions* of the world the body inhabits. You are experiencing a fundamental polarity which is your body and the world. Feeling and perception.

- Now recognise that your feelings and your perceptions are the two poles of an essential unity, because they are both aspects of your *sensual experience*.

- If you look at your experience of sensation as a unified whole, you will become conscious of another fundamental polarity within your experience, which is *imagination* and *sensation*. You are presently experiencing both your 'inner' world of thoughts and your 'outer' world of sensation.

- Now recognise that your inner and outer worlds are also poles of an essential unity, because they are both aspects of your *experience*.

- If you look at all your experiences as a unified whole you will become conscious of being awareness witnessing a flow of appearances.

- Finally, recognize that awareness is not separate from that which it witnesses but one with all that is. This is gnosis.

Contemplation

The more you understand Gnostic philosophy intellectually, the easier it becomes to go beyond the words and experience gnosis. To grasp the teachings of lucid living you need to hear them again and again, so that you progressively penetrate the ideas more deeply:

- Choose a book of Gnostic teachings and read a small section which interests you.

- Stop and carefully consider the ideas you have encountered.

- Don't settle for a partial understanding. Push and pull the ideas you are contemplating to see if they fall over. Question your assumptions. Think things through thoroughly.

Here are ten Gnostic ideas which can form the basis of contemplation, each of which is pregnant with endless insights:

- You have a dual nature. You appear to be a person, but essentially you are awareness.

- Lucid living is adopting a both/and perspective in which you are conscious of both your apparent nature and your essential nature.

- As awareness you are a spacious emptiness which contains the world. You are a timeless presence which witnesses the flow of experiences we call 'time'.

- Life is like a dream in which one awareness is becoming conscious through infinitely various forms.

- We are unconsciously one and consciously many. Gnosis is becoming conscious that all is essentially one.

- Awakening to oneness is the experience of big love. Knowing you are one with all you find yourself in love with all.

- The purpose of life is to love being this moment. When you are driven solely by other desires you miss the point and become engrossed in the life-dream.

- The foibles which keep you unconscious in the life-dream are your qualities which have become distorted because you presume yourself to be an isolated individual.

- The way to love appearing to be a person is to become conscious of your impersonal essential nature as awareness.

- Lucid living is a state of enlivenment. It is loving being human.

Loving Unconditionally

This practise is the philosophical exercise we explored in chapter 10 reduced to four simple steps to enable you to remember and practise it more easily. It will help you cultivate the habit of compassionate thinking and so experience unconditional love for all. By changing how we think we can change how we feel:

- **Love being this moment:** Appreciate the miracle of existence. This world is a wonder. As a body you exist in the world. As awareness the world exists in you. Amazing!

- **Love others:** Other people exist within you as awareness. Hold everyone—friends and enemies alike—within unconditional big love. If you find this difficult with a particular person, remember that loving has got nothing to do with liking someone. Bring to mind the person you find difficult to love and reach through their personality to connect with their essential nature, which is also your essential nature.

- **Love yourself:** You are a wonder. As a body you are a visible object. As awareness you are a mysterious subject. Be awareness embracing all you like and dislike about your personal nature with big love.

- **Live in love:** Imagine the suffering and joy that is happening throughout the world in this one moment and embrace it all with big love. Ask yourself how your life would change if you lived from love today.

Looking with Love

This practise can help you recognise the difference between living with the knowledge that all is one and living as just an isolated separate individual:

- Choose an object to focus on. Become conscious of how it feels to view that object as separate from yourself.

- Now become conscious of your essential nature as awareness.

- Become conscious that this object exists within you as awareness.

- Recognise that as awareness you are one with the object.

- Be the oneness of awareness embracing this object with big love.

- Feel the difference between being an isolated individual just looking at a separate object and looking with love by realising that 'the seer and the seen are one'.

Once you can experience looking with love, try touching with love, listening with love, tasting with love and thinking with love.

Connecting

This is a wonderful technique to practise with a friend to help you see beyond the superficial separateness which divides us:

- Sit opposite your partner and look into each other's eyes. Don't stare out from your body into your partner's eyes; rather be spacious awareness embracing your partner's apparent nature within your essential nature.

- Become conscious that when you look at your partner all you actually see is a series of shapes and coloured patches. If you focus on the pupils of their eyes all you see are black holes. Quite literally!

- You can't see your partner's essential nature, because they don't exist within the life-dream any more than you do. Just like you, they appear to be a person, but subjectively they are awareness witnessing the life-dream.

- The word *person* originally meant 'mask'. See through the mask of your partner's personality to the mystery of awareness.

- Become conscious that your apparent nature is separate from your partner's apparent nature, but as awareness you are one. See that your individual identities are different masks worn by the one awareness.

Listening with Love

In the ancient world it was traditional to explore ideas with a philosophical partner. You can do this informally through conversation, which is a wonderful way to wake each other up. But it can also be powerful to formalise a philosophical dialogue using this simple technique of listening with love:

- Decide who is partner one and who is partner two. Then select a profound question you both want to explore, such as 'What is love', 'Who am I', 'What is it that stops me waking up', and so on.

- Sit opposite your partner and become conscious of being awareness.

- Partner one now asks the question of partner two.

- Partner two then spontaneously responds with whatever thoughts arise. Don't censure what you say, simply allow your thoughts to flow. Don't feel uncomfortable about just being silent if no response arises.

- Partner one should practise silent witnessing and embrace partner two within unconditional big love. If there is a long pause and you intuitively feel it appropriate, you may like to ask the question again. But otherwise stay quiet. Don't interfere with the process by offering your opinions. Have faith in your partner's ability to find their own intuitive wisdom if you give them the space to do so.

- You may find that as you are listening your attention becomes caught up with your own thoughts. If this happens return to listening with love. It can be fascinating to observe that often your partner's flow of thoughts is directly affected by how well you listen. When you become distracted you may find your partner dries up or becomes confused, but when you give them your undivided loving attention they become more lucid and eloquent.

- After practising this exercise for five to ten minutes, swap roles. Then, after another period, swap again. Repeat this as many times as you wish.

Initially it may be best to practise this exercise for about twenty minutes, but it can be practised for hours with amazing results. When the exercise is performed for a long time you will find you go beyond superficial answers to the question and make conscious some remarkable insights. Sometimes less and less is said as the exercise goes on, but if you stay focused the silence can be wiser than words.

A Wake-up Club

It is very helpful to have others around you who support your adventure of awakening. This may happen naturally through a network of like-minded friends, but it can be fun to formalise this into a Wake-up Club. You need to find your own unique way of running your Wake-up Club which suits the people who attend, but here is a simple way of getting things started that has worked well for us:

- Choose a time and place you are going to meet. You may want to begin with a one-off event as an experiment, and then, if everyone enjoys it, start meeting on a regular basis.

- Ask everyone to bring a question which they want to explore. You can fix an overall theme or leave this open. We started by asking people to choose a philosophical question rather than a personal dilemma. This avoids the session becoming group therapy, which can also be enlivening but may not be the place to start.

- Put all of the questions in a hat. Pull out one and read it aloud. Ask the questioner to enlarge on their question should they wish to.

- Then ask the group to contribute their insights. Remind everyone that you aren't looking for the right answer, because that doesn't exist! You are sharing your collective wisdom to find deeper and deeper responses to the question. Remind everyone to practise listening with love. Disagreements can be enjoyable and enlivening if they are within an atmosphere of mutual trust and respect. Keep things playful.

- When the group feels that it is done with one question, move on to the next. If you can cover all the questions in one session, that's great. If not, return to the other questions another time.

Communing

This exercise is a group version of the previous partner practise of connecting. In our experience it is an extremely powerful exercise to do with a group of people and a beautiful way to bring proceedings to an end if you are running a wake-up club. It is a type of group meditation, but with distinct advantages over most other group meditations. Normally when people meditate together they pay no attention to each other, but rather close their eyes or focus on an object of meditation such as a candle. In this exercise we focus on each other. This means we can practise witnessing whilst connecting with each other in love beyond our apparent separateness.

- Sit in a tight circle so that you can all see each other's eyes.

- Put everyone's name in a hat and pull them out one at a time.

- When someone's name is read out everyone should focus their attention on that person by looking at their eyes and holding them within spacious awareness and big love.

- The person whose name is called should now go around the group making eye contact with each person in turn for a brief moment, reaching through the veil of appearances to the mystery of awareness.

- Continue this until everyone has been held in oneness and love.

- Be still for a period enjoying the experience of being both one and many. This is lucid living.

Become Part of the ALL

You can connect with other people who are awakening by becoming part of the Alliance for Lucid Living. The ALL will also let you have information about our experiential seminars exploring gnosis.

For information visit www.timothyfreke.com or contact:

The Alliance for Lucid Living
P. O. Box 3733
Glastonbury
Somerset
BA6 9WZ
England

Notes

Part 1, 'The Bathwater', presents an argument about historical facts, so we have annotated this when appropriate. We have not annotated Part 2, 'The Baby', because it is a philosophical journey and we don't want the reader to become distracted by unnecessary notes.

1: Gnostic Spirituality and Literalist Religion

[1] *2 Corinthians* 3.6.

[2] See *The Apocalypse of Peter*, NHC (The Nag Hammadi Codex), *The Second Treatise of the Great Seth*, NHC, Robinson J. M., *The Nag Hammadi Library* (HarperCollins paperback 1978), 377, 365.

[3] *The Gospel of Truth* 22:13–20, quoted in Jonas, H., *Gnostic Religion: The Message of the Alien God* (Beacon Press 1958). Hans Jonas says of Gnostic metaphors for the human condition: 'Of the most constant and widest use is probably the image of sleep. The Soul slumbers in Matter'. See 'Numbness, sleep, intoxication,' 68–73.

[4] *Apocryphon of James*, NHC, 29.

[5] *The Concept of Our Great Power*, NHC, 311.

[6] *The Teachings of Silvanus*, NHC, 379.

[7] *The Gospel of Truth*, NHC, 38.

2: A Religious Detox

[1] Quoted in Maalouf, A., *The Crusades Through Arab Eyes* (Al Saqi Books 1984), 37.

[2] Ibid, 39.

[3] Samuel Usque quoted in Netanyahu, B., *The Origins of the Inquisition in Fifteenth Century Spain* (Random House 1995), xiv–xv.

[4] Kertzer, D. I., *Unholy War: The Vatican's Role in the Rise of Modern Anti-Semitism* (Pan Books 2001), 282. Kertzer presents overwhelming evidence that the Nazi persecution of the Jews was merely a continuation of Catholic persecution that had endured for centuries. He reviews the major tenets of the modern anti-Semitic movement: There is a secret Jewish conspiracy to conquer the world; the Jews have already seized control of the financial centres of Austria, Germany, France and Italy; Jews are by nature immoral; Jews care only for money; Jews control the press; Jews control the banks and are responsible for the economic ruin of Christians; Jews are responsible for communism; Jews murder Christian children and drink their blood; Jews seek to destroy the Christian religion; Jews are unpatriotic; Jews must be segregated; Jewish rights must be limited. Kertzer writes, 'The Church played an important role in promulgating every one of these ideas that are central to modern anti-Semitism. Every one of them had the support of the highest Church authorities, including the popes. If the Church bore major responsibility for the inculcation of a dozen of the major ideological pillars of the modern anti-Semitic political movement and a thirteenth came from other sources, are we to conclude that the Church bears little or no responsibility for the flowering of modern anti-Semitism in those areas where the Church had great influence?' We have only touched on this subject here but anyone doubting Christianity's role in the rise of modern anti-Semitism and its contribution to the Holocaust must read Kertzer's book.

[5] *John* 15.6.

[6] *Matthew* 27.25, *John* 19.15, *John* 8.44, *Revelation* 2.9.

[7] 'God Gave U.S. "What We Deserve" ' by John F. Harris, *Washington Post* staff writer. Friday, September 14, 2001; page C03. http://www.washington post.com/ac2/wp-dyn?pagename=article&contentId=A28620-2001Sep14& notFound=true. The comments came as Falwell was appearing as a guest on Robertson's daily *700 Club* program.

[8] Ali, T., *The Clash of Fundamentalisms: Crusades, Jihads and Modernity* (Verso 2002), 157–165.

[9] Ibid, 162–165.

[10] Ibid, 251.

[11] http://www.prop1.org/inaugur/85reagan/85rrarm.htm. 'It is hard to believe that the President actually allows Armageddon ideology to shape his policies toward the Soviet Union', the *New York Times* editorialized. 'Yet it

was he who first portrayed the Russians as satanic and who keeps on talking about the Final battle'.

[12] http://www.prop1.org/inaugur/85reagan/85rrarm.htm

[13] In *Matthew* 16.28 Jesus asserts, 'I assure you there are some among those standing here who will never taste death before they see the Son of Man coming in his monarchy'. In *Matthew* 24.34 he tells his listeners, 'I assure you that this generation will not go by before all this happens'. In *Luke* 21.12–36 Jesus' claims are even more extravagant: 'I tell you truly, that there are some of those standing right here who will never taste death before they see the kingdom of God. And there will be signs in the sun and moon and stars, and on earth an anxious mass of people in confusion over the roar of the sea and the tides, with people dying of fear and apprehension about what's coming over the world. Yes, the powers of Heaven will be shaken. And then they will see the Son of Man coming on a cloud with power and great glory. When these things start to happen, look up and raise your heads, because your redemption is approaching. When you see these things happening, you know the kingdom of God is close. I assure you that this generation will not pass away till it all happens'.

[14] Torrey, R. A. (ed.), *The Fundamentals: A Testimony to the Truth*, 1909.

[15] John Shelby Spong, quoted in Leedom, T. C. (ed.), *The Book Your Church Doesn't Want You to Read* (Kendall/Hunt Publishing Company 1993), 16.

3: The Word of God?

[1] *Jeremiah* 8.8 quoted in Sturgis, M. *It Ain't Necessarily So: Investigating the Truth of the Biblical Past* (Headline 2001), 186.

[2] Thompson, T. L., *The Bible in History: How Writers Create a Past* (Pimlico 1999), preface xv and 164.

[3] Finkelstein, I., Silberman, N. A., *The Bible Unearthed: Archaeology's New Vision and the Origin of Its Sacred Texts* (The Free Press 2001), 36, 175.

[4] *Exodus* 12.37. See commentary in Finkelstein, I., Silberman, N. A., *The Bible Unearthed*, ibid, 51–60.

[5] '. . . one of the best clues to the fact that the story does not describe events happening in the 13th century BCE.' Sturgis, M. *It Ain't Necessarily So: Investigating the Truth of the Biblical Past* (Headline 2001), 54.

[6] Available online at: http://www.library.cornell.edu/colldev/mideast/jerques.htm

[7] Sturgis, M., *It Ain't Necessarily So*, ibid, 7.

[8] Ibid, 129.

[9] Ibid, 132–133.

[10] Ibid, 128–129.

[11] Thompson, T. L., *The Bible in History: How Writers Create a Past* (Pimlico 1999), 205.

[12] Thompson, T. L., *The Bible in History*, ibid, 206, and see Sturgis, M., *It Ain't Necessarily So*, ibid, 133.

[13] Daniel Lazare, "False Testament: Archaeology refutes the Bible's Claim to History," *Harper's*, March 2002, vol. 304, no.1822: 40.

[14] Davies, P. R., *In Search of 'Ancient Israel'* (Sheffield Academic Press 1992), 58. Sturgis, M., *It Ain't Necessarily So*, ibid, 82.

[15] Davies, P. R., *In Search of 'Ancient Israel'*, ibid, 60.

[16] Ze'ev Herzog quoted in Sturgis, M., *It Ain't Necessarily So*, ibid, 58.

[17] Thompson, T. L., *Early History of the Israelite People: From the Written and Archaeological Sources* (Brill undated), 418.

[18] Bickerman, E. J., *The Jews in the Greek Age* (Harvard University Press 1988), 6.

[19] Momigliano, A., *Alien Wisdom: The Limits of Hellenization* (Cambridge University Press 1975), 78.

[20] Hengel M, *Jews, Greeks, and Barbarians: Aspects of the Hellenization of Judaism in the Pre-Christian Period* (SCM Press 1980), 17.

[21] Pseudo-Aristeas. See Bickerman, E. J., *The Jews in the Greek Age* (Harvard University Press 1988), 149.

[22] *2 Maccabees* 4 v 7ff records how the high priest Jason set up a gymnasium and that soon 'the priests no longer showed any enthusiasm for their duties at the altar.'

[23] Josephus, *Against Apion*, 1.165.

[24] Clement, *Stromata*, 1.72.4.

[25] Josephus, *Against Apion*, 2.163–168.

[26] Eusebius, *Praeparatio Evangelica*, 13.12.1. See also Clement, *Stromata*, 1.22, 'And Aristobulus, in his first book addressed to Philometor, writes in these words "And Plato followed the laws given to us, and had manifestly studied all that is said in them".' Aristobulus includes Socrates with Pythagoras and Plato among those whose reference to a divine voice in contemplating the creation of the cosmos derives from the words of Moses. Eusebius, *Praeparatio Evangelica*, 13.12.3–4.

[27] In *On the Sublime* 9.8, attributed to Longinus.

[28] *Isaiah* 66.19. See Bickerman, E. J., *The Jews in the Greek Age*, ibid, 14.

[29] Eusebius, *Praeparatio Evangelica*, 9.26.1. See Gruen, E. S., *Heritage and Hellenism: The Reinvention of the Jewish Tradition* (University of California Press 1998), 153.

[30] Ibid, 9.9.27.3–4.

[31] Ibid, 9.27.6. Gruen, E. S., *Heritage and Hellenism*, ibid, 155.

[32] See *1 Maccabees* 8.17. See Momigliano, A., *Alien Wisdom*, ibid, 113. See also Alexander Polyhistor ap., Eusebius, *Praeparatio Evangelica*, 9.17.1–9.

[33] Ibid, 9.17.8. See Gruen, E. S., *Heritage and Hellenism*, ibid, 148.

[34] Ibid, 9.18.1.

[35] Josephus, *Antiquities of the Jews*, 11.304–339.

[36] *Daniel* 8.21.

[37] E. J. Bickerman calls it a 'silly story that Judaizes Greek tales of a similar nature.' Bickerman, E. J., *The Jews in the Greek Age*, ibid, 5. E. S. Gruen calls it an 'outright fabrication' whose purpose is to infer that the prophecy of Alexander's triumph in the east 'came not from Delphi, Dodona or Didyma, but from the God of the Jews.' Gruen, E. S., *Heritage and Hellenism*, ibid, 195–196. M. Hengel asserts that 'Least historical value of all is to be attributed to the legend of Alexander's visit to the holy city and his sacrifice in the Temple after the conquest of Gaza.' Hengel, M., *Jews, Greeks, and Barbarians*, ibid, 7. V. Tcherikover agrees that 'It is a historical myth designed to bring the king into direct contact with the Jews, and to speak of both in laudatory terms.' Tcherikover, V. *Hellenistic Civilization and the Jews* (The Jewish Publication Society of America 1959), 45. Tcherikover goes on, 'Here is material for research worthy not of the historian, but of the student of literature.'

[38] Alexander's visit is not mentioned by either Arrian, Diodorus, Curtius or Plutarch. As Gruen notes there is no reason for Greek sources to have suppressed a visit to the holy city as they regularly reported Alexander's arrival at key shrines and sacred places, where he honoured native gods and performed public acts of sacrifice. See Gruen, E. S., *Heritage and Hellenism*, ibid, 195.

[39] Ibid, 192.

[40] See Wallis, R. T., *Neoplatonism and Gnosticism* (State University of New York Press 1992), 111ff, which reconstructs parts of Porphyry's argument from the internal evidence found in the many Christian works written to attack it. Christian authors including Methodius of Tyre, Apollinaris of Laodicea, Eusebius of Caesaria and Philostorgius wrote many volumes in response, a clear testimony to the alarm created by Porphyry's book. It was banned and burned when the empire became Christian and was still being censored as late as the 440s. See Wallis, R. T., *Neoplatonism and Gnosticism* (State University of New York Press 1992), 126, and Lane-Fox, R., *Pagans and Christians* (Alfred A. Knopf 1987), 586.

[41] For example in Jesus' prophecy about the dismantling of the Temple of Jerusalem stone by stone. It is on the basis of its lack of faith in this

'prophecy' that Higher Criticism, followed now by most Biblical scholars, regard *Mark* as having been written post 70 CE. The fact that the temple was not completely dismantled until 135 CE suggests that the date for *Mark* could be much later than 70 CE.

[42] *Letter of Aristeas*, 201.

[43] Marlowe, J., *The Golden Age of Alexandria* (Victor Gollancz 1971), 83.

[44] Davies, P. R., *In Search of 'Ancient Israel'* (Sheffield Academic Press 1992), 26.

[45] See Thompson, T. L., *The Bible in History*, ibid, preface xv, 254, 293. Other evidence that points to the rededication of the Temple under the Maccabees as a pivotal date is the chronology now evident in the Masoretic text. See Davies, P. R., *In Search of 'Ancient Israel'*, ibid, 154.

[46] Josephus, *Antiquities of the Jews* 13.249.

[47] Thompson, T. L., *The Bible in History*, ibid, 297. 'The clerks of the Ministry of Yehud were already claiming their tiny province to be the relic of a once mighty empire, indeed claiming some kind of jurisdiction over the entire satrapy . . . of "Beyond the River", the land promised to Abraham in Genesis and ruled over by David and Solomon. Was it on the basis of this fictional claim, which a Persian king, no less, has been made to endorse . . . that later Judean kings, the Hasmoneans, aimed to re-create what they took to be the boundaries of historical Israel, including in their kingdom those kindred "half-Jews" from Idumaea and Transjordan?' See Davies, P. R., *In Search of 'Ancient Israel'*, ibid, 87.

[48] Thompson writes, 'More than one recent book of biblical scholarship has explored the possibilities of radical political parties forming around a Taliban-like Fundamentalist core of religious bigots. This work is very promising'. Thompson, T. L., *The Bible in History*, ibid, 297. Josephus accounts of Hyrcanus' military conquests echo the stories of *2 Kings* and deal with the realities of forced conversions in a religiously politicised environment.

[49] Davies, P. R., *In Search of 'Ancient Israel'*, ibid, 56.

[50] Josephus, ibid, *The Jewish War* 1.305–316. See Hengel, M. *Jews, Greeks, and Barbarians*, ibid, 73.

[51] *Numbers* 31. This seems doubly unfair as in *Exodus* 2.15 when Moses fled from the Pharaoh he dwelt in the land of Midian where he helped the shepherds to water their flock.

[52] *2 Maccabees* 2.13 '. . . so Judas has collected all the books that had been scattered', see Davies, P. R., *In Search of 'Ancient Israel'*, ibid, 151.

[53] 'The development of "tradition" over a matter of a few generations, and more or less simultaneously, is a model to which I hope scholars will devote

much attention in future'. Davies, P. R., *In Search of 'Ancient Israel'*, ibid, 124. *4Qtestimonia*, a Dead Sea Scrolls (DSS) text, gives a good example of how to create a new text by stitching together verses from other texts. The DSS show that the texts were still evolving, and *4Qtestimonia* should really be called a new text in its own right. See Thompson, T. L., *The Bible in History*, ibid, 275. 'The Dead Sea Scrolls show that quite complex literary developments can occur over an apparently short period of time'. See Davies, P. R., *In Search of 'Ancient Israel'*, ibid, 97.

[54] Thompson, T. L., *The Bible in History*, ibid, 270.

[55] Table of dates modelled after that of Thompson, ibid, 73–75.

[56] Turcan, R., *Cults of the Roman Empire* (Blackwell Publishers 1992), 18–19.

[57] Ibid, 28.

[58] *Exodus* 6.3.

[59] Thompson, T. L., *The Bible in History*, ibid, 210 and 271.

[60] '*1 Maccabees* claims consanguinity between Spartans and Jews as both nations claimed Abraham as an ancestor. This tale does not occur in epic, drama, or a work of romantic fiction, instead it appeals to ostensible documents and diplomatic correspondence. Bonds between friendly cities and nations, often deriving from a common, usually legendary, ancestor was a staple item in Hellenic folklore and the Jews readily seized upon that fiction. The Judeo-centric quality of all this is unmistakable. The fact that Abraham, the Hebrew patriarch, appears as ultimate ancestor of both Spartans and Jews makes the point without ambiguity'. See Gruen, E. S., *Heritage and Hellenism*, ibid, 264.

[61] Thompson, T. L., *The Bible in History*, ibid, 256.

[62] Rabbi Professor Jonathan Magonet, the principal of Leo Baeck College, considers this confusion of names to lead back to the Bible's origins. See Sturgis, M., *It Ain't Necessarily So*, ibid, 170.

[63] Seals and bronzes from the Persian period in the Archaeological Museums of Jerusalem show Athena, Heracles, satyrs and other Greek deities. See Momigliano, A., *Alien Wisdom*, ibid, 79. A coin in the British Museum belonging to the Persian period bears the inscription 'Judea' (YHD) and shows a figure on a winged throne confronting a Dionysiac mask. See Kanael, B., *The Biblical Archaeologist*, 26 (1963), 40 and fig. 2. Even more intriguingly, a coin found in an archaeological site less than forty miles from Jerusalem depicts Yahweh as the founder of the Mysteries of Eleusis. See Macchioro, V. D., *From Orpheus to Paul* (Constable and Company 1930), 189.

[64] *Jeremiah* 11.13.

[65] Voltaire suggested (c.1760) that the Orphic hymns were evidence of a secret monotheistic doctrine among the Greeks. See Bickerman, E. J., *The Jews in the Greek Age* (Harvard University Press 1988), 227. Orphism is synonymous with Pythagoreanism and Platonism is the philosophical codification of Pythagoreanism. This philosophical stream, although often underground, should be thought of as a kind of ancient Freemasonry that exerted a profound influence on all the great thinkers of the Greco-Roman world. Christian propaganda has largely succeeded in obscuring this tradition in order to bolster its own supposed originality.

[66] 'The wise is one alone, unwilling and willing to be spoken of by the name of Zeus'. Heraclitus' aphorisms are full of references to monistic ideas, e.g., 'From all things one and from one thing all', and 'It is wise, listening not to me but to the Logos, to agree that all things are one'.

[67] Antisthenes, following in the track of Xenophanes, declared that the popular gods were many, but the god of nature was one, *'Antisthenes . . . populares deos multos, naturalem unum esse dicens'.* Cicero, *On the Nature of the Gods* 1.13.32. The sentiment had also been articulated by Socrates. The Stoics inherited the idea from the Cynics and, without making it a formal dogma, they constantly assume it by using the singular term 'God'. See Arnold, E. V., *Roman Stoicism* (Routledge & Kegan Paul Ltd 1911), 220.

[68] See Hengel, M., *Jews, Greeks, and Barbarians,* ibid, 96. Yahweh's self-definition in *Exodus* 3.14 is replaced by 'I am who I am', *'ego eimi ho on'.*

[69] Josephus, *Contra Apionem* 2.163–168.

[70] The Bible itself records Solomon's penchant for foreign wives and for foreign gods. Among the deities whom he honoured was Astarte, the goddess of the Sidonians. *1 Kings* 11.1–6.

[71] Diana Edelman, archaeologist of the Department of Biblical Studies at Sheffield University. See Sturgis, M., *It Ain't Necessarily So,* ibid, 180.

[72] The Bible tells us that King Josiah harboured a particular hatred for the Asherah, and persecuted her cult. Other passages in the Bible refer to the Israelites as being distressed that they are no longer allowed to worship their 'Queen of Heaven', and blaming their present suffering on the prohibition of her cult. See Sturgis, M., *It Ain't Necessarily So,* ibid, 186, and see *Jeremiah* 17–19, 'But we will certainly do whatsoever thing goeth forth out of our own mouth, to burn incense unto the Queen of Heaven, and to pour out drink offerings unto her, as we have done, we, and our fathers, our kings, and our princes, in the cities of Judah, and in the streets of Jerusalem: for *then* had we plenty of victuals, and were well, and saw no evil. But since we left off to burn incense to the Queen of Heaven, and to pour out drink offerings unto

her, we have wanted all *things*, and have been consumed by the sword and by the famine'.

[73] According to the Qur'an, Sad 15–25.

[74] *Philippians* 3.5–6. Paul gives a full account of his justification according to Jewish law—circumcised on the eighth day, Israelite by race, of the tribe of Benjamin and a zealous Pharisee—'by the law's standard righteous without fault.' Startlingly, he says in verse 8 that he counts all this as 'dung' (KJV translation). As the Greek word *skubalon* can mean any refuse, including the excrement of animals, we feel justified in rendering this as 'crap', even though we are aware that it might offend some readers. In *Hebrews* 8. 13 Paul writes that 'Calling this the "new" agreement already makes the first one the "old" one, and something so antiquated and creaky won't be around much longer'.

4: The Most Famous Man Who Never Lived

[1] Hippolytus, *Elenchos* 5. 9.5. See Segal, R. A., *The Gnostic Jung* (Princeton University Press 1992), 70.

[2] Justin Martyr, *First Apology* 54, and *Dialogue with Trypho*, chapter 69. Justin claims that the wicked demons 'imitated what was said of our Christ' 'to deceive and lead astray the human race.' See Guthrie WKC, *Orpheus and Greek Religion* (Princeton University Press 1952), 266, and see King, C. W., *Gnostics and Their Remains* (David Nutt London 1887), 122–123.

[3] 'The Devil, whose business is to pervert the truth, mimics the exact circumstances of the Divine Sacraments. He baptises his believers and promises forgiveness of sins from the Sacred Fount, and thereby initiates them into the religion of Mithras. Thus he celebrates the oblation of bread, and brings in the symbol of the resurrection. Let us therefore acknowledge the craftiness of the Devil, who copies certain things of those that be Divine'. Tertullian quoted in Kingsland, W., *The Gnosis* (Phanes Press 1937), 99.

[4] Gibbon, E., *The Decline and Fall of the Roman Empire* (Penguin Classics), 529 footnote 36. Gibbon regarded the forgery to have taken place 'between the time of Origen and that of Eusebius'.

[5] Schweitzer, A., *The Quest of the Historical Jesus*, quoted in Wilson, I., *Jesus: The Evidence* (Harper SanFranciso 1997), 37.

[6] Graham, P., *The Jesus Hoax* (Leslie Frewin 1974).

[7] 'James son of Joseph brother of Jesus'. The ossuary was not discovered by archaeologists and is of unknown provenance. Witnesses claim to have

seen it in the Jerusalem antiquities market as far back as the 1970s but it was then without the second part of the inscription 'brother of Jesus'. The Israeli Antiquities Authority has declared it to be a fake, as has an expert in ancient Aramaic inscriptions. See: http://www.bibleinterp.com/articles/Official_Report.htm

[8] Wells, G. A., *Did Jesus Exist?* (Pemberton Publishing 1975), 20. See also Stanton, G., *Gospel Truth?* (HarperCollins 1995), 131, where Stanton remarks that 'Paul's failure to refer more frequently and at greater length to the actions and teaching of Jesus is baffling'.

[9] Wells, G. A., *Did Jesus Exist?* (Pemberton Publishing Company 1975), 20–21.

[10] *Galatians* 1.12.

[11] *Colossians* 1.25–28.

[12] *Galatians* 3.26–29.

[13] *Romans* 6.4–6.

[14] *Romans* 6.6.

[15] Marcion composed a treatise called the *Antitheses*, a juxtaposition of Old and New Testament texts designed to prove that the 'Just God' of the Old Testament cannot possibly be the 'Good God' of the New.

[16] 'All who depend upon works of the Law are under a curse', *Galatians* 3.6–11. 'Christ redeemed us from the curse of the Law, *Galatians* 3.13–14. For Paul, as for the Gnostics, through sharing in Christ's suffering and resurrection the Christian initiate can be redeemed from the Law and set free. Paul writes, 'Now, having died, we are out of the purview of the Law that kept us down', *Romans* 7.6.

[17] *2 Corinthians* 3.6.

[18] *Joseph and Aseneth*, the story of the conversion of an Egyptian girl to Judaism written in the second or first century BCE, is considered by Momigliano to be the oldest Greek novel in existence. See Momigliano, A., *Alien Wisdom*, ibid, 117. It was extremely popular among early Christians.

[19] Pagans condemned the Jews' unwillingness to work on the Sabbath, their circumcision and their dietary taboos as superstition. They were especially harsh about those laws that prevented Jews from associating with their Pagan neighbours or acknowledging their gods. See Balsdon JP, *Romans and Aliens* (University of North Carolina Press 1980), 67. See also Apul. *Flor 6*; Strabo 16, 2, 35ff; 760f. Horace *Sat* 1, 4, 143. Plutarch, *On Superstition*. Apollonius Molon of Rhodes in the first century BC called the Jews *atheoi* and *misanthropoi*, because of their way of life in the Greeks cities. He claims that they are 'the most stupid of the barbarians' and have failed to produce a

'single invention which is of any use for living'. The same charge is made by Apion, Josephus, *Contra Apionem* 2.148 and 135, and Celsus in Origen *Contra Celsus* 4.31. See Hengel, M., *Jews, Greeks, and Barbarians*, ibid, 80.

[20] Cicero, *Pro Flacco* 28, 67.

[21] *Exodus* 21.24–26.

[22] *John* 8.44.

[23] *Luke* 11.52.

[24] See the discussion of the extent of Gnosticism in the East in Price, R. M., *Deconstructing Jesus* (Prometheus Books 2000), 24ff.

[25] Quoted by Lacarrière in Lacarrière, J., *The Gnostics* (City Lights 1989), 100.

[26] Pagels, E., *The Gnostic Gospels* (Random House 1979), 121–122. Unlike Hippolytus and Irenaeus, Tertullian was not beatified, presumably because he apostated to Montanism in 207 CE. See Gibbon, E., *The Decline and Fall of the Roman Empire*, ibid, 523, where Gibbon records how after his apostasy Tertullian proceeded to attack the morals of the church which he had previously so resolutely defended.

[27] Irenaeus, *Adverses Haereses* 1.1.

[28] *Second Treatise of the Great Seth*, 60, 20. Robinson, J. M., *The Nag Hammadi Library* (HarperCollins paperback edition 1978), 362.

[29] Irenaeus, *Adverses Haereses* 1.11.8.

[30] Professor Wilhelm Wrede (1859–1906) of Breslau University was the first to show that the supposedly 'primitive' gospel of Mark had undergone extensive theological rewriting and editing. In 1919 Karl Ludwig Schmidt demonstrated that the gospel had been composed from previously existing fragments and that the connecting links between these were the author's own invention.

[31] Wilson, I., *Jesus*, ibid, 36.

[32] For further information on *Mary Magdalene: Author of the Fourth Gospel?* see the Web site of Ramon K. Justino at www.beloveddisciple.org

[33] 130 Many Gnostic schools were named after women, such as Helen, Salome, Mary, Marcellina and Martha. See Hoffmann, J., *Celsus on the True Doctrine* (Oxford University Press 1987), 42, where the author observes that 'One cannot but be impressed by the number of women-founded sects known to Celsus'.

[34] Wilson, I., *Jesus*, ibid, 39.

[35] Lüdemann, G., *Heretics* (SCM Press 1995), 196. Irenaeus traces all heresies from Simon Magus and quotes *Acts* to show that the heretic had been amply repudiated by Peter. Justin repeatedly mentions Simon Magus but strangely

makes no reference to *Acts*. Lüdemann asserts that the reason for *Acts'* sudden appearance between Justin and Irenaeus is 'self-evident'. The German theologian Hans van Campenhausen states, 'We do not find testimony to the *Acts of the Apostles* before Irenaeus', quoted in Lüdemann, G. *Heretics* (SCM Press 1995), 315. Harnack's view is insightful: '*Acts* is the key to the understanding of the Catholic canon and at the same time shows its "novelty" '. Tertullian himself admits that *Acts* was rejected by the 'heretics'.

[36] Wells, G. A., *Did Jesus Exist?* (Pemberton Publishing 1975), 141. The twelve are mentioned in the opening chapters of *Acts*. In chapter 9 we hear they are the leaders of the Jerusalem church. By chapter 15 they are sharing this leadership with the 'elders'; and from chapter 16 onwards we hear no more of them, and the Jerusalem church is run by James and the 'elders'.

[37] *Acts* 1.21f. See Lüdemann, G., *Heretics*, ibid, 104.

[38] *Acts'* account of Paul's visit to Jerusalem contradicts the testimony of Paul in his *Letter to the Galatians*. According to *Acts*, after his visionary experience on the road to Damascus, Paul is told to seek out a disciple called Ananias in Damascus who will tell him what to do (*Acts* 9.10). He then goes to Jerusalem where Barnabas introduces him to the Apostles (*Acts* 9.27). In the temple at Jerusalem he experiences a second vision of Jesus and receives his vocation to preach to the Gentiles (*Acts* 22.17–21). Yet this is quite different from Paul's own account, in which he makes no mention of Ananias and claims he went to Arabia and had nothing to do with Christians in Jerusalem for three years after his conversion experience (*Galatians* 1.15–17). He even emphatically writes, 'What I write is plain truth; before God I am not lying'. So who is lying?

[39] *John* 1.42. Jesus does not give any of the other disciples nicknames, and doesn't explain why he has done this to Simon. But even more inexplicably, having gone to all the bother of renaming him as Cephas, he is never referred to in this way again.

[40] See Wells, G. A., *Did Jesus Exist?*, ibid, 124ff. As Wells notes, 'There is nothing in Paul's letters to support the view that the Cephas he mentions had the career and connection with Jesus alleged of Peter in the gospels'.

[41] See Pagels, E., *The Gnostic Paul* (Trinity Press International 1975), 104.

[42] Pagels notes that Irenaeus strikingly opens his treatise claiming 'the apostle's authority to oppose the Gnostics—by citing both *Timothy* and *Titus*'. Pagels, E., *The Gnostic Paul*, ibid, 5. Tertullian admits that the heretics dared to impugn the validity of the pastorals but insists that the 'same Paul' who wrote *Galatians* also wrote *Titus*.

[43] *1 Timothy* 6.20. *Acts* and the pastorals were rejected by the Gnostic Marcion. See Lüdemann, G., *Heretics*, ibid, 196.

[44] *1 Timothy* 6.13.

[45] Irenaeus admits that the Gnostic teacher Marcus had attracted 'many foolish women', including the wife of one of his deacons, but claims that this was because Marcus was a diabolically clever seducer. However, his later admission that the Marcosians worshipped the feminine element of the divine being, 'She who is before all things', and encouraged women to prophesy and act as priests must surely be the real reason. Irenaeus, *Adverses Haereses*, 1.13.5, 1.13.1–2, and Hippolytus, *Refutationis Omnium Haeresium* 6.35. See Pagels, E., *The Gnostic Gospels* (Random House 1979), 80. Tertullian writes, 'The very women of these heretics, how wanton they are! For they are bold enough to teach, to dispute, to enact exorcisms, to undertake cures—it may be even to baptise'. Tertullian, *De Praescriptione Haeresicorum*, 41.

[46] *1 Timothy* 2:11–12.

[47] The pastoral letters, *2 Thessalonians*, *3 Corinthians* and other documents were forged to refute specific Gnostic/Pauline doctrines in the apostle's own name. See Lüdemann, G., *Heretics*, ibid, 201.

[48] *2 John* 7.

[49] A fact observed as long ago as 1699 by the leader of the Deist movement in England, John Toland, who wrote, 'There is not a single book of the New Testament not refused by some of the ancient writers as being unjustly attributed to the apostles and as actually forged by their adversaries'. See Metzger, B. M., *The Canon of the New Testament* (Oxford University Press 1987), 13.

[50] *Malachi* 3.25.

[51] Tertullian, *De Praescriptione Haeresicorum*, chapter 1.

[52] Lane Fox R., *Pagans and Christians* (Penguin Books 1986), 439.

[53] Pagels, E., *The Gnostic Gospels*, ibid, 106. Those who are enthusiastic to be martyrs are the 'foolish' who simply say the words 'we are Christians' yet who do not know 'who Christ is'. They are 'empty martyrs, since they bear witness only to themselves'. Theirs will be only a 'human death' and will not lead to the salvation which they expect, for 'these matters are not settled in this way' and 'they do not have the Word which gives life'.

[54] *Apocalypse of Peter* 78.1–2.

[55] Turcan, R., *Cults of the Roman Empire* (Blackwell Publishers 1992), 126, quoting Eunapius, *Lives of the Sophists*.

[56] Fideler, D., *Jesus Christ, Sun of God* (Quest Books 1993), 180. St. Augus-

tine likewise stated, 'I would not believe the Gospel if the authority of the Catholic church did not compel me'. See ibid 320.

5: Muhammad: From Mystic to Mobster

[1] Qur'an Sura 2 The Cow verse 79.

[2] Armstrong, K., *Islam: A Short History* (Modern Library 2000), 15.

[3] Von Harnack defined Islam as 'a transformation on Arab soil of a Jewish religion that had itself been transformed by Gnostic Judaeo-Christianity'. Adolf von Harnack, *Dogmengeschichte* 11.537, quoted in Corbin, H., *Cyclical Time and Ismaili Gnosis* (Kegan Paul International 1983), 66.

[4] Qur'an Sura 4 verses 156–15.

[5] The Elchasiates were Jewish Gnostics similar to the Ebionites. They insisted on circumcision and observed the Sabbath but also practiced baptism. One of the most famous Gnostics of all time, Mani, was born amongst the Aramaic-speaking sect in Mesopotamia in 216 CE. The Church Father Epiphanius testifies that the followers of Elchasaios still existed in the land of the Moabites and the Nabataeans in the fifth century. Therefore, a century before the birth of Muhammad there were Gnostic Judaeo-Christians flourishing in the land of the Nabataeans, where Muhammad was born.

[6] Armstrong, K., *A History of God* (Alfred A. Knopf 1993), 184. Armstrong, K., *Islam*, ibid, 14.

[7] Pelikan, J. (ed), *The Qur'an* (Princeton University Press 1988.) xiv.

[8] Sura 96 The Clot, should be at the beginning.

[9] Ruthven, M., *Fundamentalism: The Search for Meaning* (Oxford University Press 2004), 81.

[10] Shaikh, A., *Faith and Deception* (The Principality Publishers 1996), 65.

[11] Sura 2 The Cow 2.

[12] Sura 2 The Cow 1. Hence English translations of the Qur'an leave the untranslatable phrase untranslated.

[13] Sura 4 The Women 82.

[14] See Manji's comments about this in Manji, I., *The Trouble with Islam: A Wake-up Call for Honesty and Change* (St. Martin's Press 2004), 45.

[15] Sura 16 The Bees 101.

[16] Sura 2 The Cow 106.

[17] Sura 111 Abu Lahab 1–5.

[18] Hadith Sahih Bokhari vol. 4. Jame Tirmzi vol. 2.

[19] Sura 3 The Family of Imran 110.

[20] Sura 43 Ornaments of Gold 1–4.

[21] Hadith 5751 Mishkat vol 3. See Shaikh, A., *Islam: The Arab Imperialism* (The Principality Publishers 1998), 113.

[22] Ibid, 94.

[23] Sura 8 The Spoils 69.

[24] The Spoils 67.

[25] Sura 33 The Allied Troops 50.

[26] Hadith 5500 Mishkat vol. 3.

[27] Our thanks to Benjamin Liu, professor of Medieval Spanish at the University of Connecticut, for this piece of information.

[28] Sura 42 The Consultation 13.

[29] Sura 2 The Cow 121.

[30] Sura 2 The Cow 256.

[31] Sura 3 The Family of Imran 19.

[32] Sura 48 Victory 28.

[33] Cattle 30. The Cow 75.

[34] Sura 22 The Pilgrimage 28, and see Sura 3 The Family of Imran 67.

[35] Shaikh, A., *Faith and Deception* (The Principality Publishers 1996), 138.

[36] Jame Tirmzi vol. 2. Shaikh, A., *Islam*, ibid, 1998), 93–94.

[37] Sura 4 The Women 51–53

[38] Sura 2 The Cow 141–143.

[39] Bokhari 147 vol. 1.

[40] Sura 9 Repentance 17.

[41] Sura 8 The Spoils 55.

[42] Sura 9 Repentance 29.

[43] Sura 9 Repentance 123.

[44] Sura 48 Victory 29.

[45] Sura 5 The Feast 57.

[46] Sura 9 Repentance 23.

[47] Sura 58 The Disputant 22.

[48] Sura 8 The Spoils 65.

[49] Hadith 4363.

[50] Hadith 4366. See Shaikh A, *Islam*, ibid, 140.

[51] Hadith 4364. See ibid, 96.

[52] Sura 5 The Feast 33.

[53] 'Now one can see that it is the basic principle of Islam that the Muslims remain merciful to one another and cruel to the non-Muslims. It is a doctrine of extreme social conflict, and yet Muhammad claims to be the Ambassador of Mercy to the whole of mankind!' Shaikh, A., *Faith and Deception*, ibid, 1996), 96.

[54] Ibid, 94.

[55] Ali, T., *The Clash of Fundamentalisms: Crusades, Jihads and Modernity* (Verso 2002), 163.

[56] Sura 33 The Allied Troops 36.

[57] Shaikh, A., *Islam,* ibid, 72.

[58] Sura 82 The Splitting 19.

[59] Sura 3 The Family of Imran 77.

[60] Sura 98 The Clear Proof 6.

[61] Sura 4 The Women 56.

[62] Sura 22 The Pilgrimage 19–22.

[63] Sura 14 Abraham 16–17.

[64] Sura 8 The Spoils 24.

[65] Sura 83 The Defrauders 20–25.

[66] Sura 78 The Announcement 31–34.

[67] Hadith Tirmzi vol. 2 35–40.

[68] Hadith Mishkat vol. 3 83–97.

[69] Hadith Tirmzi vol. 2 138. See Shaikh, A., *Faith and Deception*, ibid, 50.

[70] Hadith 6390, see ibid, 89.

[71] Hadith 4621.

[72] Sura 39 The Small Groups 36–37.

[73] Sura 6 The Cattle 125.

[74] 'The last hour would not come unless the Muslims fought and killed the Jews'. Hadith 6985.

[75] Shaikh, A., *Islam*, ibid, 142–145.

[76] Sura 33 The Allied Troops 21.

[77] Manji, I., *The Trouble with Islam*, ibid, 58.

6: The Dream of Awakening

[1] Ibid, 162.

[2] Ali, T., *The Clash of Fundamentalisms*, ibid, 324.

[3] *Excerpts of Theodotus* 35. See Foerster, W., *Gnosis: A Selection of Gnostic Texts* (Clarendon Press 1972), 222–233.

[4] Einstein, A., *The World as I See It* (Philosophical library 1949), 24–28.

[5] Kirk and Raven, *The Presocratic Philosophers* (Cambridge University Press 1957), 168. In *Phaedrus* 243, Plato hints that Homer's blindness was a punishment for his heresy in making up such myths.

[6] Kirk and Raven, *The Presocratic Philosophers*, ibid, 168–169.

[7] Ibid, 179.

[8] Pagels, E., *Adam, Eve, and the Serpent* (Random House 1988), 124.

[9] See Freke and Gandy, *The Hermetica* (Piatkus Books 1997), 12.

[10] Maalouf, A., *The Crusades Through Arab Eyes* (Al Saqi Books 1984), 54.

[11] Armstrong, K., *Islam, ibid*, 47.

[12] Ibid, 59.

[13] Ibid, 88.

[14] Copernicus, *De Revolutionibus Orbium Coelestium*, quotes Aetius III 13, 1–3, the heliocentric theory of the Pythagoreans Philolaus, Heraclides and Ecphantus. See Guthrie WKC, *History of Greek Philosophy* (Cambridge University Press 1962), 327.

[15] *Joshua* 12–13.

[16] Carl Jung, *Collected Works* 2.148.

[17] *The Treatise on the Resurrection NHC*. Robinson, J. M., *The Nag Hammadi Library*, ibid, 54.

[18] Theodotus, *Excerpta ex Theodoto*, 57. See Foerster, W., *Gnosis*, ibid, 222–233.

Suggested Further Reading

Judaism

Davies, P. R., *In Search of 'Ancient Israel'*, Sheffield Academic Press, 1992

Finkelstein, I., and Silberman, N. A., *The Bible Unearthed: Archaeology's New Vision and the Origin of its Sacred Texts*, Free Press, 2001

Sturgis, M., *It Ain't Necessarily So: Investigating the Truth of the Biblical Past*, Headline, 2001

Thompson, T. L., *Early History of the Israelite People: From the Written and Archaeological Sources*, Brill, 1992

———. *The Bible in History: How Writers Create a Past*, Pimlico, 1999

Christianity

Doherty, E., *The Jesus Puzzle: Did Christianity Begin with a Mythical Christ?*, Canadian Humanist Press, 1999

Freke, T., and Gandy, P., *The Jesus Mysteries: Was the Original Jesus a Pagan God?*, Harmony Books, 1999

Jesus and the Lost Goddess: The Secret Teachings of the Original Christians, Harmony Books, 2001

Price, R. M., *The Incredible Shrinking Son of Man: How Reliable Is the Gospel Tradition?*, Prometheus Books, 2003

Robinson, J. M., *The Nag Hammadi Library*, HarperSanFrancisco paperback, 1978

Wells, G. A., *Did Jesus Exist?*, Prometheus, 1986

———. *The Jesus Legend*, Open Court, 1996

———. *The Jesus Myth*, Open Court, 1999

Islam

Armstrong, K., *Islam: A Short History*, Modern Library, 2000

Manji, I., *The Trouble with Islam: A Wake-up Call for Honesty and Change*, Mainstream Publishing, 2004

Shaikh, A., *Faith and Deception*, The Principality Publishers, P.O. Box 918, Cardiff, UK CF5 2N, 1996.

———. *Islam: The Arab Imperialism*, The Principality Publishers, P.O. Box 918, Cardiff, UK CF5 2N, 1998.

Gnostic Scientists

Wilber, K. (ed.), *Quantum Questions: Mystical Writings of the World's Great Physicists*, Shambhala, 1984

Index

God *(cont.)*
  as mysterious source of all, 197
  names for, 43, 44, 46–47
  omnipotence of, 16, 88, 197–201
  personal image of, 200
  self as, 176
  and spirituality without religion, 189, 197–201
  surrender to will of, 10, 83, 91
  traditional images of, 197–201
  as true "I," 140
Godmen, 55–58, 63, 64, 66, 77, 80
"Good" Book, 49–51
Gospels, 80, 171, 201–2, 205, 209, 212
Greeks, 34–39, 40, 45, 46, 47, 55–56, 63, 113–15, 116, 117, 118

Hatred, 102–4, 110, 208
Heaven, 55, 56, 77, 83, 99, 100–102, 104, 147, 157–59, 160, 164, 198, 212
Hell, 100–102, 157–58, 160, 164
Heretics, 13–15, 111–20, 217–18
Holocaust, 162, 199
Holy war, Islamic, 95–98
Homosexuality, 15, 16, 101, 198, 216

I-perspective, 134–35, 136, 137, 138, 140, 141, 171, 191, 192, 200
Ignorance, 163, 174, 205, 212
Indifference, 153, 154, 162, 163, 180
Inquisition, 7, 13–14
Intuition, 195, 196–97
Irenaeus, 68, 69, 70, 71, 72, 73, 74, 77
Islam
  and awakening to oneness, 8
  beginning of, 52, 83
  and Christianity, 84, 90, 92–95, 100
  and Heaven and Hell, 100–102
  and heretical heritage, 115–18, 119
  and homosexuality, 101
  and Inquisition, 13
  and Jerusalem, 94–95
  and Jews/Judaism, 84, 90, 92–95, 100
  and love or law, 201
  meaning of term, 83, 91
  Muhammad as godfather of, 89–92
  as new religion, 93
  as one true religion, 83, 92
  as personality cult, 98
  sacred scriptures of, 8
  sectarianism in, 90

spread of, 7
umma of, 83–84, 89, 90, 91
and violence, 7, 10, 90–91, 95–98
women in, 85, 87, 91, 101, 118, 201
See also Allah; Islamic Fundamentalism; Islamic Gnosticism; Islamic Literalism; Muhammad; Qur'an
Islamic Fundamentalism, 12, 15, 17, 18–19, 103, 104, 118
Islamic Gnosticism, 83, 88
Islamic Literalism, 11–12
Israel, 11, 15–16, 27, 30, 31, 32–33, 40, 48, 65, 103, 162
It-perspective, 134–35, 136, 141, 161, 171, 191, 192

Jerusalem, 13, 72, 108
  Abraham in, 83
  and Christians, 103
  derivation of name, 33
  destruction of, 59, 65
  history of, 27, 32–36, 38, 39, 42–45, 47
  and Islam/Muhammad, 83, 85, 94–95, 102–3
  and Jesus, 55, 59, 60, 67, 83
  and Jews, 103
  in modern times, 103
  Moses in, 83
  re-founding of, 67
  temple in, 27, 39, 42–43, 45, 65
Jesus, 11, 50, 110, 118, 133, 137, 209
  and awakening, 178, 181
  birth of, 54, 70, 81
  death and resurrection of, 55, 58, 61, 62, 70, 80, 81, 85, 108–9, 130, 157–58
  disciples of, 54
  genocidal, 64, 65
  gentle, 64
  and God, 104
  as Godman, 56–58
  as historical figure or myth, 54–81, 106, 160, 203
  inconsistencies in sayings of, 106
  as invisible man, 58–60
  and Islam/Muhammad, 83, 84, 85, 92, 98, 104
  in Jerusalem, 55, 59, 83
  Joshua as, 63–64
  and love, 64, 178, 181, 201–2, 212
  as "man of sorrows," 4

258   INDEX

miracles of, 54–55, 58, 61, 81
as perfect person, 203, 205
similarities between Pagan myths and story of, 55–58, 61–62, 66–67, 80
and spirituality, 197, 201–2
See also laughing Jesus; *specific topic*
Jewish Fundamentalism, 15–16, 17, 20, 40
Jewish Gnosticism, 52–53, 63, 64, 118
Jewish Literalism, 11, 62, 64–65, 108, 178
Jews/Judaism
and Arabs/Palestinians, 50–51
as chosen people of God, 92, 94
and Christianity, 15, 56, 64, 65–66, 67, 81, 92–95
as cursed by God, 103
in Egypt, 7, 26, 28, 29, 32–34, 37, 42, 44, 45, 46, 53
and Greeks, 34–39, 40, 45, 46, 47, 63
hatred of, 64
and heretical heritage, 115, 119
history of, 25–33, 36–41
and Islam/Muhammad, 84, 85, 90, 92–95, 96–97, 103
and laughing Jesus, 162
and Literalism, 65
and Messiahs, 65, 67
as monotheists, 46–48
as mystery religion, 63
and myths, 32–34, 52, 63, 65, 115
and Paganism, 81
persecution/plundering of, 7, 13, 14–15, 26, 63, 65, 90, 96–97
and religion as Devil's greatest achievement, 13, 14–15
return to Israel of, 32–34, 103, 162
and Romans, 39, 40, 45, 63, 65
sacred scriptures of, 8, 21, 52
and spirituality without religion, 201
See also Jewish Fundamentalism; Jewish Gnosticism; Jewish Literalism; Tanakh; *specific topic*
John, 68–71, 74, 158
John, 14, 69, 70, 71, 72, 73
Josephus, 35, 36, 37, 40, 47–48, 59, 60
Joshua, 26, 29, 40, 44, 52, 62–65, 80, 120

Knowing/knowledge, 129–35, 146, 147, 167, 182, 193, 194, 196, 197, 213, 216–17

The Ladder to the Source exercise, 225
Laughing Jesus
and Big Idea, 218
and death, 163–64
and pronoia, 164–67
reasons for, 9
and suffering, 160–62
suppression of image of, 4
as symbol of awakening, 3–5
as symbol of gnosis, 162
and waking the dead, 159–60
Law, 64, 201–3
Laws of nature, 189–90
Life
as expression of shared nature, 211
game of, 183–85
as good, 164–65, 167
and laughing Jesus, 158, 160, 164–65, 167
love of, 158, 160, 179
mystery of, 110, 131–32, 145–46, 171, 194, 200–201, 203, 218
purpose of, 143–44, 171, 183
theories about, 188–93
See also Life-dream; *specific topic*
Life-dream
and awakening, 3, 122, 171–76, 180, 181, 183–84, 185, 214
and awareness, 137, 138, 139
and game of life, 183–84
and gnosis, 128–29, 132, 137–44
and laughing Jesus, 158, 160–66
and love, 142, 180, 181, 184, 185, 210, 211
and loving being human, 151–54, 156, 163
and movie metaphor, 168
and oneness, 3, 173, 174
and philosophical workout, 227, 230
and purpose of life, 143–44
and reality, 146–54, 156
source of, 139
and spirituality, 190, 192–97, 199, 200, 203, 205
See also specific topic
Listening with Love exercise, 229, 231–32

Literalism
  characteristics of, 5
  decline of, 187
  definition of, 5
  divisiveness in, 13
  fear as tool of, 100
  and Gnostic spirituality, 3–9, 53
  as nightmare, 23
  as threat to world peace, 12
  See also Christian Literalism;
    Islamic Literalism; Jewish
    Literalism; *specific topic*
Looking with Love exercise, 229
Love
  being, 178–83
  big, 141–42, 147, 150, 158, 160, 161,
    162, 164, 182, 184, 212, 217, 226,
    228, 229, 231
  and death, 160, 164
  of enemies, 181
  and essential nature, 142, 155, 178,
    180, 181, 185, 202, 211
  exercises about, 228, 229, 231–32
  falling out of, 179
  and Islam, 201
  and Jesus, 64, 178, 181, 201–2, 212
  and Jews, 201
  and laughing Jesus, 158, 160, 161,
    162, 164, 166
  or law, 201–3
  of life, 3, 158, 160, 179
  listening with, 229, 231–32
  and living in love, 147, 171, 182–83,
    184, 213
  and loving being, 178–83
  and loving being human, 151–56
  of the moment, 171, 179, 184
  and oneness, 3, 5, 8, 202, 203
  of others, 178, 180–81, 184, 213
  and philosophical workout, 221,
    226, 227, 228, 229, 231, 234
  politics of, 210–13
  and purpose of life, 227
  self-, 178, 182
  and sex, 152, 155–56
  and spirituality, 201–3
  unconditional, 142, 161, 178–79,
    180–81, 182, 183, 228
  See also specific topic
Lucid living
  and awakening, 171, 173–74, 175,
    178, 184
  and Big Boss, 200

and Big Idea, 211, 217
and choice, 174, 175
and death, 163, 164
and enlivenment, 149–50, 151, 227
Gnosis as experience of, 129
Gnostic teachings of, 220
and hip-gnosis, 134, 135, 136, 137,
  141, 144
and I and It perspectives, 134, 135
and laughing Jesus, 158–59, 160,
  161, 162, 163, 164, 166, 167
and love, 178, 184, 211
and loving being human, 151, 152,
  153, 154, 155–56, 163
and movie metaphor, 167–69
and oneness, 173–74
and philosophical workout, 220,
  221, 227, 234, 235
and pronoia, 166, 167
and purpose of life, 144
and reality, 149–50, 151, 152, 153,
  154, 155–56
and selfishness, 153–54
and sex, 155–56
and spirituality without religion,
  200
and suffering, 160, 161, 162
teachings of, 226
Luke, 68–71, 73

Mark, 68–71, 73
Martyrs, 11, 76–77, 104
Matthew, 68–71, 73, 178, 181
Mecca, 82, 85, 89, 94–95, 102
Media, mass, 195, 217
Messiahs, 59, 63, 64, 65, 67, 185
Miracles, 54–55, 56, 58, 61, 202
Monotheism, 46–48
Morality, 49–51, 201–3, 209, 212
Moses, 11, 21, 98, 103, 107, 118
  and Ark of the Covenant, 46
  Books of, 43–44, 46
  in Egypt, 37
  and Greek-Jewish relationship, 36,
    37
  as historical figure or myth, 63, 80
  in Jerusalem, 83
  and monotheism, 47–48
  and Muhammad, 83
  as patriarch, 46
  stories about, 26, 28–29, 41
  tablets of, 44, 45
  and Tanakh, 41, 44, 45, 46

Movie metaphor, 167–69
Mrs. God, 48–49
Muhammad, 11, 12, 107–8
  birth of, 82
  and channelling God, 85–89
  and Christianity/Jesus, 84, 85,
    92–95, 98
  as Gnostic, 84–85, 87
  as godfather of Islam, 89–92
  God's relationship with, 83, 84,
    85–89, 90, 91, 94, 95, 99–100, 104
  as God's secretary, 21
  hate legacy of, 102–4
  and Heaven and Hell, 83, 99,
    100–102
  and heretical heritage, 117, 118
  as historical figure, 83
  and holy war, 95–98
  and Jerusalem, 83, 85, 102–3
  and Jews/Judaism, 84, 85, 92–95
  as megalomaniac, 98–100
  as military leader, 83, 90–91, 97
  as prophet, 82, 83, 94, 98, 99, 100
  revelations of, 84, 85–86, 87–88, 90,
    93, 94, 95, 98
  sayings and stories about (Hadiths),
    86, 89
  in wilderness, 82–83, 84
Muslims. *See* Islam; Islamic
  Fundamentalism; Islamic
  Gnosticism; Islamic Literalism;
  Muhammad; Qur'an
Mysticism, 55–58, 63, 64, 112, 188,
  214
Myths, 7, 63, 75
  Devil in Western, 12, 13
  Gnostic, 52–53
  and Greek-Jewish relationship,
    36–39
  Jesus as historical figure or myth,
    54–81, 106, 160, 203
  Jesus story and Pagan, 55–58, 61–62,
    66–67, 80
  and Jews, 32–34, 63, 65, 115
  Tanakh as collection of, 27, 28–32
  See also specific myth

Nationalism, 41, 48, 52–53, 64, 90,
  207
New Age, 41–43
"New Learning," 119, 120
New Testament, 11, 15, 68, 73, 78–79,
  80, 105

contradictions in, 75
and Fundamentalism, 17
heroes of, 64
and "Holy" Bible, 74, 75
inconsistencies in, 106
and Jesus as historical figure or
  myth, 59, 64, 70, 72, 73, 106
misrepresentations in, 105–6
as nonsense, 102
Noah, 25, 27, 42, 49–50, 52

Old Testament, 15, 17, 19, 25–27, 52,
  64, 75, 79, 197
  See also Tanakh
Oneness
  awakening to, 3–4, 5, 8, 110, 162,
    165, 166, 172–74, 175–76, 178,
    182, 184, 206, 211
  of awareness, 8, 138–39, 146–47,
    148, 150, 153, 159–60, 172, 178,
    197, 199, 211
  and laughing Jesus, 159–60, 162,
    163, 165, 166, 167
  and love, 3, 5, 8, 142, 178, 182, 184,
    202, 203, 210, 211, 213
  and loving being human, 152, 163
  and philosophical workout, 221,
    225, 226, 229, 230, 234
  and spirituality without religion,
    191, 197, 199, 202, 203
  See also specific topic
Osiris, 29, 55–56, 66, 80

Pagan Gnosticism, 175–76, 203
Pagans
  and Christianity, 7, 22, 68, 78–79,
    81, 108–9
  destruction of libraries of, 22
  and first monotheists, 48
  and heretical heritage, 116, 119
  and nationalist propaganda and
    Gnostic myths, 53
  and religious insanity, 108–9
  similarities between Jesus story and
    myths of, 55–58, 61–62, 65,
    66–67, 80
  and violence, 7, 78–79
  See also Godmen; Pagan
    Gnosticism
Palestine, 11, 26–27, 32–36, 39–41,
  43, 45–46, 50–51, 55, 65, 69,
  162
  See also Jerusalem

Paradox of our predicament, 139, 140–41
Paul, 3, 52, 66, 202
  and awakening, 173, 175–76
  and death, 159–60, 163
  as Gnostic, 61–62, 63, 64, 71–72, 73
  and "Holy" Bible, 74
  and Jesus as historical figure or myth, 61–63, 65, 71–72, 73–74
  and laughing Jesus, 159–60, 163
  as Literalist, 61, 73–74
  pastorals of, 73–74
  and Peter, 71–72
  Romanization of, 74
Perennial philosophy, 5, 112
  See also gnostics/Gnosticism
Perfect people, 203–5
Peter, 65, 71–73, 74, 83
Philo, 52, 59, 63
Philosophical workout, 219–35
Plato, 36, 42, 47, 48, 66, 105, 106–7, 112, 113, 117, 118, 119, 134, 163, 164
Plotinus, 68, 107, 118, 128, 132, 135, 136, 139, 141, 158, 172
Porphyry, 38, 118, 134
Prayer, 200
Pronoia, 164–67, 218
Prophecies, 19–20, 38
Prophets, 84, 98, 104, 197, 198, 203
  See also specific person
Protestant Reformation, 22
Ptolemy, 35, 38, 115
Pythagoras/Pythagoreans, 36, 47, 63, 66, 112, 116, 117, 119, 205

Qur'an, 18, 105, 109, 117, 201
  ambiguity of, 86–87
  and Christians and Jews, 92, 94
  differences between Bible and, 84
  and Gnostic Muhammad, 84
  and Heaven and Hell, 100, 101, 102
  and Hebrew prophets, 84
  and holy war, 95–96, 98
  inconsistencies in, 87
  and Jesus, 84
  misrepresentations in, 105–6
  and morality, 50–51
  and Muhammad, 85–86, 87–88, 89, 90, 98, 99, 100, 102, 103, 104
  as myth, 88
  as nonsense, 102

  as revelations from God, 82, 83, 85–86, 87–88
  as Word of God, 50, 94, 104
Quresh tribe, 89, 93, 94

Rationality, 195–97
Re-emergence, 147–49
Reality, 145, 159, 168
  and awakening, 146, 147, 148, 150, 151, 152, 153, 154, 156, 172, 175
  and awareness, 137, 138, 146–47, 148, 149, 150, 152, 153, 154
  and Big Idea, 210, 214, 217
  and certainty and doubt, 193, 194
  and enlivenment, 149–51
  and hip-gnosis, 131, 132, 134, 135, 137, 138, 140
  and I and It perspectives, 134, 135
  and love, 147, 150, 152, 153
  and loving being human, 151–56
  and lucid living, 149–50, 151, 152, 153, 154, 155–56
  and oneness, 146–47, 148, 150, 152, 153
  and re-emergence, 147–49
  and sex, 155–56
  and spirituality without religion, 190, 193, 194, 195
  and us versus them, 210
Reincarnation, 148, 150
Religion
  benefits of, 8
  decline in, 186
  as Devil's greatest achievement, 12–15
  future of, 187
  nightmare of, 11–12
  as nonsense, 102
  and science, 119–20, 188–93
  spirituality without, 186–205
Religious insanity, 107–11
Repentance, 170–71
Resurrection, 159–60.
  See also Jesus: death and resurrection of
Return of the Israelites, 32–34
Romans/Roman Empire
  and Christianity, 4, 59, 66, 75, 76, 77–79, 115
  collapse of, 75–76, 79
  and Godman, 56
  and Jesus as historical figure or myth, 55, 58, 70

and Jews, 39, 40, 45, 46, 63, 65
and Literalist heresy, 67–68
as unholy, 77–79
Rumi, 105, 107, 155, 166, 200

Sacred scriptures
"all-or-nothing" nature of, 106
ambiguity of, 87
authority of, 23, 197
creation of, 21
as dangerous, 22–23
functions of, 201
inconsistencies in, 106
as justification for actions, 7, 15, 21
and Literalism, 20–22
as man's creation, 8
misrepresentations in, 105–6
mystical meanings of, 53
need for assault on, 23–24
See also Bible; New Testament; Old Testament; Qur'an; Tanakh
Science, 119–20, 146, 162, 187, 188–93, 195, 196–97, 198–99, 208
Second Coming of Christ, 103
Selfishness, 152, 153–54, 177, 180, 202, 211, 216
Separateness
and awakening, 3, 172, 173, 175, 177, 180, 181, 182, 184
and death, 160, 164
and laughing Jesus, 158, 160, 161, 162, 164, 165, 166–67
and love, 180, 181, 184, 202, 211, 212, 213
and loving being human, 155
and spirituality without religion, 199, 200, 202
See also Oneness; specific topic
September 11, 2001, 11, 15, 16–17, 23–24, 111, 206, 208–10
Septuagint, 38–39, 41, 47

Sex, 104, 152, 155–56, 198
Sin, 170–71, 194
Sitting exercise, 223–24
Solomon, 26, 27, 31–32, 40, 42, 51, 80
Spirituality without religion, 186–205
Suffering, 153, 154, 158, 160–62, 166, 181, 182, 184, 206, 210, 211, 213
Sufis, 83, 107, 116–17, 200, 201

Taliban, 16, 17, 40, 79, 106
Tanakh, 25–33, 37–53, 62–65, 75, 102, 105–6.
See also Old Testament
Ten Commandments, 44, 51
Tertullian, 57–58, 68, 72, 73, 76, 77, 159, 196
Transcendence, 172, 175–76, 182
Transformation, 151, 152, 153, 160, 163, 169, 175–78, 181, 195, 196, 211, 214
Truth, 191, 193, 194, 195, 207

Universe, you are the, 139–40
Us versus Them, 8, 208–10

Violence, 7–8, 12, 13–15, 65, 75–79, 106, 110, 201–2, 207, 215
and ethnic cleansing, 15, 40, 96
and Fundamentalism, 16, 22, 118
and heretical heritage, 114, 115, 117, 118, 120
and Islam, 10, 90–91, 95–98

Wake-up Club, A, 233, 234
Witnessing, 171–72, 175–76
Women, 16, 48–49, 70, 73–74, 85, 87, 91, 101, 118, 198, 201
World crisis, 7, 11–12, 13, 19, 206, 208–10

You are the universe, 139–40

About the Authors

Timothy Freke has an honours degree in philosophy and is the author of more than twenty books on world spirituality, including *Lucid Living* (Books for Burning, 2005). He lectures and runs experiential seminars throughout the world exploring gnosis. For more information, see www.timothyfreke.com.

Peter Gandy has an MA in Classical Civilisation and is an internationally respected authority on the ancient Pagan Mysteries and early Christianity.

Freke and Gandy are the authors of five previous books, including the international bestseller *The Jesus Mysteries* and *Jesus and the Lost Goddess*.